W9-BVZ-964

DISCARD

Valparaiso Public Library
103 Jefferson Street
Valparaiso, IN 46383

Overheated

Overheated

The Human Cost of Climate Change

ANDREW T. GUZMAN

PORTER COUNTY PUBLIC LIBRARY

Valparaiso Public Library
103 Jefferson Street
Valparaiso, IN 46383

DISCARD

NF   363.738 GUZ   VAL
Guzman, Andrew T.
Overheated : the human cost of
33410012272532

01/30/13

OXFORD
UNIVERSITY PRESS

OXFORD
UNIVERSITY PRESS

Oxford University Press is a department of the University of Oxford.
It furthers the University's objective of excellence in research, scholarship,
and education by publishing worldwide.

Oxford   New York
Auckland   Cape Town   Dar es Salaam   Hong Kong   Karachi
Kuala Lumpur   Madrid   Melbourne   Mexico City   Nairobi
New Delhi   Shanghai   Taipei   Toronto

With offices in
Argentina   Austria   Brazil   Chile   Czech Republic   France   Greece
Guatemala   Hungary   Italy   Japan   Poland   Portugal   Singapore
South Korea   Switzerland   Thailand   Turkey   Ukraine   Vietnam

Oxford is a registered trademark of Oxford University Press
in the UK and certain other countries.

Published in the United States of America by
Oxford University Press
198 Madison Avenue, New York, NY 10016

© Andrew T. Guzman 2013

All rights reserved. No part of this publication may be reproduced, stored in a
retrieval system, or transmitted, in any form or by any means, without the prior
permission in writing of Oxford University Press, or as expressly permitted by law,
by license, or under terms agreed with the appropriate reproduction rights organization.
Inquiries concerning reproduction outside the scope of the above should be sent to the Rights
Department, Oxford University Press, at the address above.

You must not circulate this work in any other form
and you must impose this same condition on any acquirer.

CIP data is on file at the Library of Congress

ISBN 978–0–19–993387–7

1 3 5 7 9 8 6 4 2
Printed in the United States of America
on acid-free paper

To Nicholas and Daniel,
Whose Generation Will Face The Consequences

CONTENTS

PREFACE

Climate change is a subject that is at once familiar and mysterious. It would be hard to find an adult who is unaware of the issue, yet discussions of the subject are so full of misinformation and uncertainty that most of us are not sure what to believe. Scientists who study the climate know a great deal more than the public realizes, and their questions about climate change are not at all the ones that seem to make the news or get included in political debates.

Some of the confusion surrounding climate change can be explained by the complexity of the science involved. Understanding the workings of the earth's climate is a massive task that remains a work in progress in even the most sophisticated scientific circles. That said, public debates about climate and climate change often do an exceptionally poor job of presenting and considering what we do know about the science. This means that while climate change is a critical subject for scientists, they are not the only ones who should be, or must be, talking about it.

I am certainly not a scientist. I am trained as an economist and a lawyer, and I work as a law professor. Much of my career has been spent thinking and writing about how international legal and political systems work (or, sometimes, don't work). A few years ago, I started to think about climate change, in part because it is perhaps the single greatest international challenge of this century and beyond. How could I be a student of the international system without examining this critical issue? This seemed a little like being an expert on terrorism in 2001 and yet ignoring Al-Qaeda.

When I started working on climate change, I had no intention of writing this book. The plan was to produce academic articles, which are, ultimately, the main currency by which those in my profession are evaluated. But as I worked on the subject, I became more and more convinced that the most important hurdle to meaningful action on climate change is the fact that people have not come to accept how serious it is. A great deal has been written and discussed about the subject, but the basic message of how changes in the world's climate will affect virtually every human being on the planet has not been communicated effectively. Unless and until regular people understand the seriousness of the threat, it is unlikely that our politicians will make serious efforts to respond.

This pushed me to investigate more specifically how climate change will affect all of us. Rather than focusing on debates about whether climate change is real or getting distracted by the (important) details of whether temperatures will rise by 2° C or 3° C or 4° C, I tried to understand more clearly what would happen to people on the ground. Over time, I found myself putting together a story about how a seemingly modest increase in temperature of a couple of degrees is enough to make the seas rise, food production collapse, nations go to war, and disease spread virtually unchecked. It was becoming clear, in a way that I felt was not widely appreciated, that the consequences of these changes will be measured in the hundreds of millions of lives, if we are lucky. If we are unlucky, perhaps billions.

This book, then, is an attempt to tell this story. It represents a gathering of a wide range of scientific information and study of human systems and human beings. I am fortunate to work in an institution and a context that not only allow me to do this work but also encourage it. To talk sensibly about how climate change will affect human beings requires an interdisciplinary excursion into climate science, economics, politics, international relations, and much more. Nobody can be an expert in everything, so it inevitably requires working outside one's comfort zone. In many parts of a research university, this sort of cross-cutting work is discouraged and branded as dilettantism. In fairness, this reluctance to work across disciplines or to venture into topics in which one is not expert is part of what makes the best scientists good at their jobs. It also offers a partial explanation for why climate scientists, who know more about climate change than anyone else, often refrain from explaining the connections between their own research and human well-being. A similar, if perhaps more flexible, set of norms makes it difficult for social scientists such as economists and political scientists to use the predictions of climate scientists as a starting point to explain how people will be affected. The connection between the scientific outputs and the real-life impacts are too complex to analyze fully without exposing oneself to the charge of being overly speculative. There are good reasons for this commitment to academic rigor, and I am certainly not trying to criticize it here. The problem of climate change, however, is at once scientific, economic, political, social, and institutional. It cannot be fully understood without going beyond the normal boundaries of individual academic disciplines and without accepting a certain degree of informality in the discussion.

In writing the book, I developed an ever deeper appreciation for the complexity of the climate-change challenge. The task of presenting an accurate and reasonably general account of how humans will be affected by climate change was even more difficult than I anticipated. I relied on my experience in writing about and studying human and legal institutions and systems. I turned to my training in economics to understand the consequences of climate change for resource issues such as the food supply or access to water. Perhaps more than anything, I drew on years of academic work spent evaluating and challenging theories and arguments as I tried to extract from the enormous amounts of available material the most reliable predictions about the earth's natural and human systems. Even with my best efforts, I am certain that I have only scratched the surface. The implications of a changing climate are far-reaching, and I have yet to find a field of human endeavor that will not be affected. Perhaps that is the most important message of the book. Climate change will turn the world as we know it upside-down. Each chapter of the book presents one way in which it will do so and considers some of the consequences for the human race.

I cannot imagine completing a project of this size and scope without assistance from many people. From the very earliest stages, when writing a book was no more than a distant possibility, I have had the benefit of outstanding help. Working with young, energetic, and brilliant students is one of the great joys of an academic job, and this project gave me the opportunity to do so in a more concentrated way than at any other time in my career. Law students and undergraduates who made major contributions to the book include Brenda Au, Leslie Bryant, Sarah Cohen, Jalle Dafa, Matt DalSanto, Earth Duarte-Trattner, Karis Anne Gong, Ryan Lincoln, Scott Lindlaw, Holly Mariella, Elaine Meckenstock, Andrew Robertson, Sabrina Solange, Sophie Turell, Lindsay Walter, and Andrew Wang. I also received valuable editing assistance from Christine Sinnott.

For financial assistance, I am grateful to Berkeley Law School; the Center for Law, Energy, and the Environment; and the Undergraduate Research Apprentice Program at the University of California, Berkeley.

My academic colleagues endured many hours of discussions and questions, including time spent educating me on issues I knew little about. They also provided invaluable comments on earlier drafts and represent an academic community without which this work would have been impossible. I cannot name all of those who were of help, but a few of the most important were Jeff Atik, Eric Biber, Dan Farber, Jody Freeman, Deborah Lambe, Katerina Linos, Timothy Meyer, and John Yoo. For this and every project I have undertaken for many years, I am indebted to my assistants, Jennifer Zahgkuni and Don Johnson, who not only make the entire enterprise run smoothly but also serve as the last line of defense for proofreading and editing.

Oxford University Press and David McBride have provided wonderful support throughout the process. My agent, Susan Schulman, has guided me through the publishing thicket with grace and effectiveness.

My greatest debts are personal ones: to my parents, Danilo Antonio Guzman and Carole Guzman, whose influence is palpable in anything I accomplish; to my wife, Jeannie Sears, whose friendship and love are the foundation of all of my achievements; and to my children, Nicholas and Daniel, who inspire me to think about the future and who will always be the greatest thing I have done.

Overheated

1

KerPlunk! and Planet Earth

*"We have already shot ourselves in the foot. Our immediate problem is
not to shoot ourselves in the head."*
                                        —Robert Strom, *Hot House*[1]

This book's lesson is easy to state and is worth making explicit up front. As
we make decisions about how to respond to climate change, we must not lose
sight of the very real possibility that it will have a cataclysmic impact on the
way we live. I do not mean that there will be serious economic effects or that
there will be modest numbers of additional deaths—these impacts are already
happening. I mean that we should be worried that climate change may kill tens
of millions or hundreds of millions and severely disrupt the lives of perhaps
billions.

This all sounds alarmist, and I suppose it is. But that is because we should be
alarmed. Nobody knows with certainty (or with great confidence, for that matter) exactly what the impact of climate change will be, and I am no exception.
We do know some things, however, and they are not comforting. We know that
the expected changes in our climate are significant, and the projections seem
to grow more dire with each passing year. We know that the oceans are rising
and will continue to do so for at least the next century, causing deadly flooding
in many parts of the world. We know that agriculture will be disrupted as temperature and precipitation patterns change and as mountain glaciers melt. We
know that the stresses generated by climate change will increase tensions in
many parts of the world and are likely to trigger violent conflict. We know that
rising temperatures will increase the incidence of disease and illness around
the world. We know that even if the changes turn out to be on the mild end of
existing projections, there will be great suffering—and that is if we are lucky. If
fate is unkind and climate change is on the severe end of our best predictions,
then we are all in deep, deep trouble.

Whether or not we are lucky, the consequences of climate change will
be felt by billions of people around the world. This is obvious, but it is also

often ignored in our public debates. We talk about environmental changes, scientific evidence, ice sheets, ocean levels, and droughts, but we do not always get around to talking about people. In writing this book, I have tried hard not to fall into this familiar trap. I have written it with the human impact of climate change in mind. The book is about how people will be affected by climate change, rather than how science and climate interact.

A focus on the human cost of climate change is critical, because that is what will persuade people to act. Scientific debates are important, but acknowledging the science is not, by itself, enough to get our political systems to react. Discussing possible policy responses to climate is important, but these responses will happen only if people are persuaded that something must be done. I am convinced that the most important barrier to a sensible and determined response to climate change is a lack of public understanding about the ways in which our lives and the lives of our children will be affected. Hearing that global average temperatures will increase by a couple of degrees is not enough for most people to support aggressive government action in response. Recognizing that this change in climate will lead to tens of millions or hundreds of millions of deaths and that it will harm billions of people, on the other hand, may motivate people to demand action from their political leaders.

There is no way to avoid a discussion about science entirely, but I have tried to keep that material to a minimum. I ask that you bear with me for a few pages in this introduction as I address the predictions of scientists just enough to get the ball rolling. Chapter 2 then explains the basic science of climate change, because some understanding of the science is necessary to appreciate the consequences for humans. The remainder of the book, however, is focused on how human beings, our communities, and our social structures face a threat unlike any we have ever seen before.

There is no way to think about the future without predictions, and so there is no way to think about the challenge of climate change without predictions about the world's future climate and its consequences. You can think of scientists making predictions about the likely impact of climate change the same way you think of making bets on the roll of two six-sided dice. If you have to bet on the outcome of a roll of the dice, you should bet that they will add up to seven. This is the most likely of all outcomes. You will, however, be wrong much more often than you are right. There is one chance in six that the roll will be a seven, so you will be wrong five out of six times. When climate scientists make a prediction—for example, when they predict that the earth will warm by 2° C during this century—they are making a prediction the same way you are when you are betting on the dice. That is, they are offering their best guess, even though they are more likely to be wrong than right. This is not a criticism of the science or the scientists but rather a reflection of the complexity of the earth's climate system. The best scientists are not the ones who get it right all the time—there are no scientists like that—but rather the ones who have the best understanding of the probabilities involved. These scientists will get it right more often than anyone else, but they will still be wrong a lot.

The fact that we do not know exactly what the future holds does not, unfortunately, relieve us of the need to make policy decisions. Should we tax carbon emissions? Implement a cap-and-trade scheme? Enter into an international agreement on mitigating greenhouse-gas emissions? Invest in geoengineering projects to try to cool the earth? To talk sensibly about any of these options—or any of the dozens of other issues relevant to climate change—we need to take our best guess about what the future holds, even if our best guess is wrong more often than it is right.

Fortunately, we have some tools for making policy in areas, such as climate change, where there is a lot of uncertainty. Knowing that a seven is the most likely result when you roll the dice is useful for gamblers, even though that prediction is wrong more often than it is right. In a similar way, the best guess of scientists about what climate change will bring is useful for political leaders deciding what policies to implement.

Human conduct is causing the earth to warm, and we have to decide what to do about it. We are locked into playing a game of dice with the world and with humanity. If there was ever a time when we could have chosen not to play, it is long past. The challenge we face, then, is not deciding whether or not to play but, rather, how to place our bets. Should we enact policies that are a little less expensive but cause more warming in the future, or should we opt for policies that cost more today and cause less warming later? Either way, we are placing a bet on how the climate will react to our actions and how we—humanity—will be affected by the changes in the climate. And we are playing with the highest possible stakes.

These questions always bring us back to the scientists for answers. Scientists can tell us which outcome is, in their view, most likely. There are, of course, disagreements within the scientific community. Disagreement is at the very heart of scientific inquiry. But despite the ever-present debates and competing claims, scientists have reached a broad consensus on climate change that is sufficient to let us make sensible decisions.

So, just as the gambler knows that the most likely roll of the dice is a seven, scientific research has given us some sense of the most likely changes to the earth's climate. We also know a lot about the likelihood that the changes will be greater or less than expected and about how serious the impacts will be if existing climate predictions prove to be wrong. This is essential information if we are to make responsible choices about how to respond to a warming world.

Given what we know about how the climate is likely to change, and even with the uncertainty surrounding that information, we need to consider how those changes to our climate will affect the way we live. To understand how our lives will be affected, it is not enough simply to note the ways in which the climate will change or even how those changes will affect the natural world around us. We need to have some appreciation for how we, ourselves, will be affected. How will our lives be changed? How will we actually feel the consequences of climate change? Climate scientists can tell us only a small part of that story. They know something about how our environment will change, but we also want to know how humanity will react, how our infrastructure will hold up, how food supplies will be affected, how our health will be compromised, and more. In short, we need a sense of how our way of life will be changed along with the climate.

Ideally, we would not only want to know how our lives will be affected by the most likely consequences or the most likely changes to the climate. We would also want to know how we will be affected by all of the possible outcomes and, of course, have a sense of how likely each one is. The chances of even the most likely impacts, after all, may be no greater than the likelihood that a seven will appear when you roll two dice. In light of the substantial uncertainty involved, we do not have the luxury of assuming that the most probable outcome will actually come about. The gambler certainly wants to know what happens when a seven is rolled, but he also needs to know what happens if some other number comes up.

Despite the desire to know about all possibilities, I have chosen to look at just one of the potential outcomes, because doing so helps to make my message clearer. It means that you do not have to try to keep track of a whole range of possibilities as you read this book. In addition, focusing on just one scenario allows me to discuss the coming challenges in more depth, something that is necessary to get a sense of how human lives will be affected.

The question, then, is what degree of climatic change I should focus on. If I assume a relatively large change, I risk exaggerating the effects of climate change. The book would be a cautionary tale but would not describe the most likely set of events. If I assume too modest a change in the climate, I will be understating the likely harms and providing an overly, and perhaps naively, optimistic picture of what the future holds. You might think that the best thing to do would be to pick the most likely outcome. This presents two problems. First, although it is the most likely, that prediction is also quite likely to be wrong—just as predicting a seven on the roll of two dice is likely to be wrong. More important, nobody knows just what the most likely outcome is.

With all of that in mind, I have chosen to focus on an outcome that is within the range of likely outcomes based on current predictions but that lies near the bottom of that range. The book will operate on the assumption that we can expect an increase in temperature of 2° C by the end of this century. This is a very conservative choice, as I explain more fully in chapter 2. I opted for a fairly low estimate for a couple of reasons. First, as I already mentioned, my goal with this book is to convey the seriousness of what climate change will do to humanity. It turns out that even if we make a fairly optimistic assumption about how the climate will change, the effects will still be enormous—certainly large enough for me to make my point. Second, one of the things I most want to avoid is making an overly pessimistic assumption about the climate. Doing so would undermine the force of the book. I do not want to discuss future events that are merely possible. I want to discuss events that are likely. Assuming a rise in average temperatures of 2° C allows me to do so.

Even with a conservative assumption about how the climate will change, there is, of course, some chance that the actual outcome will be something less. It is possible that the fates will smile upon us and things will turn out to be better than I have assumed. I certainly hope that is the case. Not only that, but I will be the first to admit that when we think about how to respond, we have to take into account both good and bad outcomes. Let's return to the example of rolling two dice. Assuming an increase in temperatures of 2° C is a little like investigating what will happen if we roll a six. A six is possible, but lots of higher outcomes (analogous to larger changes in temperature) are also possible. Some lower outcomes are also possible, but they are less likely. The chances of rolling a six or higher are about 72 percent, so by choosing a number a little less than the most likely, it is possible to capture most of the possible outcomes.

By making a conservative prediction, then, I have rigged the game against myself. The outcomes I describe are less severe than what I think is most likely. As the rest of the book shows, however, they are still enormous. Choosing an increase of 2° C does not, of course, eliminate the uncertainty surrounding climate change. It is still possible that we will see less than 2° C of warming. It would be a mistake, however, to take much comfort from this fact. In addition to my intentional choice of a modest temperature increase over the next century, there are two reasons it would be foolish simply to hope for a bit of unlikely good fortune without taking action in response to the more likely and more frightening alternative outcomes.

First, our experience to date has been that the scientific community has consistently underestimated the speed of climate change. In 2008, for example, climate-change expert Nicholas Stern stated that emissions "are growing much faster than we'd thought, the absorptive capacity of the planet is less than we'd thought, the risks of greenhouse gases are potentially bigger than more cautious estimates, and the speed of climate change seems to be faster."[2] A different study found that "carbon-cycle feedbacks could significantly accelerate climate change over the twenty-first century."[3] Although past performance does not guarantee future results, as financial advisers say, one cannot help but get the sense that scientists are playing catch-up in the climate-change game. Humanity has never witnessed such rapid changes to our climate, so there is no precedent to guide science. Add to this the fact that the climate is a staggeringly complex system with a seemingly endless number of influences all interacting with one another. To give just one simple example, because clouds can both trap heat and reflect sunlight back into space, they cause warming of the planet in some circumstances but cooling in others. Furthermore, we do not understand how clouds form and dissipate. You can see how difficult it is to incorporate this one variable into climate models. Overall, I think it is amazing that science has done as well as it has in coming to grips with the problem. Nevertheless, I cannot help thinking that there remain so many forces pushing us toward a warmer world that we may still be underestimating what is coming.

Second (and more important), the climate-change cost curve is, as economists put it, convex. In plain English, this means that costs rise more quickly as the earth warms. So if a temperature increase of 1° C causes a certain amount of harm, an increase of 2° C will cause more than twice as much harm—perhaps a lot more than twice as much. This is important because, even if we conclude that, for example, we can manage not only an increase of 1° C, but harm that is twice as much, it does not necessarily follow that we can handle an increase of 2° C. The latter may be much more than twice as bad.

There are a lot of instances in everyday life in which we encounter costs that rise at an ever-increasing pace. Anyone who runs, swims, cycles, or participates in any other type of exercise with an endurance component has experienced this situation. Suppose you go for a jog. As long as you do not choose too fast a pace, running is initially almost effortless. After a time, however, you start to feel some strain. It is no longer quite so easy, but it is still possible to maintain your pace. As you keep running, the effort you have to exert increases. The first ten minutes is easier than the second ten minutes, which is easier than the third ten minutes, and so on. Unless you are an experienced distance runner (even for these runners, the same holds true, but it may take longer for them to wear down), it will eventually become almost impossible to maintain your pace for yet another ten minutes. And even if you succeed, the ten minutes after that will be harder still. At some point, you will simply have to slow down; your body will be incapable of continuing at your pace. If you keep running, even this slower pace will become too difficult. Eventually, you will have to stop; another ten minutes will simply not be possible. One can describe the effort required to continue running as a convex cost curve: as you run, it gets harder and harder to continue.

Figure 1.1 illustrates how the impact of climate change rises at an accelerating pace as temperatures increase. Suppose, for example, that the expected increase in temperature is 2° C. As indicated in the figure, this corresponds to a certain level of impacts. These include impacts on the economy, health, national security, agriculture, and more. If the warming we actually experience is somewhat less than anticipated—if it is 1.5° C instead of 2° C—you can see that the corresponding impacts are reduced. If, on the other hand, climate change is more severe than expected and the change in temperature is 2.5° C, the impacts are greater. The key thing to notice is that the difference between the impacts felt at 1.5° C and at 2° C is much smaller than the difference between 2° C and 2.5° C.

Because the harm from climate change increases at an accelerating rate as temperature changes, the difference between what is predicted and what actually happens is much bigger if we underestimate climate change than if we overestimate it. Even a small underestimation of the changes coming to our climate might cause us to overlook enormous impacts. It is better to face the reality now that these terrible events might come to pass, while we still have a chance to do something to avoid them, than to seek the false comfort that comes from ignoring them, only to realize in the future that they have become inevitable.

In Al Gore's famous 2006 movie, *An Inconvenient Truth*, the former vice president used the familiar metaphor of boiling a frog to describe the crisis of climate change. The story, which you have likely heard many times applied in many instances, goes like this: If a frog is placed in a pot of cold water that

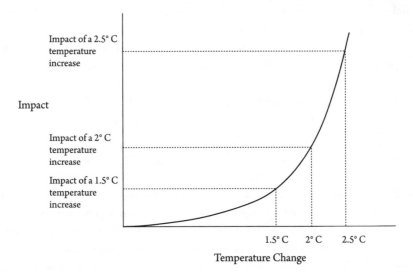

Figure 1.1 Impacts accelerate as temperature increases.

is then gradually brought to a boil, the frog stays put. The temperature of the water increases so slowly that the frog is unaware of the impending danger, whereas a sudden change in temperature would have prompted the frog to jump out of the pot. By failing to react, the frog is boiled to death (although in Gore's more humane version, the frog is rescued before it is harmed).[4]

Although a frog placed in water that is slowly heated apparently will, in fact, jump out (I have never tried it, but that is what I am told), the use of the metaphor is now so widespread that it has a life of its own, quite apart from what an actual frog would do in an actual pot. It is a wonderfully apt metaphor for climate change for the obvious reason that in both the metaphor and the real world, things are getting hotter, and in both the metaphor and the real world, the heating might go unnoticed until it is too late. The boiled-frog analogy is effective to make the point that if we wait too long to act, we will not be able to prevent a variety of harms, including higher sea levels, increased storm activity, drought, conflicts over environmental resources, and so on. In fact, the metaphor works so well that it has become a familiar part of climate-change discussions.[5]

When I think of climate change, however, I think of a different metaphor. As a child, I played a game called *KerPlunk!* A generation later, my children played it, too. The game consists of a clear plastic tube with thin sticks, like pick-up sticks, pushed through holes in the sides of the tube so that they stick out on both sides. When all of the sticks are put in, they form a kind of platform. Marbles are then dropped in from the top of the tube and rest on the sticks. Once the sticks and the marbles are in place, the game begins. During your turn, you must remove one stick. If any marbles fall when you remove a stick on your turn, you keep them. Once all of the marbles have fallen, the winner is the player who has collected the fewest.

At the start of a game of *KerPlunk!* things are easy. You can pull out just about any stick and be confident that no marbles will fall. Before long, however, you have to pay attention and select the stick you are pulling out with care. Even at this point, however, an examination of the position of the sticks usually allows you to pull one out without collecting even a single marble. As the game proceeds to the stage in which no player can avoid collecting some marbles, the stakes remain relatively low for a few turns. There are a lot of marbles in the game, and a few marbles are unlikely to make a difference in the final outcome. As long as the sticks still create some sort of serviceable platform, even if the platform has small gaps, there is no cause for panic. The game gets more serious as more sticks are pulled out and the platform erodes. This happens slowly at first, but things get progressively worse with the removal of each stick. Eventually, somebody pulls out a stick and a whole bunch of marbles—sometimes all that remain—come tumbling down. The loss of that one stick causes a collapse.

Figure 1.2 KerPlunk!

Sometimes it is clear that the next stick to be removed will cause an avalanche of marbles. At other times, it seems as if a stick can be removed safely, but this turns out to be an illusion as the marbles cascade down.

The dynamic of climate change resembles that of the game of *KerPlunk!* Think of the marbles in *KerPlunk!* as representing the harm caused by climate change and the removal of the sticks as representing the continued emission of greenhouse gases (GHGs) into the atmosphere. When one first thinks about a warming world, it seems as if there is nothing to worry about. Just as we can remove some sticks early in the game of *KerPlunk!* without much concern, adding GHGs initially seems harmless. Even if we add enough to cause a change in the concentration of GHGs in the atmosphere, the impact on the climate initially seems so small that it is easy to ignore. The planet was at this stage toward the start of the Industrial Revolution, when greenhouse gases started being released in dramatically higher quantities. Indeed, we were also at this stage fifty years ago, at which time we had not yet experienced much of an increase in temperatures. By that point, human activity had raised the level of GHGs in the atmosphere, but without much consequence for the climate or the way we lived our lives. Even if we had fully understood the impact of sending GHGs into the atmosphere, the imperceptible effects on temperature and precipitation would not have seemed worth worrying about.

By the late 1970s and into the 1980s, the situation was changing. By this time, GHGs had accumulated enough to start warming the planet. The changes were small and hard to measure, and their cause (or even their existence) was controversial. Our limited understanding of the climate system and how we were affecting it made it difficult to consider whether to restrain GHG emissions. Even if we had understood the rise in temperature, the changes might not have been large enough to cause much concern.

Like the few marbles that fall in the middle of a game of *KerPlunk!,* the small temperature changes that were taking place were perhaps not ideal but did not cry out for a dramatic response. While we would have preferred, for example, not to contribute to damaging weather events such as hurricanes, the world ran, as it continues to do today, on fossil fuels and other sources of GHGs, and it would have been both difficult and expensive to change our ways. It was better to let a few *KerPlunk!* marbles fall than to undertake large-scale changes in how we lived.

More recently, however, it has become clear, and seems to become more so with each passing year, that the later stages in this global game of *KerPlunk!* are either fast approaching or already upon us. We have added enough GHGs to the atmosphere that the situation is now very much like the stage of a game of *KerPlunk!* at which many sticks have already been removed. We are already able to identify marbles that have fallen. Sea levels are higher, temperatures have risen, and the frequency of storms has increased. Glaciers are disappearing from mountains, and the ice in the Arctic is melting. The twelve hottest years on earth from 1880 to 2011 have been (not in this order): 1998, 2001, 2002, 2003, 2004, 2005, 2006, 2007, 2008, 2009, 2010, 2011. I bet you can see a pattern.[6] There has also been a toll in human suffering. The best estimate we have puts the death toll from climate change at 300,000 per year, with an even larger number of people made worse off in small or large ways.[7]

As we continue to emit GHGs, more sticks from this game of *KerPlunk!* will be removed, and more marbles will fall. By 2030, it is expected that 500,000 people will die each year as a result of climate change, and 660 million people could be negatively affected.[8] This represents a dramatic acceleration of the harms caused by global warming. The marbles are starting to fall more quickly.

Even these estimates assume a certain "continuity" in the system; they assume that a small change in the factors that affect the system will *not* lead to an abrupt change in the magnitude of their effect. But in the game of *KerPlunk!* the marbles do not always fall at a continuous rate. There comes a point at which the removal of one more stick will cause an avalanche of marbles. If the game is indeed a good metaphor for our climate, it is this reality that should frighten us most. At what point will a further increase in GHGs (the removal of one more stick) trigger a sudden increase in harm (the avalanche of marbles)? The truth is that we simply do not know. We know that the harms will increase more quickly as temperatures rise, which is bad enough. We do not know if we are heading toward a sort of "tipping point" where there will be a very sudden and dramatic increase in consequences. We do not know, for example, what the risk is that the melting of the permafrost in the Arctic will release GHGs sufficient to cause further warming, melt more permafrost, and release more GHGs—creating a vicious cycle that will accelerate warming.

We also do not know how humans will respond to the stresses of climate change. Existing estimates of the impact of climate change, including the one mentioned above indicating that 500,000 people per year might die as a result of climate change by 2030, assume that human and natural systems will continue to work more or less as they do now. On the contrary, there are many ways in which those systems could break down, leading to much greater harms. The already fragile coexistence of nations in the Middle East could collapse as states in the region compete for limited and shrinking water resources. Agricultural production is likely to be slashed by drought or the melting of mountain glaciers whose summer runoff is currently used to irrigate crops. Rising seas will flood major population centers and displace millions. As these things happen and as other threats materialize, the death rate from climate change will shoot up in much the same way the marbles in *KerPlunk!* fall down when the wrong stick is removed.

With so much uncertainty, it is essential to return to what we do know. We have reasonable estimates of how much temperatures will increase in the future, for example. My assumption of 2° C may not seem like very much, but as I discuss throughout this book, such an increase will cause immense damage. If we are unlucky and the change is larger, however, the damage will be much greater.

We also know something about where we are. There is no doubt that we are at the stage in the game where marbles have started to fall, and we have already begun to feel the consequences of climate change. Worse still, we are finding it difficult to stop playing or even to slow the game down. As we continue to emit GHGs, we are still pulling sticks out of the game. Humans emit GHGs with virtually everything we do, making dramatic reductions in emissions an enormous challenge. Even with global recognition of the fact that a reduction in emissions is imperative, the trend is in the opposite direction: humans are sending more GHGs into the atmosphere each year. To date, neither domestic nor international efforts have done much to reduce emissions. If we fail to slow the rate at which GHGs are released into the atmosphere, we will continue to pull sticks from the game, and the pace at which marbles fall will continue to increase.

We face a real risk of the collapse of human institutions that we take for granted—agricultural systems, water-distribution systems, health-care systems, national borders, and international peace, to name a few. This would have seemed impossible just a few decades ago, but if we do not react properly to climate change, it is a genuine possibility. This fact has become clearer as the concentration of GHGs in the atmosphere has increased. Once a certain number of sticks are removed in *KerPlunk!* players can see that the platform of sticks is eroding badly and will soon fail. In a similar way, we have seen the early signs of how climate change will affect us, and it is not encouraging. If we continue to pull out sticks, sooner or later (and there is mounting evidence that it will be sooner), we will see marbles falling much more quickly. Unfortunately, in our game of global *KerPlunk!* instead of paying the price in falling marbles, we will see human lives cut short or upended and entire ways of life lost. Not only that, but just as the removal of a few key sticks can transform what was once a platform into a few stray sticks, unable to support more than a few leftover marbles, we may find that climate change threatens to dismantle the physical and social structures that form the platforms of our society. If we do not find a way to reduce the rate of GHG emissions, we may find our very way of life transformed.

This book explains how that might happen and why it might happen faster than many people realize. It considers the potential impact of climate change and asks how important aspects of the lives of billions of people who share the planet might be affected.

We are so used to the way our systems and institutions work that we forget that they have not always been there. In my own state of California, for example, we recognize that there are droughts and water issues, but we do not often consider that if our children want to live in California as adults, there may no longer be enough water to support them. By this, I mean that there may not be enough even if the population does not grow. Future population growth will make the challenge much greater.

In other parts of the world, the problems are sometimes easier to grasp. For many small island nations (e.g., Tuvalu, the Maldives), climate change may cause the entire country to disappear beneath the waves. In other places, rising seas will flood large tracts of land, displace people, and interfere with existing infrastructure. In Bangladesh, for example, it is likely that millions will be displaced from their homes, very possibly creating the largest humanitarian crisis the world has ever faced. With nowhere else to go, they will no doubt try to move to already overcrowded cities. Some will try to leave the country in search of a better existence, creating international tensions. Makeshift camps may crop up to house some of these displaced persons, creating a permanent class of people living on the edge of subsistence. Rising seas will also interfere with food production, making it difficult for some nations to feed themselves.

Even in rich nations such as the United States, the infrastructure is not in place to deal with seas that are a meter or more higher than today.

The food problem created by rising seas will be exacerbated by other changes. Billions of people around the world rely on mountain glaciers to serve as massive water-storage facilities. Rain that falls in the mountains freezes to form glaciers. In the summer, some of this stored water melts, and the runoff is used to grow crops and support human existence. When these mountain glaciers melt—as they are already doing—there will be no natural storage system. When rain falls, it will immediately run down the mountains, creating flooding during the rainy season and drought during the dry season. Existing irrigation and agricultural systems that rely on the runoff from glaciers will not work properly, and agricultural yields will fall—in some places catastrophically. While water-storage issues create crises in some parts of the world, the simple absence of water will be the problem elsewhere. A changing climate means changing patterns of precipitation, and some parts of the world will experience much less rainfall in the future. This is a problem because human beings have come to rely on existing patterns. Population centers have been built up based on where water is available. When drought and other disruptions of water availability come to pass, the best we can hope for is an expensive adaptation process, and the worst is a major crisis.

Unfortunately, the impact of climate change will not be limited to natural systems. Humans are constantly interacting with one another, and changes in our environment have an effect on those interactions. There is already a major effort under way within American national-security circles to consider how climate change will affect the security and interests of the country. The main concern is that climate change creates additional tensions among and within countries. Where tensions already exist within or between countries, climate change may tip the relationship into violence. We have already seen this in Darfur, where existing tensions were managed in a peaceful way until a drought tipped the situation into violence and, ultimately, genocide. It does not require an overly active imagination to see that strains in other areas—including the Middle East, the India-Pakistan region, and various parts of Africa—could descend into war and violence.

Although there is a lot we cannot say for sure about climate change, one of the effects that can be predicted is a worsening of human health. It is virtually certain that more people will get sick at a younger age, although there is no way to know precisely how bad the impact will be. Health may also be affected in a different and more frightening way. Climate change will generate conditions that are ideal for the spread of contagious disease. Experts can testify that they are always concerned about the potential for a large-scale outbreak of a deadly disease. If we decided we wanted to trigger such an outbreak, we could hardly do better than what climate change promises. A combination of rising seas, higher temperatures, changing precipitation patterns, and lack of access to water will displace enormous numbers of people. These people will find their way to already crowded cities or perhaps be housed in refugee camps. In either case, very large numbers of people will live in cramped and unsanitary spaces without proper infrastructure such as sewage systems or access to clean water. They will live in precisely the conditions that are suitable to the outbreak and spread of disease. The combination of a lack of proper prevention strategies, a shortage of medical care, and the frequent movement of people from one place to another (from camps to cities, from one camp to another, from country to country) will make it easy for disease to travel and find new victims.

The first step to understanding the threat of climate change is adjusting your mind to appreciate the meaning of an increase in global average temperatures of 2° C, 4° C, or 6° C. Although I now live in Oakland, California, I grew up in Ottawa, the capital of Canada. Compared with where I live now and, indeed, compared with most places, Ottawa has "real" weather. Winters are colder and summers are hotter than in Oakland. The average high temperature in July is a little more than 26° C (79° F), and the average low in January is –15° C (5° F). The record high is 38° C (100° F), and the record low is –36° C (–33° F). In the context of these extreme temperature swings, a change of two or even four degrees can seem like a trifle. After all, if people can happily go about their lives in places where the temperature can change by more than 40° C over the course of a year, why would a global increase of a few degrees matter?

This misconception is understandable. A few degrees certainly does not seem like much. Most people in the world experience larger shifts than that from morning to afternoon in their daily lives. And in many parts of the country, the local weather will vary by more than 2° C from one place to another. This is true in the San Francisco Bay Area, where there are bizarre microclimates. Places within thirty minutes of each other by car might differ in temperature by 10° C (18° F) or more. When I first moved to Oakland, there was more than one warm summer day when I hopped into my car and took the twenty-minute drive into San Francisco without realizing that, while shorts and a T-shirt suited the weather in Oakland, I needed, and had failed to bring, long pants and a jacket for San Francisco. Our everyday experiences with changes in the weather shape how we think of changes in temperature and make a global shift of a few degrees seem trivial.

The problem is that we are used to thinking in terms of weather, the day-to-day variation in temperature or precipitation. Climate is something different. A particular climate will experience changes in weather from day to day, and both humans and nature are able to adapt to these changes. But a change in the climate itself affects us much more. Humans, human systems, and natural systems are much less able to adapt to climatic changes, at least when they happen quickly enough. What sound like small changes to the climate can turn out to have enormous consequences.

For example, the difference in average temperature from the last ice age to now is about 5° C.[9] If an average decrease of 5° C means the difference between the world we live in today and an ice age, it is suddenly much easier to believe that an increase in average temperatures of 5° C could lead to dramatic changes, including the melting of mountain glaciers, rising sea levels, and so on.

In reality, we don't need a temperature increase anywhere near 5° C to trigger major changes. Looking farther back, into prehistory now, an increase in average global temperatures of 2° C would make the earth as warm as it was 3 million years ago. This seemingly modest difference in temperature is enough to explain why sea levels were about 25 meters higher at that time than they are today.

This disconnect between our intuition and the reality of global temperature changes comes about in part because the changes we are talking about are *averages*. If the average temperature goes up by 2° C or 3° C, the temperatures that we experience may vary by considerably more. Our instincts about climatic change are also misleading because the world is much more sensitive to changes in climate than our everyday experiences suggest. Even before the invention of many of the technologies that make our lives comfortable today, humans were able to live in many different climates around the world, giving the impression that small changes in climate do not cause problems. Summer temperatures in Port Sudan, Sudan, for example, reach into the mid-to-high 40s C, with an average in the summer of 41° C (106° F). In contrast, winter temperatures in Yakutsk, Russia, are below –30° C (–22° F) from December to February, and it is not unusual for temperatures to fall below –40° C (–40° F). These two places have wildly different climates, yet humans are able to live in both.

Contrary to our instincts, however, a change of just a few degrees can have a major impact on a number of critical systems on our planet. These include, for example, the level of the oceans, when and where water is available for humans to use, and the types of flora and fauna that exist. Nor is it only temperature that is at stake when GHGs cause changes to the climate. Precipitation patterns also change, posing challenges to all manner of human activity, from agriculture to energy to human health. Even the small changes we have already seen have been fatal for many species. Just one example is that "at least 70 species of frogs, mostly mountain-dwellers that had nowhere to go to escape the creeping heat, have gone extinct because of climate change. . . . Between 100 and 200 other cold-dependent animal species, such as penguins and polar bears, are in deep trouble."[10]

The reality is that even modest changes to the climate can have major impacts on our lives and our world. Because of this, climate change threatens the very fabric of our global system. It has the potential to cause loss of prosperity, calamity, and dramatic suffering on a scale humanity has never seen.

Before moving on to the heart of this book, I need to comment on the continuing debates about whether climate change is real and whether it is the result of human action. I have more to say about this in the next chapter, but I must acknowledge the question here. If one listens to the popular media, it often seems as if there are two important and opposing views about climate change. The first is that the earth is warming and is doing so as a result of human activity. The second, often portrayed as a minority scientific view, is that climate change is not a serious threat.

These opposing views frame and dominate many books and articles on the subject and often frame the way the media present the issue. Believers in climate change argue that there is a widespread consensus among scientists to support their view, and they lobby for one form of government action or another. Skeptics claim that the consensus among scientists is more illusory than real and that we are in the grip of climate-change hysteria.

Presenting the issue of climate change in this way is misleading. It is simply not the case that climate-change debates feature two comparable groups, each with its own strong arguments. Those of us who are persuaded that the threat from climate change is real do not simply differ from deniers in our view of the science involved. Many of us, myself included, find it difficult even to believe that anyone is persuaded by the arguments of skeptics. The skeptics flit back and forth between claims that the scientific community agrees with their position and complaints that science itself cannot possibly give us answers. They claim to want a sober and rational debate but then refuse to engage, in a serious way, the mountains of evidence that climate scientists have provided (some of which is presented in chapter 2). When one examines the arguments of deniers, they turn out to be little more than a mix of conspiracy theories, misrepresentations of the science, and unfounded assertions.

Although I believe that climate-change deniers are dangerous and undermine efforts to undertake a serious discussion about how to respond to climate change, my objective is not to engage in a debate with this group. I firmly believe that climate change is real. Indeed, I am among those who believe that a good-faith examination of the evidence cannot lead to any other conclusion. I will spend some time (mostly in chapter 2) laying out the reasons for my views and the reasons scientists are about as unanimous on this question as they ever are on any issue. Chapter 2 also explains why the arguments of deniers are so deeply flawed. But I am under no illusion that the contents of that chapter will convert any true climate-change skeptics.

Although our understanding of climate change seems to be growing by the day, the most important evidence is well known. As far as I am concerned, we are well past the point where there is serious doubt about whether humans are causing the globe to heat up. I do not deny that the arguments of skeptics must be challenged to prove that they are misleading and without scientific basis so that critical policy decisions can be made without the confusion created by deniers. For this reason, I applaud those who take on these skeptics in public and who fight to make discussions of climate change as transparent and honest as possible.

As important as it is to explain the science of climate change and to convince the public and political leaders of the reality of this threat, it is equally important to examine what will happen if our response is inadequate. We cannot let deniers hijack this most important debate. At some point, we have to ignore the unfounded claims of skeptics and turn to the evidence so that we can understand, as well as possible, what the consequences of inaction are likely to be. This book does that, explaining in clear and straightforward language what we need to worry about as we make decisions on climate policy, both domestically and internationally.

Although I do not intend to get bogged down in a skirmish with climate-change deniers over their all-too-successful attempts to manufacture controversy, I cannot ignore the real uncertainty that exists in our understanding of global warming. The fact that the earth is warming is clear, but there remains substantial uncertainty with respect to many important questions: the rate at which humans will continue to put GHGs into the atmosphere, the precise way in which the climate will respond to those GHGs, how natural systems will respond to a changing climate, how human institutions and practices will respond, and how all of these changes will affect the well-being of humans. Despite this uncertainty, we have to do our best to look forward so that we can decide what to do today.

Predictions about the future are essential, yet getting such predictions right is almost impossible. As Mark Twain once said, "The art of prophecy is very difficult, especially about the future." Fortunately, the problem is not quite so serious if you remember the earlier discussion about predicting what number will come up when you roll two dice. It is impossible to predict what the dice will do on a given roll, but we have a good sense of what is likely. It is in that spirit that this book considers the potential impacts of climate change.

I do not and cannot claim that all of the events I describe here are inevitable. I do not aspire to that level of precision. Throughout the book, I try to be clear about which events are virtually certain (e.g., the loss of some low-lying island states to rising seas, an increase in extreme weather events, major challenges for agricultural systems that rely on mountain glaciers for water storage, increased security threats, and more); those that are likely if climate change is as bad as (or worse than) what most experts predict (e.g., major population displacements, dramatic food shortages, deadly heat waves); and those that might be caused by climate change and would be so terrible that we need to keep them in mind even if they may not happen (e.g., worldwide spread of a deadly disease, extreme increases in sea level).

The fact that I cannot avoid the uncertainty associated with climate change makes it impossible for me to anticipate precisely what we have to look forward to. I am not the only one who has to deal with this uncertainty, however. Policy makers who have the power to decide how we respond to climate change face the same problem, as do the voters who put those policy makers into positions of power. We have no choice but to make decisions in the face of this uncertainty.

To decide what to do in the face of uncertainty, however, we have to know what might happen. This book presents a picture of what is likely to be waiting for us in the warmer world that we are creating.

A Message from Climate Scientists

*"The debate on the authenticity of global warming and the role played by
human activity is largely nonexistent among those who understand the
nuances and scientific basis of long-term climate processes."*
— Peter T. Doran and Maggie Kendall Zimmerman,
"Examining the Scientific Consensus on Climate Change"[1]

If you feel that the subject of climate change continues to provoke an apparently endless debate, you are not alone. Sometimes there is so much contradictory and angry dialogue that it is difficult to understand the key issues and evaluate how much evidence there is on each side. Most of us are fed up with over-the-top rhetoric that seems to be more about scoring points than getting to the facts. This reality makes the entire issue unnecessarily hard to understand and makes trying to learn about it frustrating and off-putting. You should not need a Ph.D. to understand the basics of climate change, and learning about the relevant issues should not require that you wade through a never-ending stream of information. Furthermore, deciding what you think about the issue should not be a political act of either loyalty or betrayal. Climate change is an important public-policy issue, but it is one that can be talked about calmly and sensibly. Doing so, however, requires some understanding of what we know, including the relevant scientific information.

This chapter is written for those who are interested in climate change (if you are reading this book, you qualify) but who are not specialists in it. You can think of it as a simple tour of what we know about climate change. The idea is to help us understand the fundamental scientific forces at work and what they are doing. I have not tried to include everything we know, because the goal is to keep the discussion as straightforward as possible. On the other hand, I believe that I have included the key information you need and that, after reading the chapter, you will have an accurate and practical sense of the science of climate change and how scientists view the problem.

The chapter has five parts. In the first part, I explain the remarkable degree of consensus that exists in the scientific community. If you pay only casual attention to climate-change reports and stories, it is easy to get the impression that the scientific world is in the midst of a battle about whether climate change is happening and how humans are contributing to that change. In fact, there is almost no disagreement among climate scientists that it is happening and that humans have contributed to it. This is important to understand, because it puts a different light on the debate. Those who deny climate change are asserting that virtually the entire scientific community has gotten it wrong. Deniers, then, must explain how the observed facts lead them to a contrary view and why so very few scientists agree with them. Despite a broad consensus within the scientific community, the general public remains much more skeptical about climate change. The first section of the chapter also addresses the public discussions of climate change and how I think those should be viewed.

The second part of the chapter explains what we know about past climatic changes and considers what might happen in the future. I use the projections of climate scientists to get a sense of what the climate might look like decades from now.

The third part presents the science that explains why the world is warming. Basically, as human activity emits increasing amounts of greenhouse gases (GHGs), the concentration of those gases in the atmosphere increases. GHGs reduce the amount of energy that escapes into space, so adding more of them to the atmosphere leads to more energy in the earth's system, causing temperatures to rise.

In the fourth part of the chapter, I address the most common arguments of climate-change skeptics. As I said in chapter 1, I think it is important to avoid getting bogged down in a battle with skeptics. The science on the subject is compelling, and the skeptics' arguments have been addressed many times over. The consensus among climate scientists illustrates that when people look carefully at the relevant science, the reality of climate change is clear. Nevertheless, I want to spend a little time addressing the claims made by skeptics for two reasons. First, it is helpful to get a sense of why skeptics continue to advance their claims and why they have refused to be convinced by the existing evidence. Second, I want to present the most common claims made by skeptics so that you can understand the weaknesses of the claims and the ways in which those claims have been disproved.

In the last part of the chapter, I explain why even someone who is skeptical about climate change should support efforts to address the issue.

I. As Much Consensus as a Political Issue Can Get

Climate change can be a polarizing political topic, especially in the United States. Many of those who speak about it have a political ax to grind, and it can be hard to know what to believe. Climate change remains part of the culture wars in the United States. To believe that human behavior is causing warming is to betray one side of the political divide, and to reject that notion is to betray the other.

To pick an admittedly extreme example, Melanie Phillips, a columnist at Britain's *Daily Mail*, wrote in 2006: "The theory that global warming is all the fault of mankind is a massive scam based on flawed computer modeling, bad science and an anti-western ideology.... The majority of well-meaning opinion in the Western world believes a pack of lies and propaganda."[2] Similarly, Steven Milloy, a Fox News commentator, described the very idea of fighting climate change as "an attack on our standard of living."[3] These comments raise the stakes: apparently, we are not simply trying to decide if the climate is changing, but we are also deciding whether to be "anti-western," to believe "a pack of lies," and to join an "attack on our standard of living."

Those who believe that man-made climate change is a serious problem have not been immune to using extreme rhetoric. Al Gore, for example, has said, "The people who dispute the international consensus on global warming are in the same category now with the people who think the moon landing was staged on a movie lot in Arizona."[4] Others make Gore's comments seem downright charitable. The United Nations special climate envoy, Gro Harlem Brundtland, declared in 2007 that "it's completely immoral, even, to question...whether we need to move forward at a much stronger pace as humankind to address the issues."[5] Not to be outdone, the executive secretary of the Framework Convention on Climate Change, Yvo de Boer, stated that it would be "criminally irresponsible" to ignore the urgency of climate change.[6] Here again, a scientific and policy issue is suddenly something about which we cannot even ask questions without invoking immorality and criminal irresponsibility.

The political drama surrounding climate change has also leaked into the media and general public discussions. If you pay attention to discussions of climate change in the media, it is easy to get the impression that there is a significant and widespread debate on the question of whether climate change is actually happening and, if it is happening, whether it is the result of human activity. However, if you listen to these debates carefully, and especially if you investigate them on your own, it soon becomes clear that "believers" in climate change make their case by trying to point to the science that is involved, while "deniers" spend much more time criticizing the views of believers. It is difficult to find denials that involve their own scientific investigation and analysis.

The debate takes this form because the scientific evidence for man-made climate change is overwhelming. It is so overwhelming that believers continue to point to it as if to say, "Look, here it is, clear scientific evidence that we are right. What else do you need before you believe us?" Because the science is fairly clear, deniers retreat to a rhetorical strategy of poking holes in the believ-ers' claims. This is essentially the same tactic used to resist the scientific evi-dence that tobacco and asbestos are dangerous. Science works because people ask hard questions. They challenge one another's findings and take nothing for granted. That is all good and terribly important. But it is equally important not to ignore where the evidence points. The evidence on climate change points clearly and consistently in the direction of a hotter future.

Although climate-change deniers do not believe that the world is heating up (or do not believe that it is heating up very much), they do agree that the issue is ultimately a scientific question. It is not something that can be determined by political ideology, economic interests, popular opinion, or, as comedian Stephen Colbert would say, "gut." It is either a scientific fact that the earth is warming, or it is a scientific fact that it is not. This point of agreement—how-ever limited—is a good place to start the conversation.

If you had some indication that there was a problem with your car's trans-mission, you would take it to a mechanic. You would hope that nothing was wrong, but it would be a bad idea simply to rely on that hope. You might even have a friend who, despite a lack of automotive expertise, opines that the trans-mission is fine. Even so, you would want to hear from a mechanic, because he is an expert on this question. If the mechanic gave you bad news, explaining that in his opinion the transmission would give out within the next thousand miles, you would be wise to take that opinion seriously. Of course, if you had doubts about the ability or the honesty of the mechanic, you might seek a second opin-ion before spending the money to fix the transmission. If a second mechanic said the same thing, you would be pretty sure that you had a problem. If a third, and then a fourth, also agreed, you would presumably accept that your trans-mission was shot. If you had hundreds, or even thousands, of mechanics all agree that you had a problem, though perhaps disagreeing on the question of whether you had five hundred, one thousand, or two thousand miles left before the transmission failed, it would seem self-evident that you should accept the fact that your transmission was in trouble. If your friend continued to insist that there was no problem, you would be wise to dismiss or at least discount his opinion, since he does not know anything about cars. You would also not let your own hopes about the transmission override the information you were getting from these many mechanics.

For the same reason you would ask a mechanic about your car, we should seek out experts to tell us what is happening to our climate. These experts are climate scientists.

Before examining what scientists say, I want to acknowledge that climate scientists disagree on many issues. This is what scientists do—they debate the available evidence. Through this process, they reach more reliable conclusions. Just because they disagree on some things, however, does not mean that they disagree on everything. There are areas of strong agreement among scientists, and when that is the case, we are wise to listen to them, much as you would be wise to listen to what mechanics believe about your car. Investigating what scientists believe can be difficult, because each individual researcher has his or her own views. Fortunately, we are interested in a relatively simple question that allows us to get a good sense of what the community of scientists believes. We want to know if the earth is warming and, if so, if humans are causing it to do so.

Despite the many uncertainties and disagreements about the climate and climate change, we have a very clear answer to this question. There is no longer any serious doubt that the earth is, indeed, getting warmer and that human activity is a major contributor. These are facts that scientists know. When I say that scientists know that man-made climate change is real, I mean it in the same way that we say scientists know that cigarettes and asbestos cause cancer. I mean that there is no serious dispute within the community of climate scientists.[7] These are questions that were once the subject of scientific debate but are now settled.

The best way to get a sense of what scientists believe is to look at scientific writings. The currency of science is the publication of research in peer-reviewed journals, where scientists evaluate submissions and select the best ones for publication. These journals are where scientists tell the world about their research and their discoveries. They are the gold standard of scientific inquiry.

In 2004, Naomi Oreskes from the University of California, San Diego, went looking for climate-change skepticism in the American scientific community. She was unable to find any. She examined more than nine hundred scientific articles about climate change published in peer-reviewed journals between 1992 and 2003. Of these, exactly zero disputed the notion that climate change was real and was caused by humans.[8]

This is a stunning result, especially when contrasted with the public debate about climate change. The peer-review system of publication, used by all academic disciplines, ensures that only the highest-quality work gets published. It is also a system that encourages debate, because a researcher can become famous by successfully challenging or debunking a well-established theory. If the claim that the earth is warming as a result of human activity were full of holes, there would be a rush of scientists eager to make the opposite case. That is how careers are made in the academic world. What Oreskes found, however, is a complete lack of disagreement on this most fundamental point. Unanimity of this sort is just about the best evidence one can imagine in support of the notion that humans are causing a change in the world's climate.

Oreskes also found that "all major scientific bodies in the United States whose members' expertise bears directly on the matter have issued...statements" concurring with the message that humans are causing the earth to warm.[9]

A more recent study, released in 2010, examined the work of 1,372 climate researchers and found that about 97 percent of those most actively publishing in the field believed that human activity was causing climate change.[10] This survey does not quite allow us to say that literally every climate researcher believes that man-made climate change is happening, but it comes awfully close. The old television commercial for sugarless chewing gum used to say that four out of five dentists recommend sugarless gum. Well, it turns out that climate scientists share a much stronger agreement on climate change than dentists do about sugarless gum. There are far more dentists (at least according to the commercial) who recommend gum with sugar than there are climate scientists who doubt climate change.

When we add up the scientific evidence, then, it is hard to imagine a clearer signal coming from the scientific community. The relevant scientific bodies all agree that climate change is real and is man-made, the peer-reviewed scientific literature has fully accepted the same conclusion, and virtually all climate scientists agree. Whatever debate exists outside the scientific community, the scientists themselves are in agreement.

You might think that if the scientists agree that human activity is contributing to climate change, everyone else would believe them. This might be how it should work—who better to judge the scientific question than scientists trained to do so? But that is not the world we live in. In his book *Denialism*, Michael Specter reminds us that the general public, or at least significant portions of it, often refuses to believe what science has shown to be true. The expertise of scientists and researchers is sometimes dismissed in favor of views and opinions that have no basis in science and/or can be shown to be false.

The lack of faith in science is aggravated by the fact that scientists are not always good at explaining science to the public. When the conversation turns to "emissions models," "radiative characteristics," or "thermohaline circulation," many of us tune out. Even when the problem is presented clearly, the reality of climate change is not uplifting. A genuine crisis is looming, and sometimes it is easier to avoid focusing on bad news. All of us, after all, have plenty to do in our everyday lives as we study for school, work for a promotion, struggle to take care of our kids, worry about paying bills, and so on. The last thing we want is something else to fret about—especially a problem as big as changes to the earth's climate that no single person, or even a group of people, can solve.

Any serious response to climate change will inevitably cost money and will involve a reduction in GHG emissions. It is hardly surprising, then, that people and businesses that stand to lose as a result of sensible climate-change policies will look for ways to delay action as long as possible. Gore makes this point with a quote from Upton Sinclair that has become almost a mantra of advocates for stronger climate-change policies: "It is difficult to get a man to understand something when his job depends on him not understanding it."

In short, there are many powerful economic and political forces that have an interest in denying climate change's existence, regardless of what the evidence says. Prominent members of this camp are the oil, coal, and auto industries, all of which stand to lose if governments get serious about addressing climate change. Money has poured into systematic campaigns aimed at promoting the views of skeptics. Despite the absence of scientific support, these groups have put out the message that climate change is not happening, is not caused by humans, is not a threat, is not worth fighting, or all of these things. This has been a fantastically successful effort, as it has prevented the public from recognizing the deep agreement among climate scientists.

All of the above reasons explain why skeptics have had an influence on the climate-change debate within the general public that is far greater than the influence they have had in the scientific community.

The disconnect between scientific and popular opinion creates a challenge for this book, and for any book on climate change. I want to emphasize that the science of climate change is clear, but to do so in a comprehensive way would take up so much space that there would be no room left to discuss the human impacts of global warming. Fortunately, there have already been several careful efforts to present what we know on the subject and to debunk the skeptics' arguments. These other books and articles persuasively demonstrate that climate change is, indeed, real, man-made, and threatening.[11]

I will not, therefore, review the debate about the existence of climate change in full detail. I will not chase down every skeptic's claim about why the science and scientists are wrong or why the evidence is imperfect. And I will not try to respond to all of the assertions of deniers or the conspiracy theories used to explain why virtually all top scientists are convinced that our world is warming. Instead, I try to present the key scientific evidence we have in an accessible and even-handed way.

It is also worth noting that while the public debate has nothing like the consensus that can be found in the scientific community, skepticism does not run nearly as deep as it sometimes seems. Although skeptics are often given a voice in the media, for example, the usual stance of major media outlets is to accept that humans are causing climate change. The *Economist* magazine, hardly a bastion of left-leaning thinking, put climate change on its cover in March 2010. The treatment focused on the ambiguities in the science, but it treated the question of whether humans have caused the planet to warm as a settled one. In fact, it went even further, recommending serious action to combat the threat.

The *Economist* is a British publication. What about American media on the right of the political spectrum, where doubts about climate change tend to be more common? Here, too, editorial views are clear: climate change is happening, and it is man-made. To be sure, the media cover the claims of skeptics. For example, not too long ago, the *Wall Street Journal* published an op-ed piece by well-known climate-change skeptic Patrick Michaels, in which he questioned the science of climate change along with the character of climate-change scientists[12]—but the newspaper itself recognizes that the world is warming. Such examples illustrate that while it is easy to find people with some doubts about whether the world is warming, those doubts are not credible enough or common enough to be reflected in most major media outlets (Fox News being a possible exception). Although the media understandably focus on areas of disagreement, we should not lose sight of the fact that here, too, there tends to be an acceptance of the idea that humans are causing the planet to warm.

How does all of this reflect itself in the attitudes of the general public? While there are certainly people with doubts about climate change, there is less serious skepticism among the public than it may seem. In 2009, a Gallup poll found that 41 percent of Americans polled felt that the seriousness of global warming was exaggerated in the news. Fifty-seven percent thought the news got it about right or underestimated the danger. So by this measure, about two in every five Americans could be counted as skeptical. But we should be careful in interpreting polls. This is not skepticism about the fact that the world is warming. Rather, it is skepticism about the seriousness of the issue. Many people believe that human activity is, indeed, causing the earth to warm but are not convinced that a small increase in temperature is something to worry about. That group is also included in the above 41 percent.

In the first chapter of this book, I discussed why an increase of a couple of degrees seems so modest. The most important message of this book is that, in fact, a change of that magnitude will have devastating impacts. I do not expect to convince hard-core climate-change deniers who refuse to accept the clear scientific evidence. I do not think any evidence would convince them. I do hope to demonstrate how catastrophic a warming of a couple of degrees would be. I want to speak both to those who recognize the threat we face and those who accept the science but wonder why two degrees is so dangerous. Many of those people are among the 41 percent who say the news overstates the danger. My hope is that when someone in that group reads this book, he or she will be convinced that the problem really is deadly serious.

Turning from popular opinion to the opinions of politicians, views on climate change have been unstable recently. The science of climate change has not undergone a revolution in the last few years, but there has nevertheless been a great increase in the voice of climate-change deniers among national political figures. At the time of the 2008 presidential election, both major political parties in the United States had come to the conclusion that climate change was happening. Of the two parties, there is no doubt that the Democratic Party has historically been less skeptical about climate change than has the Republican Party. Indeed, it is easy to get the impression that the Republican Party does not believe climate change is happening at all. This impression, however, is wrong—or at least, it was wrong in 2008. Just the opposite was true at the time. If one judges from their official party platforms, the Republicans and the Democrats had both come to the conclusion that human activity was causing our planet to warm.

During the 2008 presidential campaign, Senator John McCain, the Republican candidate, was on the record as believing that climate change was indeed man-made. Within his party, McCain was hardly alone. The official party platform stated:

> The same human economic activity that has brought freedom and opportunity to billions has also increased the amount of carbon in the atmosphere. While the scope and long-term consequences of this are the subject of ongoing scientific research, common sense dictates that the United States should take measured and reasonable steps today to reduce any impact on the environment. Those steps, if consistent with our global competitiveness, will also be good for our national security, our energy independence, and our economy. Any policies should be global in nature, based on sound science and technology, and should not harm the economy.
>
> As part of a global climate change strategy, Republicans support technology-driven, market-based solutions that will decrease emissions, reduce excess greenhouse gases in the atmosphere, increase energy efficiency, mitigate the impact of climate change where it occurs, and maximize any ancillary benefits climate change might offer for the economy.[13]

Although it is couched in economic rather than environmental terms, this language accepts the reality of man-made climate change.

Party platforms are political documents rather than scientific ones. They are intended to attract voters during an election campaign. This means they are a good place to get a sense of what each party and its supporters believe. They can be viewed as a sort of political weathervane. My point here is that in 2008, the Republican Party's platform stated that climate change posed a real threat (though perhaps not a serious enough one to justify actions that come with significant economic costs). So while there were still voices that disputed the very existence of climate change, including the voices of some politicians, both political parties could be counted as believers.[14]

Just a few years later, things have changed. Deniers in Congress have been more outspoken of late, and Republican politicians appear much more hesitant to acknowledge publicly the reality of climate change. To be sure, there have always been doubters in Congress. In 2003, for example, Senator James Inhofe from Oklahoma, another prominent skeptic, stated that "the claim that global warming is caused by man-made emissions is simply untrue and not based on sound science.... With all of the hysteria, all of the fear, all of the phony science, could it be that man-made global warming is the greatest hoax ever perpetrated on the American people? It sure sounds like it."[15] Speaking on the floor of the U.S. Senate on March 15, 2010, he confirmed that the ever-mounting evidence demonstrating that the climate is changing has not altered his view. In fact, he uttered almost exactly the same words (though with apparently a little more confidence): "The notion that anthropogenic gases are causing global warming is the greatest hoax ever perpetrated on the American people."[16]

The apparent increase in the number of skeptics in Washington may be the inevitable result of an economy in recession; nobody wants to talk about long-term problems that may cost money when the economy is on the skids. Whatever the reason, both individual politicians and congressional hearings have featured strong statements by deniers. On March 25, 2009, for instance, during hearings on climate change before the House Subcommittee on Energy and the Environment, Lord Christopher Monckton, a prominent climate-change skeptic with no scientific training, testified that the planet was "carbon starved" and answered in the affirmative when asked by Representative John Shimkus, "If we decrease the use of carbon dioxide, are we not taking away plant food from the atmosphere?...We could be doing the opposite of what the people who want to save the world are saying." Even if one were skeptical of climate change, there is absolutely no evidence that reducing emissions of carbon dioxide would be harmful because it would be "taking away plant food."[17] The exchange had no pretense of trying to bring serious science to bear on policy making. It is an embarrassing indictment of our decision-making process that this sort of political posturing, without a shred of scientific foundation, is carried out at the highest levels of government.

On June 26, 2009, during debate on a climate-change bill in the House of Representatives, Representative Paul Broun from Georgia stated that "climate change is nothing but a 'hoax' that has been perpetrated out of the scientific community."[18] These statements demonstrate either a willingness to make claims that the speakers know to be false or a wildly exaggerated sense of the scientific community's capacity to perpetrate a "hoax." Strangely, while Inhofe argues that the scientific community has perpetrated a hoax, he simultaneously claims that hundreds of scientists "challenged man-made global warming claims."[19] Surely, deniers must choose between the claim that scientists should be listened to and the claim that they are part of a vast conspiracy.

II. Two Degrees Too Much

Whatever the politicians or experts say, the best way to appreciate that climate change is real might be simply to observe some of the dramatic changes that are happening in the world. For example, all over the globe, ice is melting as it has not done in hundreds, thousands, or even hundreds of thousands of years. Arctic sea ice has lost nearly half its average summer thickness since 1950, and by 2050, it may fully melt for the first time in more than a million years. Montana's Glacier National Park expects to lose its glaciers by 2030. Growing seasons have lengthened in many parts of the Northern Hemisphere. The ranges of birds, insects, and other animals are moving farther north. In the Canadian Arctic, for example, birds that had not previously been present have arrived.

Seas are rising before our eyes. In 1983, for instance, the British government built a set of floodgates on the Thames to protect London from ocean-storm surges. The expectation at the time was that the gates would have to be closed once or twice each year. From the late 1990s to 2010, however, the gates had to be closed ten times per year on average. Even if the gates are used more often, rising seas are expected to reduce the protection they offer by 50 percent by 2030.[20] Furthermore, the decade from 2000 to 2010 was the hottest ever recorded. The years 2005 and 2010 tied for the warmest on record.[21] What is in third place? Take your pick from several years that were all about the same: 1998, 2002, 2003, 2006, 2007, and 2009.[22] The next four hottest years were (from hottest to coolest) 2004, 2001, 2011, and 2008. The records against which we are comparing these temperatures go back to 1880. So in the last 130 years, the hottest twelve years have all been within the last fifteen years, and *every* year from 2001 to 2011 is on the list. Another indication of this same warming trend is the fact that world average temperatures have found a new "normal." In each of the last thirty-four years, the average global temperature has been higher than the twentieth-century average. The most recent news as I write this is that the first half of 2012 was the hottest ever in the United States (at least since record keeping began in 1895) and more than a full degree Celsius hotter than the twentieth-century average.

As far as science is able to discern, this increase in temperatures is continuing. Since 1880, average global surface temperatures have increased by about 0.9° C. The last three decades have accounted for 0.6° C of this increase.[23] At the current rate, without any further acceleration, temperatures would rise by an additional two degrees over the next hundred years. That would be bad enough, but unfortunately there is every reason to expect temperatures to rise faster, reflecting the constantly increasing rate at which humans are sending GHGs into the atmosphere.

These are not matters of politics or opinion or conjecture; they are observable facts. All over the world, we can see signs that the earth is warming in a way it has not done since before the dawn of man. This warming is going on whether or not we acknowledge it.

Recognizing, first, that the earth is warming and, second, that we are causing it to warm is important, but it is hardly the whole story. We want to know lots more, including how fast the planet is changing, how long it will continue to do so, and what is causing it to happen. As we move beyond the simple question of whether the climate is changing to more subtle questions about exactly how or why, we have to confront more uncertainty and more areas in which the science is still being worked out. This is why it is so essential to get past the question of whether humans are causing climate change. We know the answer to that question is yes. Continuing to argue about it distracts us from dealing with those issues that are still uncertain and from deciding what to do about it all.

The good news here is that there is a single place to look for most of the key answers or, more accurately, the range of possible answers. The place for this one-stop shopping is known as the Intergovernmental Panel on Climate Change (IPCC). The IPCC was established in 1988 by the United Nations Environmental Program and the World Meteorological Organization. Its mission is to study and report on the climate-change problem.

The IPCC has proven to be an enormously important organization. It has made it possible to gather scientific work on climate change from around the world, and it brings together literally thousands of scientists to examine and comment on one another's work. The IPCC is a clearinghouse where the ideas and beliefs of scientists can be shared and discussed. The organization does not control the work of scientists, but it tries to synthesize the research into a coherent view.

Among the IPCC's activities, the most important for our purposes is the publication of its periodic "Assessment Reports." These are intended to give an up-to-date picture of what is known about changes to the climate. Since 1990, four Assessment Reports have been completed, and a fifth one is in progress. More than eight hundred authors and review editors are working on the project,[24] and a rigorous review process makes sure that governmental and expert concerns and comments are addressed.[25] The IPCC aims to be "comprehensive, objective, open and transparent."[26] Thus, the selection of authors is carefully regulated to ensure the most balanced report. Authors can nominate themselves for consideration and can be nominated by their governments or certain environmental organizations.[27]

Once selected, each author or reviewer is given specific responsibilities and is assigned a certain section. The authors report to the lead authors of their sections,[28] so no one person monopolizes all of the material in the report. It is the most comprehensive and representative report on climate change.

The most recent report is the "Fourth Assessment Report" (FAR), issued in 2007. It reflects the scientific consensus on the question of whether humans are causing climate change by saying that "[m]ost of the observed increase in global average temperatures since the mid-20th century is very likely due to the observed increase in anthropogenic greenhouse gas concentrations."[29] The words "very likely" are used by the IPCC to mean that the likelihood is judged to be greater than 90 percent. This is confirmation of the scientific consensus that I have already discussed.

The report contains a lot of other important information, of course. We can start with the most obvious: information on how temperatures have changed in the past. Looking at past temperatures allows us to observe the warming of our planet directly.

The easiest way to see how temperatures have changed is with a simple graph. The climate changes very slowly, so the graph has to reflect temperatures over a long period of time. The problem is determining how far back to go. If you do not look far enough back in time, you may be fooled by normal year-to-year fluctuations that make it difficult to see the longer trends. You may observe temperatures warming, for example, just because we are coming out of a short-term cooling period, or you may fail to see warming because we are entering a cooling period. The same problem exists when you look at the movement of stock prices. Even if the prices are trending upward, if you look over a short period of time, you might happen to see a period in which the prices fell. On the other hand, if you go too far back, you lose details about the most recent years. Looking at stock prices over many decades gives the impression that short-term movements are smaller than they actually are. If you are interested in recent changes (say, over the last decade), looking back over a century is not very useful.

The obvious solution, and the one I will use here, is to look at several different time periods. In the end, whatever time period you use, the message is the same: temperatures are rising at an unprecedented pace.

We are interested in the question of how much the earth has warmed as a result of human activity. It is the release of GHGs by humans that causes this warming. For most of human history, we have not released enough GHGs into the atmosphere to affect the climate in important ways. That changed with the Industrial Revolution, which started a process of ever-escalating emissions. Temperatures started rising around the same time. But before we look at the last century and a half, let's go back farther with one of the most controversial pieces of information in the entire climate-change debate: the hockey-stick graph.

This graph has it all: a dramatic message, a great name, and controversy about its creation. The original hockey-stick graph was produced by Michael Mann in 1998. Since then, a large number of similar studies have been done. The version presented here (figure 2.1) is from a 2004 article by P. D. Jones and M. E. Mann.

The hockey-stick graph presented here shows average temperatures in the Northern Hemisphere from the year 200 to the year 2000, relative to the average temperature from 1961 to 1990. The solid line shows estimated fifty-year average temperatures, which makes the long-term trends much easier to see. The shaded region, on the other hand, shows the statistical range of plausible values (known as the 95-percent confidence interval). The line and the range feature similar upward movement toward the very end of the time period.

It is a dramatic picture. Temperatures are mostly flat for the first 1,700 years. They then start to climb rapidly. The change is so sharp and rapid that the graph resembles a hockey stick—a long, flat shaft and then the upward movement of the blade. It shows clearly that temperatures in the Northern Hemisphere

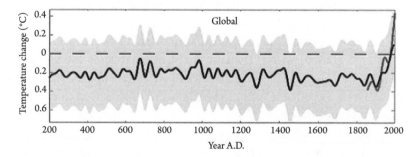

Figure 2.1 The hockey stick. Source: P. D. Jones and M. E. Mann, "Climate over Past Millennia," *Review of Geophysics* 42 (2004).

went up dramatically toward the end of the millennium. Perhaps because it is so compelling, the hockey-stick graph has been heavily scrutinized. In fact, the hockey stick is one of the major pieces of evidence that deniers sometimes advance to make the claim that climate science has it all wrong (or, worse, that the evidence of climate change is manufactured).

The bottom line, however, is that all of the scientific attention devoted to the hockey stick and temperatures over the relevant period has confirmed the basics of the graph over and over again. In order to avoid getting distracted by what is really a manufactured and artificial "debate" about the hockey stick, I have put off a more detailed discussion until I address the arguments of deniers later in this chapter. Overall, the hockey-stick graph has it basically right, and this fact has been shown in numerous studies.

The key message is that temperatures today are higher than at any point in the last 2,000 years. This is in part because temperatures rose more during the twentieth century than they had in any century going back 2,000 years.[30] Things have not gotten any better recently: over the last twenty-five years, temperatures have risen faster than during any similar period over the last 10,000 years.[31]

The long view is dramatic and alarming. Looking to a more recent period— say, the last 130 years—delivers a similar message. Since 1880, temperatures have risen by about 0.9° C.[32] Worse still, they have been rising at a faster pace. Since the early 1980s, the temperature has been rising at about 0.18° C per decade. That may not sound like much, but it means that even without any further increase in the pace of warming, temperatures would rise as much over the next 50 years as they have in the last 130. If we also take into account the fact that these changes continue to accelerate, still larger temperature increases are looming.

Among the points to be taken from temperature records is that it is simply a fact that the earth is warming and that it is doing so rapidly. The measurements are reliable and cannot be refuted. While past trends do not always continue into the future, if this one does, we face serious problems. This is another example of facts that point to serious climate-change concerns that cannot easily be dismissed by deniers. One strategy has been to claim that the temperature measurements are simply wrong, but this has been shown (over and over) to be untrue. Another approach for skeptics is to claim that the increase in temperatures will not continue. The problem here is that they have no explanation for what is causing the rise in temperatures (since they refuse to accept that GHG emissions are responsible). If they cannot explain why temperatures are going up, they cannot give any reason to think that they will stop doing so. Finally, some skeptics claim that this is simply a natural process of temperature fluctuation. Even if this were true, we should still be very worried about such large changes in the climate. Whatever the cause, the rise in temperature is changing the world around us in important and danger-ous ways.

Once the fact of rising temperatures is acknowledged, several other critical questions come up. How fast will the earth warm in the coming years? What is causing the warming? What will be the consequences? Because the climate is an incredibly complex system and because there are still many things we do not understand about that system, the answers to some of these questions are not as precise as we would like.

Part of the problem is that there is so much information available that relates in some way to how we can expect the climate to change in the future. So many people are talking about climate change that it is hard to know whom to focus on. One reason for this cacophony of voices is that there is no single "truth" to the question of what is going to happen. Different climate projections reach different results because they make different assumptions about the climate system or about how humans will behave in the future. Furthermore, each of the projections is more accurately described as a range of possible outcomes and a statement about how likely those outcomes are. The best we can hope for is to get a sense of what possibilities are likely.

The place to start, once again, is the IPCC and its 2007 Fourth Assessment Report. That report predicts that there will be an increase in global average tem-perature of between 1.1° C and 6.4° C by the end of this century.[33] Obviously, this is a very wide range. An increase in temperature of a little more than 1° C would be harmful, but an increase of more than 6° C by 2100 would be noth-ing short of apocalyptic. To get a sense of how terrible a swing of 6° C would be, recall from chapter 1 that a difference of just 5° C is about the same as the difference in temperature between the last ice age and the present. As far as I know, nobody disputes the notion that a rise of 6° C would be an unmitigated disaster for the planet and all of its inhabitants.

The IPCC estimates cover such a large range because they have to deal with two distinct sources of uncertainty. The first is uncertainty about the science and the climate. For any given increase in GHGs, for example, how much will temperatures rise, and how fast? We do not have precise answers to these sorts of questions, and so we have to work with estimates. The second source of uncertainty is not scientific, but human. What happens in the future depends on what humans do in the future. Since we do not know how humanity will behave over the next hundred years, we cannot predict exactly how the climate will respond.

To deal with both types of uncertainty, the IPCC produced six distinct esti-mates of future climatic outcomes. Each was based on a set of assumptions about what would happen in society. These assumptions were about things such as population growth, economic growth, technological change, and so on. Basically, the various estimates went from very optimistic to very pessimistic assumptions about how things would change during the century. Each of these six estimates led to a possible range of outcomes, which reflected the scientific uncertainty. For example, the two middle estimates had ranges from 1.4° C to 3.8° C and from 1.7° C to 4.4° C.

All of this leads to six different estimates, each of which has a range. The range from 1.1° C to 6.4° C mentioned above represents the lowest and highest points of those ranges. This creates a lot of numbers to worry about—too many, perhaps, to give us a feel for the situation. You can see that even the briefest inquiry into future global average temperatures has tossed up a blizzard of estimates and assumptions. It would take a good part of a book to explore each of the estimates in detail, and that is without even starting to talk about regional variations in outcomes, aspects of climate other than temperature (e.g., precipitation patterns), or "tipping points" that might create a terrible spiral of higher temperatures. All of this also helps to explain why talking about climate can be difficult. By varying the assumptions we make about future human activity and about how the climate responds to that activity, we can generate many different predictions. Fighting about different predictions can become a sport.

I very much want to avoid getting lost in this world of alternative predictions. To that end, I have picked a single, conservative estimate of how much temperature will change, and I use that estimate throughout this book. Doing so allows me to talk about how climate change will affect people without constantly worrying about a laundry list of alternative climatic scenarios. I have chosen 2° C because that estimate is toward the bottom of the range. The IPCC estimates suggest that we will avoid an increase of 2° C only if everything goes just right—population does not grow too fast, the global economy becomes more service-oriented and less production-oriented (leading to lower emissions), economic growth is not too high, and we benefit from rapid technological shifts that allow us to use alternative energy sources. Climate change will have a sufficiently large impact that even with a temperature increase of only 2° C, changes to the world will be frightening. As you continue reading, keep in mind that I am probably underestimating future warming and that the resulting damage grows very quickly if temperatures rise above an increase of 2° C.

It is possible that in assuming an increase of 2° C, I am dramatically underestimating what the future has in store for us. There is evidence, for example, that a doubling of CO_2 above preindustrial levels—something we are well on our way to achieving—is likely to produce a temperature increase of between 4.5° C and 6.0° C.[34]

So I feel very comfortable saying that unless we are incredibly lucky *and* we move incredibly fast, we are almost certain to see temperatures rise by more than 2° C by the end of this century. I already mentioned that from 1981 to 2005, temperatures increased at about 0.18° C per decade. Even without any acceleration, this would generate an increase of 1.8° C over a century. But we know that the pace of change is accelerating. Just by looking at past trends, then, it is clear that an estimate of two degrees is quite conservative. There are strong signs that the actual increase will be larger.

Before moving on, let me offer one more piece of evidence that an increase of 2° C is likely. I reached the 2° C figure by choosing something close to the bottom of the range identified by the IPCC. In the spring of 2009, a team of climate experts met in Copenhagen to discuss the climate-change problem.[35] Many of these experts had contributed to the IPCC FAR. The report that emerged from the conference states that "greenhouse gas emissions and many aspects of the climate are changing near the upper boundary of the IPCC range of projections…or, as in the case of sea level rise, at even greater rates than indicated by IPCC projections."[36] In other words, the IPCC projections that I have been discussing are more likely to have underestimated the danger than to have overestimated it. This makes my choice of a figure near the bottom of the IPCC range even less likely to overstate and more likely to understate the problem.

Is it possible that we could see temperature increases of less than two degrees during this century? Of course it is. I cannot say with absolute certainty that temperatures will rise by more than 2° C. I am, however, comfortable saying that the chances of rising by 2° C or more are much greater than the chances of not doing so. To stay below that threshold would require an incredible streak of good luck, and even that might not be enough. No bank would make a loan to a business if the path to profitability required a similar streak of extreme good fortune. No employer would hire an applicant whose likelihood of success was so low. Nobody would bet on a horse whose prospects for winning were so faint.

III. Why Is It Getting Warmer?

When thinking about climate change, it is helpful to understand the central forces behind the warming of the world. It turns out that the basic reason that the earth is getting hotter is not so very complicated.

We all know from (sometimes painful) experience that the balance in a bank account can go up, or it can go down. If you earn more than you spend, the balance goes up. If you earn less than you spend, the balance goes down.

The earth's energy can be thought of in much the same way. At any moment, there is a certain amount of energy in the system. This is like the balance in your bank account. If the earth takes in more energy from the sun than it loses to space, the total amount of energy in the system rises, just as your balance rises if you earn more than you spend. If the planet takes in less energy than it loses, the amount of energy falls. This is sometimes referred to as the earth's "energy budget." The total amount of energy in the system determines the average global temperature. More energy means higher temperatures.

The earth's atmosphere has a critical influence on how much energy is kept in the system; it controls how much of the energy is returned to space. Without the atmosphere, the planet's energy budget would look like your bank account if an irresponsible relative was constantly making withdrawals. Your account would see large swings from when money is deposited to when it is all withdrawn, and the average balance would be very low (maybe negative if the bank allows the account to be overdrawn). Without the atmosphere, temperatures on earth would swing wildly from day to night, and the global average temperature would be below freezing.

The atmosphere affects the energy balance much the way taking away your relative's access to your bank account affects your balance. By trapping some of the energy the planet gets from the sun, the atmosphere increases the average temperature on the planet and reduces the daily temperature swings.

Like your bank account, the earth's energy budget takes into account both inflows and outflows. In the case of the energy budget, we are interested in inflows and outflows of energy rather than money. The sun is the key source of energy for the planet; it provides the "income" side of the budget. The outflow side of the budget consists of energy that escapes into space. About 30 percent of solar energy is reflected by clouds, by the ground, and by the atmosphere itself. This 30 percent is a little like taxes on your income: the energy reaches the planet but is almost immediately lost to space, just as taxes take a percentage of your income. The remaining 70 percent represents an addition to the earth's energy budget and is absorbed by land, water, and the atmosphere.[37] You can think of this as corresponding to a monthly paycheck deposited into your bank account. Whether your balance goes up or down depends both on how large this deposit is and on how much you spend. For the planet, the impact on the energy budget depends on how much energy is radiated into space. If more is lost than is received, there is less energy in the system. If less is lost than what is received, there is more energy in the system. The simplest way to think of it is in terms of what it takes to keep the energy in balance. As long as the earth takes in the same amount of energy as it loses, the total energy in the system remains the same, and temperatures remain stable.

In the early 1800s, the energy budget was in balance; the planet was neither heating nor cooling in any significant way. Since that time, humans have upset the energy budget by adding GHGs to the atmosphere. As I describe below, more GHGs in the atmosphere means that less energy escapes the earth. The energy that the earth loses to space mostly takes the form of infrared radiation. GHGs absorb some of this energy and radiate it back to the earth. More GHGs means more of that radiation is returned to the earth, and less escapes. Less escaping energy affects the energy balance just as less spending would affect your bank account. Over the last century and a half, humans have been emitting more and more GHGs. This has caused the atmosphere to retain more energy, and the earth has warmed.

Adding GHGs to the atmosphere is like reducing the rate at which you withdraw money from your bank account: more energy is retained, and the temperature goes up. So there are three steps in our understanding of climate change: (1) humans cause the emission of more GHGs; (2) the concentration of GHGs in the atmosphere increases; (3) the GHGs in the atmosphere cause the earth to retain more energy, so temperatures go up.

We have already discussed the last of these steps, how temperatures have increased over the last century and a half. It is easy to see that the other steps are also consistent with the reality during that period. There is no doubt that GHG emissions have risen, and it would be remarkable for anyone to claim otherwise. The dramatic increase in use of fossil fuels provides the most obvious example of humans sending much more of these gases into the atmosphere.

The next question is whether the GHGs have been collecting in the atmosphere. If for some reason the higher emissions have not translated into higher atmospheric concentrations, then the emissions cannot be causing the planet to warm. Here again, the answer is clear: concentrations of GHGs have risen steadily since the Industrial Revolution.

Four greenhouse gases are relevant to climate-change conversations: carbon dioxide (CO_2), methane (CH_4), nitrous oxide (N_2O), and halocarbons. Water vapor also makes an important contribution to keeping the planet warm. In fact, about 60 percent of the warmth provided by GHGs is attributable to water vapor. Discussions of climate change focus on other GHGs, and on carbon dioxide in particular, because human activity is driving up the concentration of those gases so dramatically. Water vapor has a big impact on the earth's average temperature, but its role in how that temperature is changing takes the form of a harmful feedback effect, which I will address below.

Returning to the analogy of a bank-account balance, water vapor affects the energy-budget balance the way a fixed-rate mortgage might affect a bank balance. Having a mortgage with monthly payments has a dramatic effect on the outflows each month. But mortgage payments do not change from month to month. If the balance in the bank account changes because of an increase in spending on vacations, we need to examine the vacation spending to understand what is going on. For the energy budget, water vapor affects the outflow of energy, but it is the changes in other GHGs that have caused the climate to change.

By far the most important anthropogenic GHG when it comes to changes in the planet's temperature is carbon dioxide. Carbon dioxide exists in the atmosphere in larger concentrations and contributes more to the earth's warming than the other anthropogenic GHGs.[38] Air bubbles trapped in ice for hundreds or even thousands of years have allowed scientists to determine the CO_2 levels in the very distant past. This in turn allows us to compare concentration levels throughout history. In 1750, the concentration of CO_2 in the atmosphere was about 290 ppm (parts per million). Today, the level is 387 ppm and going up by 2 ppm each year.[39] With each passing decade, the change accelerates. Even after taking into account natural year-to-year fluctuations of CO_2 that are unrelated to human activity (e.g., El Niño years tend to cause a spike in CO_2 levels), the trend is easy to see. Carbon dioxide concentrations were increasing by about 0.9 ppm per year in 1960, 1.3 ppm in 1980, 1.8 ppm in 2000, and 2.0 ppm in 2010.[40] That number continues to rise, and the IPCC projects that without some change in behavior, CO_2 levels will be between 730 and 1,020 ppm by 2100.[41]

To put these numbers into perspective, we can compare them with historical levels. Natural changes in the concentration of GHGs take place over very long periods—thousands of years or more. The changes the earth is experiencing now are both much larger and much faster than any natural changes. The level of GHGs today is higher than at any point in at least 650,000 years and is currently rising more than fifty times as fast as what would be caused by natural fluctuations.

We now have all of the ingredients to understand the relationship between human activity and our warming planet. The earth gets energy from the sun, and the temperature on the earth depends on how much of that energy is absorbed into the earth's system and how much is radiated back into space. More retained energy means a warmer planet. When humans send GHGs into the atmosphere, their increased concentration causes the earth to retain more energy. This has a direct effect on temperature because more energy means more heat. This warming causes some additional feedback effects. Most important, it causes more water to evaporate from lakes and oceans, increasing the water vapor in the atmosphere and roughly doubling the amount of warming (because water vapor is a key greenhouse gas).

During the last 150 years, the concentration of GHGs in the atmosphere has risen dramatically. Far from coming to an end, the trend seems to be accelerating. More GHGs means more energy is trapped in the earth's system, and this means more warming. As long as we continue to increase the concentration of GHGs, we can expect the planet to continue to get warmer. Our understanding of the planet lines up extremely well with the data that have been collected on GHG concentrations and temperature. Overall, the message is that everything we know about climate science and the earth's climate going back hundreds of years (or more) indicates that human behavior is changing our climate.

The last aspect of science that I want to discuss is the movement of carbon within the earth's system. Because carbon is so critical to the issue of climate change, it is useful to have a sense of how it migrates from the atmosphere to the earth and to the oceans. The flow of carbon within the system is known as the "carbon cycle."

There is a fixed amount of carbon on the earth. Humans neither destroy nor create it. All we do is change where it is. If there is more carbon in the atmosphere, there must be less somewhere else. If we want to reduce the amount in the atmosphere, it has to go somewhere else.

One way to view the climate-change problem is that as a result of human activity, more carbon is in the atmosphere, and less is elsewhere. Before the Industrial Revolution, there was about 560 billion metric tons of carbon in the atmosphere. Today there is about 730 billion metric tons, an increase of 30 percent. An easy illustration of why this increase has taken place is the burning of oil. When we burn oil, the carbon in the oil is released into the atmosphere. As you can imagine, humans have burned a lot of oil in the last 150 years and have released a lot of carbon. Looking forward, unless there is some sudden shift to other energy sources, we will continue to burn oil and continue to add carbon to the atmosphere.

Burning oil is not the only way we send carbon into the atmosphere. Virtually every human activity contributes to the problem. In addition to the burning of fuels, we release carbon stored in marine sediment when we use the rocks in that sediment to make cement. Deforestation is a huge cause of emissions because trees are important storehouses of carbon. When a tree is cut down and the wood decays, is burned, or is processed, much of the carbon stored in the trees escapes to the atmosphere. Emissions from airplanes, though a small proportion of total anthropogenic emissions, are thought to have a disproportionate impact because the emissions are released at high altitudes.[42]

Although we cannot live on this planet without adding carbon to the atmosphere, we can influence how much is released by changing our behavior. Changing the fuels we use, the amount of energy we consume, the rate at which we cut down trees, and much more allows us to change the speed at which humans add carbon to the atmosphere. To keep the concentration of carbon at any given level requires that it be removed from the atmosphere at the same rate as it is added. Reducing the rate at which we add carbon obviously helps to achieve this balance.

The other side of the carbon balance is the rate at which carbon is removed from the atmosphere. Natural processes remove some. For instance, when plants photosynthesize, they remove atmospheric CO_2 and convert it to sugar, so plants and algae are huge players in the reduction of atmospheric carbon levels. Oceans also absorb large amounts of CO_2 from the atmosphere.[43] Carbon is stored in biomass (e.g., animals), the earth itself, and sedimentary carbonate rock.[44] Just as humans can influence the rate at which carbon is released, we can also affect the rate at which it is removed from the atmosphere. The most obvious way to do this is by changing the number of trees on the planet. There are two bad effects when we burn trees. First, burning the trees releases the carbon that they store, as mentioned above. Second, killing a tree prevents it from continuing the process of absorbing carbon from the air.

As carbon moves about the earth's system—and more specifically in and out of the atmosphere—the climate is affected. Humans could not live without the greenhouse effect generated by GHGs, but we are also threatened if that effect gets too powerful. We need from our climate the same thing Goldilocks needed from the porridge she ate at the three bears' house. In that fairly tale, Goldilocks came upon the bears' house and found three bowls of porridge on the table. She was hungry and tasted from the papa bear's bowl, finding it too hot to eat. She then tasted from the mama bear's bowl but found the porridge too cold. When she tried the baby bear's porridge, however, it was just right, and she ate the entire bowl. Too little GHGs will make our world too cold. Too much will make it too hot. If the level of GHGs is just right, however, we (along with other forms of life) can thrive.

As a result of the increased concentration of GHGs in the atmosphere, our planet is in the process of moving from "just right" to "too hot." Some warming has already occurred, and more is on the way. The changing climate will have all sorts of impacts on humans, animals, and plants. Temperatures will increase, precipitation patterns will change, sea levels will rise, and more. The rest of this book examines some of these impacts.

One wonderful visual metaphor for this process is referred to as the "carbon bathtub." *National Geographic* magazine popularized this idea in December 2009; it originally belongs to John Sterman, a professor at MIT, and Linda Booth Sweeney.[45] Each year, a certain amount of CO_2 and other GHGs is released into the atmosphere. We can think of these emissions as water flowing from a faucet into a bathtub. If carbon never left the atmosphere, we would be constantly increasing its concentration, just as the level of water in the bathtub would rise if the drain was closed. In fact, a little more than half of the carbon we release each year does leave the atmosphere as it is absorbed by plants, soil, and the oceans. The problem is that carbon leaves the atmosphere more slowly than it enters. We put a little more than 9 billion metric tons of carbon into the atmosphere each year, but only about 5 billion metric tons is removed from the system. If you poured nine gallons of water into a tub each minute and drained five gallons from the same tub, the water level would obviously rise at a rate of four gallons per minute. In a similar way, the carbon in the atmosphere increases at about 4 billion metric tons per year. As water accumulates in the tub, the water level increases. As carbon accumulates in the atmosphere, the concentration of carbon increases. In preindustrial times, the carbon level was 271 ppm. Today it is 387 ppm. As long as carbon is released into the atmosphere faster than it is removed, the concentration level will continue to increase, just as a bathtub continues to fill as long as the water flows in faster than it drains out.

A concentration of 387 ppm causes the earth to retain more energy than it would at its earlier level of 271 ppm. The extra energy causes the earth to be warmer. The warming process takes time, so even if we turned off all fuel-burning machines on earth, the climate would likely warm an additional 0.5° C or more. If instead we reduced our emissions enough to remain at current concentration levels (387 ppm), then we would experience warming beyond that 0.5° C. In other words, even if we reduced our carbon output from 9 billion tons to 5 billion tons, we would still face a warming world. This is why some scientists have taken the view that we have to reduce our emissions even further. They believe that 387 ppm is too high, that the resulting warming will be too devastating, and that we must aim for a concentration level of 350 ppm.

Given that we are at well more than 350 ppm already and that our emissions continue to increase, getting down to 350 ppm is no small task. Nevertheless, 350 ppm has become the focus of a movement seeking to make that the target for policy makers around the world: "350 is the most important number in the world—it's what scientists say is the safe upper limit for carbon dioxide in the atmosphere."[46] If this view is correct (and it may well be), we have already pushed carbon concentration above what is safe. As that concentration rises, all of the associated harms—biodiversity loss, dissolving coral reefs, rising sea levels, water stresses—will grow even larger.[47] To get to 350 ppm would require a major reorientation of our way of life.

What does the future hold? Obviously, that depends on how humanity behaves. So far, there is little evidence that we are curbing our behavior. In fact, just the opposite seems to be true: the rate at which we are putting carbon into the atmosphere is increasing over time rather than decreasing. In the 1990s, an average of 3.2 billion tons of carbon was added to the atmosphere each year. From 2000 to 2005, it was 4.1 billion tons. At a time when we needed to find ways to reduce our emissions, we increased them by almost 30 percent.

If we continue on the "business as usual" path, we can expect to pass 450 ppm by the middle of this century. To put this figure into perspective, before the present period, the highest concentration of CO_2 we know of occurred 330,000 years ago and was 299 ppm, far lower than today's 387 ppm, let alone the 450 ppm we can expect in a few decades. There may have been higher levels in the distant past but not in the last 800,000 years. The best information we have from still-earlier periods suggests that you would have to go back at least 15 million years to find another time with concentration levels as high as today's. During that period, temperatures were much warmer than they are today, sea levels were 20 to 35 meters higher, and no permanent ice cap existed in the Arctic.[48]

IV. What About the Skeptics?

Despite the overwhelming evidence that climate change is happening and that humans are the cause, climate-change skeptics and deniers have found a strong voice in the media and in popular discourse. It is a great frustration to many scientists that the public fails to appreciate the scientific consensus on the issue.

What deniers lack in hard scientific evidence they more than make up for by managing their message and accusing climate scientists of all manner of misdeeds and cover-ups. Although the scientific community reached agreement on the existence of man-made climate change many years ago, the media cannot resist presenting the issue as a story with two sides. When you see climate reports on the news, pay attention to the people who speak on each side. You will often find a climate scientist from a prestigious university or a well-regarded government institution defending the thesis that climate change is real, that it is serious, and so on. On the other side, there will be someone refuting these claims, but that person is very often not a scientist at all (or not a scientist in a field relevant to the issue). It is often a politician, a pundit, a spokesperson for an interest group, or perhaps an employee of a think tank.

The presence of deniers does enormous harm to both climate-change research (scientists spend too much time defending themselves against misguided attacks and not enough on the many real uncertainties about our climate) and public policy (political leaders react to the attitudes and beliefs of the public, whose views have been influenced by deniers).

I know of only one way to respond to the claims of deniers without devoting the entire book to them. In what follows, I highlight a few of the most prominent and important claims by deniers. I then compare these claims to what we actually know about the science. This is actually a fairly simple task, because scientists are quite public with their results, and the criticisms fall pretty quickly once confronted with the evidence. It is nonetheless important, because a public that is misled about the science of climate change cannot possibly press for appropriate policy responses.

A. The Hockey Stick

Earlier in the chapter, I presented Mann's famous hockey-stick graph, which shows that the earth has warmed dramatically over the last century and a half. Although I acknowledged the fact that the graph has been criticized and stated that the criticisms were not persuasive, I held off on explaining why we should believe the basic story the graph tells about climate change. It is now time to turn to that discussion.

The criticism of the Mann graph includes several components. One is that the most recent data in the graph rely on direct readings of temperature, while the older readings rely on proxies such as tree rings. The concern here is that the tree-ring data may not be fully accurate. A second critique is known as the "urban heat island effect." The idea here is that urban centers are warmer than more rural settings, because roads, buildings, and other infrastructure cause the surrounding area to grow warmer. If modern temperature measurements taken in urban areas show that temperatures are higher than they once were, this may simply be reflecting the fact that our cities and towns have gotten warmer as they have gotten larger. Finally, it has been speculated that the upward slope toward the end of Mann's hockey-stick graph might simply be the unusually strong El Niño event of 1998.

The criticisms are at least framed as legitimate questions about the method by which Mann collected and analyzed his data. The correct response to such questions is to reexamine the graph and, where the critiques are valid, take them into account and see if the results change. That is exactly what scientists have done. In doing so, they have confirmed the basic lesson of the hockey-stick graph.

The easiest criticism to deal with is the last one, that the graph reflects a strong El Niño year. We are now many years past the 1998 El Niño, and the evidence of warming continues (recall that the hottest twelve years on record have all occurred since 1998), so there is no longer any argument that this one year distorted the results.

The second concern is the heat-island effect. It is certainty true that urban centers tend to be warmer, and it is true that temperature measurements have to take this into account. But it is a big leap from this to arguing that evidence of warming is flawed. Climate scientists have known about the heat-island effect for many years and use a variety of strategies to avoid the problem. One of these techniques, for example, is to take temperature readings over the oceans, which are obviously not subject to urban heating. Many measurements have carefully avoided any urban-heat effect, and the data continue to show warming.

Finally, the graph is criticized for using tree-ring data to calculate past temperatures. The easiest way to address this concern is not to descend into a debate about tree rings but, rather, to look at what other scientists have done. It turns out that many other studies, using many other techniques, have reached the same results as the hockey-stick study.

In 2006, the National Academy of Sciences, the preeminent scientific body in the United States, convened a panel to examine the claims made by the hockey-stick graph. Although the panel had some methodological critiques, its ultimate conclusion was to support the main thrust of the Mann study.[49]

Mann's basic conclusion was that the late twentieth century was experiencing warming in the Northern Hemisphere that was unprecedented over at least the last 1,000 years. This conclusion has subsequently been supported by an array of evidence that includes both additional large-scale surface-temperature reconstructions and pronounced changes in a variety of local proxy indicators, such as melting of ice caps and the retreat of glaciers around the world, which in many cases appear to be unprecedented during at least the last 2,000 years.[50] Support for Mann's general conclusions can also be found in a number of other scientific studies. Scientists have examined tree rings, ice cores, corals, historical records, glacier records, and ocean sediment. Each of these approaches has led to results consistent with Mann's hockey stick.[51]

When these and other similar studies are examined, the basic result of the hockey-stick graph remains: a mostly flat pattern going back a thousand years or more and a sharp rise over the last 150 years. Most important, the twentieth century is the warmest in the last 2,000 years, and the warming was much faster during that century than it has been in the past.[52]

Time and again, scientists have examined the temperature records going back hundreds of years and the basic results of the hockey stick graph have been confirmed. These results have been published in high-quality, peer-reviewed scientific journals and are widely accepted by experts in the field. So, while it may be possible to quibble with methodological details in some of these studies, no credible argument has been advanced that they are all wrong or that the upward slope of the hockey-stick blade, so consistently found to exist, is a fantasy.

B. Do Hundreds of Scientists Doubt Global Warming?

One of the key arguments in this chapter is that the scientific community has reached a consensus on climate change. There is agreement that the earth is warming and that human actions are responsible for it. There are really only two ways for climate-change deniers to respond to this claim (without capitulating). The first is to claim that science as it is practiced in the United States and throughout the world cannot be trusted. Somehow the "scientific community" has been fooled or is part of a massive conspiracy attempting to fool the public. This response also requires a claim that the speaker has some special information not only about this conspiracy but also about the science itself, and this secret information shows that the earth is not warming. That is a hard argument to make, especially when you are invited to bring forward the secret scientific information. If you listen to discussions about climate change, though, you do hear versions of this argument. Ask yourself what the speaker would have to know for the claims to be true. Why are the scientists all wrong (or in cahoots), but the speaker is not?

Scientists make their living by questioning the world around them, and it is difficult to imagine getting them all to cooperate in a campaign to mislead the public—the professional rewards for making original claims that prove to be true are simply too great. Much the same reasoning explains why it is unlikely that the entire scientific community would be fooled but a pundit, politician, or public-relations person would not. Where scientific questions are involved, scientists are rewarded for pointing out where others are wrong or mistaken and publishing evidence of their alternative views. Whatever might lead a media personality to see that the scientific community is misguided should also lead some enterprising and ambitious scientist to see the same thing and make a career out of it. In short, I find it extremely hard to believe claims that the scientists are all wrong about science but that someone who is not trained in the science has it right.

The other way to respond to the claim that I, and others, make about a consensus among scientists is to argue that, in fact, many respectable scientists disagree with this alleged consensus. If a significant minority of scientists doubts the scientific claims about climate change, then it can be said that there is a real debate about the science.

Climate-change deniers advance this argument, of course. For example, Senator Inhofe, who has long insisted that climate change is a hoax, released a report at the end of 2007 asserting, "Over 400 prominent scientists from more than two dozen countries recently voiced significant objections to major aspects of the so-called 'consensus' on man-made global warming."[53] This is an impressive claim. Certainly, if four hundred experts in the field of climate science did indeed have serious doubts about whether the world was warming or whether humans were causing it to happen, it would be difficult to claim a consensus among scientists. It turns out, however, that no reasonable person could describe all of the people on Inhofe's list as prominent scientists—or scientists at all, for that matter—and certainly not as experts in climate science. The list is populated with, among others, economists (pretty clearly not experts in climate), weather reporters (they may deal with weather, but they do not generally study climate), people without any identifiable background in climate science, employees of think tanks funded by industry groups seeking to spread doubt about climate change, and so on.

To refute Inhofe's report fully and directly would require chasing down the full list of names. This task has been completed by others, and I can report that the list loses its shine when you actually examine the individuals on it.[54] In the end, however, trying to respond to each name individually is fruitless. It is possible to produce an endless parade of names of those alleged to have doubts about climate change, so it is a waste of time to try to refute each one individually.

Rather than trying to examine every name, let us look at a relatively short list of the most well-known experts to get a sense of their backgrounds and expertise. I will use a list put together by Business Insider, an online business-news magazine. I chose this list because, as far as I know, Business Insider is not itself invested heavily on one side of this debate or the other, and so the list it produces is likely to be selected fairly. In July 2009, it published a list of "The Ten Most Respected Global Warming Skeptics."[55] The lead-in to the list states, "The media portrays climate scientists as having delivered a final verdict on global warming. They haven't." This suggests that the list that follows includes the most respected voices on the subject of the science of climate change and that the author of the list believes that this group demonstrates the lack of consensus among scientists. So let's look at the list, which is shown in figure 2.2 and presented in the order used by Business Insider.[56]

Looking over this list reveals exactly one climate scientist, Patrick Michaels, and he is in last place. Michaels is a senior fellow at the libertarian Cato Institute and at the School of Public Policy at George Mason University. He has a Ph.D. in ecological climatology. Michaels does not deny that global warming is taking place, but he downplays the severity of the problem and the role of human activity. So far, so good. It turns out, however, that Michaels has received a great deal of money over many years from various groups in the energy industry, including, for example, $100,000 from the Intermountain Rural Electric

Name	Expertise	Active Writer on Climate Science?
Freeman Dyson	Physics	No
Bjorn Lomborg	Political Science	No
Myron Ebell	Think Tank Director	No
Kiminori Itoh	Chemistry	No
Ivar Giaever	Physics	No
Will Happer	Physics	No
Ian Plimer	Mining	No
Michael Crichton	Novelist	No
Alan Carlin	Economics	No
Patrick Michaels	Climate Science	Yes

Figure 2.2 Business Insider's ten most respected global-warming skeptics.

Association. He also has ties to a number of think tanks that receive funding from ExxonMobil.

Several others on the list are scientists, but they are not experts on climate. The second person on the list—Bjorn Lomborg—is no longer a denier at all. He had previously argued that efforts to combat climate change should take a back seat to other global priorities such as fighting malaria or HIV/AIDS. On the question of whether man-made climate change is real, he has long been a believer, stating that the fact that "humanity has caused a substantial rise in atmospheric carbon-dioxide levels over the past centuries, thereby contributing to global warming is beyond debate."[57] In 2010, he reached the conclusion that climate change should be a priority, and he now advocates spending $100 billion per year to fight climate change.[58] He says, "If we care about the environment and about leaving this planet and its inhabitants with the best possible future, we actually have only one option: we all need to start seriously focusing, right now, on the most effective ways to fix global warming."[59]

Two of the people on this list have hardly participated in public debates on the subject at all. Ivar Giaever, a retired physicist from the Rensselaer Polytechnical Institute and cowinner of the Nobel Prize in physics in 1973, made the list by virtue of a few comments made at a single conference of Nobel laureates. He has done no scientific work on the subject and has not written on it.

Alan Carlin is an economist who worked at the Environmental Protection Agency for decades. He became a darling of deniers because of a scandal in which it was alleged that his contrarian views on climate change had been suppressed by his superiors. It turned out that there was very little to the scandal, but the key for our purposes is that Carlin has no background in science, has not done any research on the subject, and rose to the attention of deniers for reasons having nothing to do with a contribution to climate science (or any other science).

Name	Expertise	Active Writer on Climate Science?
Stefan Rahmstorf	Oceans	Yes
John Mitchell	Climate Modeling	Yes
Rajendra Pachauri	Energy Efficiency	Yes
Myles Allen	Statistics and Modeling	Yes
Tim Lenton	Earth Systems Science	Yes
Kevin Trenberth	Global Energy and Water Cycles	Yes
Chris Rapley	Earth Systems Science	Yes
Susan Solomon	Atmospheric Chemistry	Yes
Carl Wunsch	Oceanography	Yes
Isaac Held	Climate Dynamics	Yes

Figure 2.3 Financial Times's top ten climate scientists.

My personal favorite on this list, however, is Michael Crichton. Crichton, who passed away in 2008, was a famous writer whose novels regularly populated best-seller lists. He earned a place on this list as a result of his novel *State of Fear*, the plot of which revolves around global-warming issues and ultimately delivers the message that global warming is a hoax. There is little doubt that Crichton wrote the book as a way to express his own views on the subject—he was, indeed, a denier of climate change. But why would he be on the list of "most respected" skeptics? The answer is that it is difficult to find full-throated skeptics with backgrounds in the relevant science. Crichton is here because his writing reaches many people, not because there is any particular reason to think that he knew what he was talking about.

Keep in mind that the issue here is the fundamental question of whether the climate is changing and, if so, what role humans are playing. These are questions about climate science. The fact that a list of the ten most respected deniers includes only one climate scientist and that this individual has strong ties to the energy industry speaks volumes about the scientific consensus among climate scientists.

To be fair, let's compare the above list with a list of the most respected advocates for the view that man-made climate change is happening. In November 2009, the *Financial Times* assembled its own list of the top ten climate scientists, based on the importance of their original research and their influence on scientific debates. Figure 2.3 shows its list, which does not include a single climate-change skeptic.[60]

All of these people are scientists, all have been published in peer-reviewed scientific journals, and all have deep expertise in climate issues. Among them are the director of climate science at the United Kingdom's National Weather Service, the head of climate analysis at the National Center for Atmospheric Research in Colorado, the chairman of the IPCC, a senior scientist at the

National Oceanic and Atmospheric Administration, and professors from
Oxford, MIT, and Princeton. They have published countless articles in the top
scientific journals in the United States and elsewhere. Most important, in contrast to the list of prominent skeptics, these are scientists at the forefront of
research about climate. Earlier, I analogized understanding the climate system
to understanding your car's transmission. When you want to know about the
health of your car, you seek the opinion of a mechanic because that is who
understands how your car works. The people listed in figure 2.3, and others
with similar backgrounds, are the ones we should turn to for expertise. They
are the climate's mechanics.

Even without looking at any of the information available on the subject,
which group would you find more credible? One list is overflowing with PhDs
whose expertise relates directly to the question of climate change, while the
other has only one such person. One is populated by people employed by
some of the most prestigious scientific institutions in the world, while the
other consists of people without an academic climate-science-based appoint-
ment. One is a list of climate experts who are famous for the quality of their
scientific work, while the other is a list of people who are famous primarily
because they are deniers. These two lists show that although it is possible to
assemble a group of people who are skeptical about climate change, it would
be difficult to fill a minivan with active climate scientists who count themselves as skeptics.

What if we looked at a larger group of climate scientists? Perhaps we
would find more deniers there. It turns out that somebody tried exactly
that. The scientific journal *EOS* published a survey of earth scientists on
precisely this question. The survey, directed at more than ten thousand
earth scientists, asked two simple questions: (1) "When compared to the
pre-1800s levels, do you think that mean global temperatures have generally risen, fallen, or remained relatively constant?" (2) "Do you think
human activity is a significant contributing factor in changing mean global
temperatures?"

Of the group as a whole, 90 percent answered that they believed temperatures had risen, and 82 percent answered "yes" to the second question (and a
majority of the remaining 18 percent responded that they were not sure). The
category of "earth scientists" includes a range of disciplines, and this survey
showed that as the level of active research and specialization in climate science
goes up, so does belief in man-made climate change. Among those who listed
climate science as their area of expertise and who have published more than 50
percent of their recent peer-reviewed papers on the subject of climate science,
96.2 percent answered "risen" to question one, and 97.4 percent answered
"yes" to question two.

C. How Sensitive Is the Climate?

One of the key factors affecting our future climate is the relationship between higher concentrations of GHGs in the atmosphere and temperature. If the climate is very sensitive to increases, we can expect much more warming than if it is less sensitive. This is the basis of a distinct argument from skeptics. This argument acknowledges that GHG concentrations are rising and that these gases tend to cause increased temperatures, but it claims that the effect on temperature is so small that we can ignore it.[61]

There are two ways to estimate climate sensitivity, and each has been used several times. The first is to use existing climate models, which try to represent the behavior of the climate through mathematical relationships. These models are never perfect, but they do provide some assistance in knowing what to expect. They have been used to estimate the impact on temperature of doubling the concentration of GHGs in the atmosphere. The results are fairly consistent on the low end and lead to an average prediction that temperature would rise at least 1.65° C. Each model also estimates a higher possible temperature change, and here there is more variation, ranging from just less than 3° C to almost 8° C. The average of the upper-bound estimates is 3° C.

The other way to estimate sensitivity is to examine existing physical evidence such as ice cores, ocean heat uptake, and so on. Studies using this approach suggest that a doubling of GHG levels would increase temperatures by between 1.8° C and 3.5° C—not too far from the estimates from climate models.

There is no doubt that it would be great to have a more precise understanding of climate sensitivity. What we do know, however, is that the evidence supports the view that a doubling of GHGs will increase temperatures by somewhere between 1.65° C and 3.50° C. This range is high enough to cause considerable concern and certainly not consistent with a claim that low climate sensitivity is saving us from the harms of climate change.

D. Doing Your Own Research

There is another way to get a sense of what climate scientists believe. Just go to the Web site of a university. Just about any university will do, but you might as well pick one of the best in the world, so try places such as MIT, Harvard, Yale, Berkeley, Oxford, and so on. Find the department within the university that deals with climate science. These go by various names, such as Yale's Climate and Energy Institute, Oxford's Environmental Change Institute, and MIT's Center for Global Change Science. If there are research groups about climate, see what they are saying on their Web site. You will most often not have to do much digging to find clear statements that the scientists and the institutions involved know that climate change is happening and know that humans are causing it.

I have just done this for my own institution, the University of California, Berkeley. From the home page of the university, I searched for "climate science." This produced a set of results that included the "Climate Science Department," so I clicked on that. From there, I clicked on a link that said "Research" and found a discussion of some of the ongoing research in this particular corner of my university. One of those projects is described as follows:

> *Climate Modeling.* Understanding climate change is one of the most important problems facing us all. It is a major challenge to include not just more finely resolved versions of the coarse air, sea and land models now in use, but much more detailed models of other biological and human activities that play a large role in the climate.[62]

There is no debate here about whether man-made climate change is happening. The science has moved on to understanding how it is taking place.

Wherever you look, you are likely to find similar research statements. The top climate scientists at the world's top universities are not investigating whether man-made climate change is real. They are trying to develop a deeper understanding of why it is real, to discover how to slow the pace of change, to refine their estimates of how much change we can expect, and so on. This is exactly what it means to say that there is a scientific consensus.

V. If You Still Do Not Believe the Scientists

Before moving on to discuss the impacts of climate change on the planet and on humanity, one more point about climate-change science and our attitudes toward it is worth making. I believe that anyone looking at the evidence that science provides would conclude that climate change is happening and is man-made. This is certainly the conclusion that has been reached by governments and scientists around the world. Suppose, however, that you somehow came to agree with climate-change skeptics who assert that we do not know whether climate change is happening. Even in this situation, it would still make sense to act more aggressively against the risk of climate change than we are currently doing.

When children ride bicycles, many parents insist that the children wear helmets. This is widely seen as a sensible safety precaution and is legally required in many places. Insisting that your child wear a helmet has two costs that any parent will immediately recognize. The most obvious is the cost of the helmet. Although some helmets are not terribly expensive, they still cost money. Second, it is sometimes a struggle to get children to wear helmets, creating friction and conflict that could be avoided if the parents let their children ride without them.

If we thought about bike helmets the way we often think about climate change, the case against them would seem obvious. If your child never wears a helmet, the most likely thing to happen is that you will avoid spending the money to buy it and getting the headache from making him or her wear it. It is extremely unlikely that your child will be seriously hurt as a result of not wearing the helmet. In 2004 in the United States, for example, there were about 11,000 bicycle-related head injuries that led to hospitalization.[63] This is out of a population of some 57 million people who ride bicycles in the country.[64] In other words, the probability of your child sustaining a serious head injury is less than 0.02 percent. Because the helmet cannot prevent all injuries, the chances that the helmet will save your child from an injury are actually even lower.

So why do so many kids wear helmets? Because the prospect of a head injury is sufficiently serious that we are willing to bear the costs of a helmet (including the fights with our kids) in exchange for reducing the risk of that injury. The fact that most kids will not suffer any injury is relevant, but it is not the whole story. We also care about the seriousness of the injury. Because it is serious, we take action to prevent it.

Now, think again about the climate-change debate. Those who argue for taking things slowly on climate change claim that the most likely outcomes can be managed with, at most, modest harm. I think there is strong evidence that they are wrong on this point, but even if they are right—meaning that even if the most likely outcome is not so bad—we have to ask what happens if things go badly. That is, even if they are right, we may be unlucky, and climate change may cause much more damage than is expected. If so, we could suffer enormous harms, measured in tens of millions or even hundreds of millions of lives, trillions of dollars, and major disruptions of the way all humans live their lives. Even if you believe that this is not the most likely outcome, the risk is much greater than the risk that your child will suffer a head injury while riding a bike. We need to take precautions to protect against this possible outcome. The earth needs a helmet.

3

Deeper Waters

"We are going to die."

—President Mohamed Nasheed of the Maldives[1]

I. Can the Oceans Be Higher Than Sea Level?

A. A Modern Exodus

On October 17, 2009, President Mohamed Nasheed of the Maldives summoned the leaders of his government. He and eleven cabinet members donned their scuba gear and descended to the bottom of the ocean floor (admittedly only 20 feet) to meet. At first glance, you might not think it was an especially productive meeting. The President and his cabinet spent only half an hour at the bottom of the sea and did little more than use hand signals and whiteboards. They took only one significant action, which was to sign three copies of a document calling on nations to curb their carbon emissions. This exercise was conducted in anticipation of a December 2009 climate-change conference and was an attempt to call attention to the threat of climate change and to persuade the world's nations to reduce their carbon emissions.

The Maldives has a population of 386,000 and a per capita GDP of about $4,500. By any measure, it is a tiny country. Tiny countries are so bad at influencing other states that they normally do not even try. You probably cannot think of the last time a country as small as the Maldives was a key player in some international effort. In this case, however, Nasheed had high hopes. When the topic is climate change, the Maldives has the misfortune of owning a much stronger voice than its size suggests. It turns out that the prospect of being wiped off the face of the earth gets you at least a little attention from the international community.

By meeting at the bottom of the ocean, the Maldives government sought to draw attention to the fact that the entire country may disappear as the ocean rises. Climate change presents a risk to all nations, but only a few small and virtually powerless ones expect to vanish altogether. This unfortunate club is made up of tiny bits of land that barely peek out above the surface of the water. As global warming causes the seas around them to rise, some of these nations will simply disappear beneath the waves. Others will still be visible but so badly flooded and exposed to storm surges as to be uninhabitable. The Maldives consists of nearly two thousand coral islands. The land sits an average of 1.5 meters above sea level,[2] and 80 percent of it is less than one meter above the ocean surface. A rise in the level of the oceans, even by less than one meter, threatens the very existence of this country. Much of the population lives within 100 meters of the coastline, where homes are at risk with even a small increase in sea level.[3]

A modest sea rise would be bad enough if the ocean agreed to sit motionless on the country's beautiful white beaches. Unfortunately, it refuses to do so, and not even an underwater cabinet meeting is likely to change that fact. The ocean generates waves that threaten the land above sea level even without storm surges. With storm surges, waves can be high enough to flood many of the islands completely. If storm surges are at the high end of what is predicted, even the largest islands would be inundated. And in case you remain tempted to buy real estate in the country (you could probably get a great deal), the waves and flooding generated by the regular monsoon activity in the area will make things still worse.[4]

Even the most recent United Nations Intergovernmental Panel on Climate Change (IPCC) prediction (from 2007), which is now generally considered to be overly conservative, anticipates a sea rise of up to 0.6 meter by 2100.[5] This change in the sea level, which sounds tiny, would create regular tidal inundations on most islands. If the more common predictions made by experts today of between 0.8 meters and 2.0 meters turn out to be correct, then most of the islands will be underwater.

You might ask how such a small change in the ocean level can cause so much devastation. Part of the answer is that there has already been a fair amount of damage caused by climate change. For example, almost half of the islands in the Maldives have been flooded at least once in the last six years. More than a third have experienced flooding at least once a year in that time.[6] In 2004, a tsunami flooded all but nine of the two hundred inhabited islands, and thirteen required evacuation.[7] With higher seas, events like these will become more common and more harmful. Ocean swells that used to be minor inconveniences will be disastrous, and what used to be major flooding will be catastrophic.

None of this is lost on Maldivians. Following his cabinet meeting, but before getting out of the water, Nasheed explained in clear and simple terms what would happen if nothing is done. "We are going to die," he said.[8]

Nasheed's cabinet meeting was intended to draw attention to climate change and the threat it poses to his country, but he is not so naive as to expect this publicity stunt, or anything else, to solve the problem for him. What options does the country have? It is difficult to think of historical precedents for countries being submerged. The mythical Atlantis comes to mind, but that is about it.

There seems to be only one option left for Nasheed and his country. They have to move. As strange as it sounds, the Maldives is attempting to negotiate the purchase of land so that its entire population can evacuate and resettle elsewhere.

If nothing else, this is a challenge to deniers of climate change. Small island nations are where the rubber meets the road, so to speak, for climate change. What would it take for you to agree to seek a new home for your entire nation? Certainly, history provides plenty of evidence that cultural groups do not abandon their homes and their land easily.

The Maldives and other small island nations are not only planning to abandon their homes and countries, they are also facing the prospect of losing their national and cultural existence. They have every reason to look for justifications and rationalizations that would allow them to remain in place. On the other hand, staying too long poses an even bigger threat, so they have good reason to evaluate carefully the dangers of climate change. You can bet that there is nothing the Maldives would like better than for climate change to be a hoax. The country would not be investing time, energy, money, and political capital to address the issue if it were not convinced that climate change represents a threat to its existence.

People behave differently when their own interests are at stake from how they behave when they are simply advising others. If you are getting advice on how to invest your money in the stock market, what information would be most useful to you? It is nice to get recommendations from a financial adviser, but it would be much better to know how that adviser's own money is invested. If your adviser's investments lined up with the recommendations you received, you would have a lot more confidence in that advice.

Consider another example. When people sell their homes, they typically rely on a real estate agent to help them. This is sensible, since agents make it their business to understand the housing market and are more likely than the sellers to know what to do. Yet there is a difference between what agents advise their clients to do and what they do when selling their own houses. Houses owned by real estate agents sit on the market longer than the average house, and they sell for more.[9] When selling their own houses, agents work harder to get the best possible price. Like real estate agents in this example, small island nations thinking of abandoning their homes and countries have plenty of skin in the game. They have reason to base their actions on a careful and accurate assessment of the situation, and they are certainly not ignoring the threat of climate change.

In a sense, there is nothing new about people moving in search of a more promising place to live. People have relocated to seek better lives since humanity's earliest days. This is a big part of the story of the settlement of the United States, for example. Both the arrival of Europeans to the continent and the westward movement that continues to this day have been driven by people searching for opportunity or avoiding hardship. For that matter, the story of early *Homo sapiens* moving out of Africa and spreading around the globe some one hundred thousand years ago is also a story of people moving to find better lives.

But the connection between territory and statehood is so intimate that it is a challenge even to imagine the full relocation of a country, let alone to think of historical examples. In fact, it may not be possible. It may be that only the people can move—perhaps the country itself must fade into history.

Nasheed's plan is to use tourism revenue to establish an investment fund with which to buy a haven for Maldives citizens.[10] The irony here is hard to miss. "Come visit our island paradise so that we can escape before it is swallowed by the sea."[11] Sri Lanka and India are prime targets for this effort, because they have cultural, culinary, and climatic similarities. But refugees cannot afford to be too choosy, so the president is also considering Australia.

This should not be mistaken for anything other than the desperate plan that it is. There are serious doubts about whether the country can raise enough money to buy a new home for its residents, and there is no guarantee that it will find a country willing to admit the citizens of the Maldives as permanent residents or, even less likely, as citizens. Unfortunately, there are few alternatives. "We do not want to leave the Maldives, but we also do not want to be climate refugees living in tents for decades," says Nasheed.[12]

The Maldives is not the only country worried about losing its land. Many other island nations—Tuvalu, Kiribati, Tokelau, Tonga, Fiji, Samoa, and more—face the threat of losing all or much of their land to rising seas, and some are adopting the same strategy of looking for a new home.[13]

Of all the countries facing extinction as ocean waters rise, Tuvalu is probably the worst off. It is much smaller than the Maldives. It consists of just nine atolls that collectively make up only ten square miles. Nobody in Tuvalu asks if global warming is real. If, as is sometimes said, politicians are the last to acknowledge bad news, then things must be very bad indeed in Tuvalu, where the prime minister states bluntly, "In fifty years, Tuvalu will not exist."[14] Unfortunately, many experts agree with him.

It is easy for those in Tuvalu to believe the claims made about global warming, because they are forced to watch waves splash over the islands' roads and struggle to grow food on agricultural land ruined as salt water presses in. If you want to wager on the first country to be destroyed by climate change, Tuvalu is a good bet.

So, like the Maldives, Tuvalu is considering an exodus. It has one important advantage over the Maldives: it is much smaller. The population of Tuvalu is just shy of twelve thousand people—a number one can at least imagine being accepted as a group somewhere in the world. Like the Maldives, Tuvalu considers Australia to be one possible destination. The Australians, however, have not been persuaded. In testimony before a hearing of the Australian Senate in 2008, the deputy secretary of the Immigration Department used bureaucratese that illustrates how difficult it will be for residents of these island nations to find new homes: "Should the situation come to the need for international resettlement, Australia would play a part along with other countries in facilitating that, as we do in other circumstances."[15] One does not need a Ph.D. in politics to understand that this is how immigration officials say no. Translated into plain English, the Australian statement means that if things get really desperate for Tuvalu, Australia will allow the citizens of that country to line up along with other refugees. At that point, of course, they would likely be joined by other island nations being flooded out of existence. This is hardly the orderly emigration that Tuvalu is hoping for. Clearly, Australia is not inclined to make any sort of commitment, even to tiny Tuvalu. One wonders what hope there is for the Maldives, which has thirty times as many people.

The abandonment of these island nations is probably unavoidable at this point. Even if greenhouse-gas emissions were to go to zero tomorrow, the effect of what we have already pumped into the atmosphere would continue to cause warming, and the seas would still rise. Beyond finding a new place to live, there is not much left for the residents of these islands to hope for other than that they will be able to hold on to at least some of aspects of their culture (soon to be cultural history) as they seek a new life in a new place. The following poem was written about the plight of Tuvalu, and it captures the inevitability of what is to come and the sadness felt by those who know the country.

I hear the waves on our island shore
They sound much louder than they did before
A rising swell flecked with foam
Threatens the existence of our island home.
A strong wind blows in from a distant place
The palm trees bend like never before
Our crops are lost to the rising sea
And water covers our humble floor.
Our people are leaving for a distant shore

And soon Tuvalu may be no more
Holding on to the things they know are true
Tuvalu my Tuvalu, I cry for you.
And as our people are forced to roam
To another land to call their home
And as you go to that place so new
Take a little piece of Tuvalu with you.
Tuvalu culture is rare and unique
And holds a message we all should seek
Hold our culture way up high
And our beloved Tuvalu will never die.[16]

How will the story end for these island nations? It is clear that a sea rise of one meter or more will be enough to submerge some of these nations and wreak chaos on the others. At a minimum, several of these sovereign states would become uninhabitable. It is conceivable that some form of international effort will allow for the orderly evacuation of the islands and resettlement of their populations. It is more likely that the world will act, if at all, only when there is a real crisis. This will probably be when storms hit these islands with enough force to make it impossible to live there. At that point, emergency efforts may be needed. It is hoped that international resources will be available and will be close enough to rescue most of the people as these nations disappear.

If and when they are rescued, the citizens of these former states will become refugees. History gives us some indication of what will happen next. There are few historical precedents for the peaceful resettlement of refugee communities in stable, healthy, and economically viable environments. Given the small numbers involved in the cases of at least some of these states, perhaps some nations will find the political will to allow resettlement of island states in a fashion that preserves community. If not, the most likely outcome involves refugee camps, people without a country, poverty, and suffering.

B. Island States

The disappearance of countries such as Tuvalu or the Maldives will clearly be tragic, but if this were the full extent of the damage done by climate change, we might dismiss it as the inevitable cost of progress. After all, the emission of greenhouse gases is what fuels our economic prosperity. The world's large carbon emitters are unlikely to change their ways to protect these small and politically weak island nations.

If, on the other hand, we were talking about devastating and destabilizing a big country—say, a country the size of Argentina (40 million people) or Spain (45 million people)—things might be different. Or perhaps not.

In an attempt to find strength in numbers, forty-two small states have banded together to emphasize the struggle they face as a result of climate change. They have formed an organization called the Alliance of Small Island States (AOSIS). These countries have a total population of about 41 million, and they have issued a passionate call for action on climate change. Not all of these states are going to be completely flooded, many are much larger than Tuvalu (e.g., the Dominican Republic, Cuba, and Papua New Guinea), and some are not even islands (e.g., Suriname). But they all share a concern for their future in the face of rising seas.

In addition to flooding, these states have identified four ways in which climate change and rising seas will cause major harm to their countries. First, rising seas will cause damage on their coasts. This is a serious problem, because in these small countries, most of the economic activity and population is located on the coast. Indeed, for many of them, there is precious little of the settled country that is not on the coast. Second, rising seas threaten to cause contamination of coastal aquifers with salt water, threatening both agricultural and personal water use. Third, as the amount of carbon dioxide in the air increases, the oceans absorb and dissolve more of it than they used to. This causes the ocean to become more acidic. A more acidic ocean has a range of impacts, but one of them is damage to coral reefs. For many AOSIS countries, this represents a serious economic threat, because their fisheries rely on species that depend on these reefs and because the reefs provide some protection against storms. Fourth, these countries are understandably worried about an increase in the severity of tropical storms and hurricanes. A single such storm can destroy years of development in a matter of hours. There are plenty of examples: Grenada (2004), Haiti (2004, 2008), Niue (2004), Cook Islands (2005), Cuba (2008), Fiji (2008), and others.[17]

Everybody eventually learns that the saying "If you want something done right, do it yourself" applies to a distressingly large number of situations. AOSIS, however, is unable to solve the problem of climate change by itself. These countries have contributed trivially to the problem of global warming, and there is nothing they themselves can do to change the course of the earth's climate. Nor is there much they can do to protect themselves from the harms caused by rising seas or the other effects of climate change. With the exception of Singapore, the members of AOSIS are not only small but also poor and have very limited adaptive capacity.

They have only one hope of reducing the impact of climate change on their already fragile communities: persuade the world's rich and powerful states to do something about the problem. Their main effort to get the attention of the world has been to issue a "Declaration on Climate Change" in which they call for, among other things, (1) a long-term stabilization of GHGs below 350 ppm CO_2-equivalent, (2) the limiting of global average surface-temperature increases to less then 1.5° C above preindustrial levels, (3) a peak in global GHG emissions no later than 2015, (4) reductions in global GHG emissions by more than 85 percent below 1990 levels by 2050, (5) technical and financial assistance in adapting to the impacts of climate change.[18]

This is, to put it mildly, an ambitious agenda. It is doubly so because it is difficult to point to much international progress toward these goals. One could be forgiven for suggesting that the proposal is utopian, but I think that would be a misunderstanding of the situation. For AOSIS states, the climate-change crisis is a fundamental threat. Many of these nations worry about their very survival in the face of climate change, and others face the prospect of national calamity. The criteria listed above reflect what AOSIS states believe, with reason, to be necessary to protect them from the worst of climate change. The AOSIS Declaration on Climate Change is not utopian. It is desperate.

C. Bigger States, Bigger Stakes: Bangladesh

As seas rise in AOSIS countries, we will all watch some sovereign states being swallowed by the sea, others becoming uninhabitable though remaining partly above water, and still others enduring crushing economic and political damage. We will see poverty and disease flourish and refugees flee in search of shelter and survival. If these small countries are counting on a major international response to save them, they are likely to be disappointed. The problem is that even if the international community is willing to help, the crisis in AOSIS states will have trouble getting the world's attention. The same one-meter rise in the oceans that causes crisis in these countries will inflict damage on a larger scale in other places. The world will probably fail to respond to the crisis of small island states because it will have much bigger problems to deal with.

On May 25, 2009, Cyclone Aila hit Bangladesh and eastern India at speeds of up to 110 kilometers per hour, triggering four-meter-high tidal surges and flooding low-lying regions. A half-million people in Bangladesh had to move to temporary shelters for refuge. Hundreds of thousands of homes were damaged or destroyed, and hundreds of villages were flooded.

Cyclone Aila's tidal surges and floods washed away roads and submerged fields. Many areas were left underwater and inaccessible to relief workers. Survivors in the hardest-hit coastal villages were marooned, some standing in water up to their shoulders or on fishing boats, awaiting rescue and the delivery of food and water. After reaching a village on a remote island, for example, one relief officer found fifty thousand people stranded on river embankments.

The storm was especially devastating for farmers who were preparing to harvest rice and other crops and who suddenly found their livelihoods demolished. The combination of heavy rains and gales flattened large tracts of standing crops and washed away fisheries. Salt water contaminated rice-paddy fields, tens of thousands of poultry and livestock died, and fishing boats were destroyed. Tidal seawater inundated coastal regions after the storm breached levees and washed away embankments, destroying the vast majority of potable water supplies in the area. Many people, especially children, got sick from drinking seawater. Fears about waterborne diseases became reality with an outbreak of diarrhea that spread across Bangladesh's southwest coast, affecting thousands.

Although Aila was a major storm, it was just a preview of what is coming to Bangladesh. Before examining the full extent of what will happen to the country, however, it is important to appreciate that Bangladesh is already in a precarious position. It has a population of about 150 million people, making it the eighth most populous country in the world, and it is expected to grow by another 100 million over the next few decades.[19] It is also one of the poorest countries in the world, with an income of about $1,440 per person each year. This income ranks it 180th on the list of the world's richest countries.[20] In recent decades, there has been some progress in the fight against poverty in the country. As is often the case, gains have been difficult to achieve and not always large, but they are gains nonetheless. Unfortunately, climate change threatens to do much worse than simply slow the rate of economic gain. It threatens to ravage the country, its people, and its economy.

The most important problem is that Bangladesh is extremely vulnerable to a rise in the sea level. Almost half of the population lives in low-elevation areas, including the 12.6 million who live in the capital of Dhaka, which is highly susceptible to flooding.[21] A sea-level rise of one meter will submerge as much as 17.5 percent of the country's territory.[22] This may be better than having the country disappear altogether, but it is still catastrophic for this already poor nation. I doubt if even Tuvalu is envious of what Bangladesh will face.

To get a sense of what losing 17.5 percent of a country means, think about how much of either the East Coast or the West Coast of the United States makes up 17.5 percent of the nation's territory. The entire East Coast would disappear: Maine, New Hampshire, Vermont, Massachusetts, Rhode Island, Connecticut, New Jersey, Delaware, Maryland, New York, Pennsylvania, West Virginia, Virginia, North Carolina, South Carolina, Georgia, Florida, Alabama, Tennessee, Kentucky, and Ohio. If the West Coast were lost, fewer states would be flooded out of existence, because the states in the west tend to be larger. It would, however, be the entire continental West Coast, roughly everything to the west of the Rocky Mountains: California, Washington, Oregon, Idaho, Nevada, Utah, and Arizona.

For Bangladesh, it is a good bet that half of the rice-producing land in the country would be flooded. There will also be massive displacements of people. In the fall of 2009, the foreign minister of Bangladesh said she feared that 20 million people might be forced to flee their homes.[23] It would be comforting to think that this figure—20 million—is nothing more than political hyperbole. The sad truth, however, is that it is fairly realistic.[24]

It is hard to imagine any country responding effectively to the loss of so much arable land and the displacement of so many people. It is almost impossible to imagine Bangladesh managing to do so. If you then think of the resources required to take action, it is clear that a country as poor as Bangladesh has almost no chance. Seawalls, even if they could help, are too expensive. Importing massive quantities of food to make up for the loss in local production is too costly even as a short-term strategy and cannot be a permanent solution. Relocating millions of people would be a nightmare in any country. Bangladesh is already painfully short on infrastructure such as housing, water systems, sewage systems, electrical systems, and so on. As the millions of displaced people pour into the cities that remain intact, this limited but vital infrastructure will be taxed beyond capacity. Once you realize the scale of the human displacement, it is clear that there is no chance of Bangladesh avoiding catastrophe.

In Bangladesh, as is true in most countries facing serious problems from higher sea levels, the story does not end with the submerging of land. Rising seas will also have a large impact on land that remains above water. For example, along the coast of Bangladesh and India, there are enormous mangrove swamps called the Sundarbans. These cover an area of more than 3,800 square miles and are the largest mangrove forests in the world.

This land is known for its biodiversity. It is home to all manner of wildlife, including several endangered species, most famously the Bengal tiger. Because of this biodiversity, the forests were included as two of the 176 natural sites on the World Heritage List run by UNESCO (the Indian portion was added in 1987, the Bangladeshi portion in 1997). In addition to the wildlife that lives in the Sundarbans, 2 million Bangladeshis rely on the resources of the region for survival. On the Indian side, the population is more than 4 million.

The Sundarbans are even more vulnerable than the rest of Bangladesh to sea-level rise. A rise of only 45 centimeters could destroy 75 percent of the Sundarbans mangroves. A rise of 60 centimeters would flood the entire

Sundarbans.[25] Needless to say, this alone would create a humanitarian crisis, as millions would have to relocate and find new ways to survive. But the problem extends beyond the suffering of those who live in the area.

The Sundarbans serve as a natural barrier that reduces the impact of storms and flooding on the rest of the country. You cannot normally call Bangladesh a lucky country, given the challenges that history, geography, and politics have forced upon it, but the existence of the Sundarbans is one of the few ways in which fortune has smiled upon it. This is one of the most cyclone-prone parts of the world, so the buffer provided by these forests is critical. When the seas swallow the Sundarbans, the country will not only lose the land, but it will also lose the protection that the land provides from storms. The mangroves reduce the impact of storms on the shore by dispersing their energy. The mangrove trunks and roots weaken the force of incoming waves, and the mangrove floor slows the storm.[26] Later in this chapter, I discuss how climate change is causing an increase in storm intensity. When the Sundarbans are lost, Bangladesh (and India) will face a double whammy of stronger, more damaging storms and less natural protection from them. Actually, it is probably better described as a triple whammy, because the country will also have lost a good deal of other land, leaving it more defenseless than ever in the face of extreme weather events.

So stronger storms will make land that is not flooded less hospitable. For people trying to survive in what remains of Bangladesh, there will be other problems with the land. For example, as the salt water from the ocean moves inland, it can increase the salt content of nearby land that is not submerged, greatly reducing the amount of food that can be grown. In Bangladesh, which already has serious problems related to hunger, a reduction in agricultural output is a disaster.

So some land will be lost to the sea, some will be flooded when there are storms, and even land that remains dry may be damaged. All of this will cripple agricultural output, increase hunger and starvation, and push the country further into poverty. When a society faces calamity on this scale, nothing can be taken for granted. The government itself may not be able to continue functioning as the economic and social fabric of the country is torn. The meager social services that Bangladesh currently provides will not only be stretched beyond their capacity, but they may collapse altogether. Law and order may be compromised as people struggle for a share of the country's limited resources. In chapter 5, I discuss how climate change will trigger war and violence in the world. Rising seas (even without considering other effects of climate change) will put such enormous strain on Bangladesh that it may prove to be a case study of how global warming can push a country over the edge and into violence. To be clear, no one can predict how Bangladesh will respond to the loss of so much land and the displacement of so many people. My point here is not that civil war or societal collapse is inevitable but, rather, that every aspect of social and collective life in the country will be up for grabs. It is hard to think of any source of stability that is sure to remain intact.

Bangladesh clearly faces catastrophic problems in the coming years. It is worth emphasizing that Bangladesh is just one example of a country and people for which higher seas will be disastrous. There is no space for a full list of the affected areas or a detailed discussion of any of them, but I offer one very brief example of another country, in another part of the world, that will also face major challenges. In Egypt, a sea rise of one meter will affect more than 7 million people. The city of Alexandria is home to 40 percent of the country's industry and to 4 million people. Even a rise of half a meter—much less than expected—would put two-thirds of the city's population and industrial sector underwater.[27]

D. World of Refugees

As the ocean waters rise and flood a large share of Bangladesh, the loss of land and agricultural output will obviously be a serious problem, but it will hardly be the only one. I mentioned above that millions of people will be displaced. What should or could be done about this humanitarian crisis? To get a sense of perspective, consider that there were about 16 million refugees and about 26 million "internally displaced persons," or IDPs, in the entire world in 2009. IDPs are essentially the same as refugees, except that they remain in their own countries rather than crossing international borders. So we can think of 2009 as having 42 million displaced persons (including both IDPs and refugees). The largest single population of displaced people was in Sudan, where by the end of 2008, almost 5 million people were displaced.

Compare these numbers with what is likely to happen in Bangladesh, where as many as 20 million people may be displaced. This would be a group four times larger than the biggest group of displaced people in the world today. In fact, Bangladesh by itself may increase the global population of displaced people by 50 percent. I should add that all of this assumes no population growth. At its current growth rate, the population of the country will double within the next forty to fifty years. In other words, the number of displaced people will be much larger than the "mere" 20 million I have been talking about.

Of course, Bangladesh is only one country. The good news is that no other country is likely to have as many people displaced as a result of rising seas (or climate change more generally). We would, though, like to know how many people will be displaced around the world. It is devilishly hard to come up with a reliable figure for a total number of people likely to be displaced by climate change. The International Organization for Migration (IOM), to which 127 states belong, describes the likely outcome as follows:

> There are no reliable estimates of climate change induced migration. But it is evident that gradual and sudden environmental changes are already resulting in substantial population movements.... Future forecasts vary from 25 million to 1 billion environmental migrants by 2050...with 200 million being the most widely cited estimate.[28]

One striking thing about this quote is the enormous uncertainty. The upper estimate is forty times the size of the lower estimate. This is like taking your car in for repairs and being told that the cost could be anywhere from $250 to $10,000.

It is important not to confuse uncertainty about the number of future environmental migrants with uncertainty about whether there will be a problem. Twenty-five million migrants present a serious problem. At 1 billion, it is hard to imagine how society could even continue to function in many (perhaps most) parts of the world. Even if we accept 200 million as the most likely outcome, the number is so large that it is hard to appreciate. Our brains are not very good at understanding numbers this large. If the earlier sentence had said that there would be 300 million migrants, would you have reacted differently? How about 500 million? We just don't have good instincts about such numbers.

To help get a sense of how many people we are talking about, we can think in terms of the share of the world's total population. Right now, there are a little more than 7 billion people in the world (another number that is hard to grasp). Two hundred million displaced persons is equal to about 3 percent of the world's population—three out of every one hundred people displaced. Keep in mind that this 200 million estimate is for 2050. By 2100, as climate change continues and intensifies, we could find ourselves in a world where one in ten people are displaced.

It is clear that being a climate refugee will be terrible. The world has no systems in place that could possibly handle such huge numbers. The Bangladeshi finance minister, Abul Maal Abdul Muhith, pointed out one of the only possible solutions when he stated that developed countries should "honour the natural right of persons to migrate."[29]

Ask yourself how that idea would go over in Washington, D.C. Can you imagine anyone in the U.S. government making the case that the United States has been, and continues to be, a major contributor to climate change and so should accept its share of 200 million displaced people over the next few decades? How many would that be? If the shares were allocated based on

GDP, the United States would be expected to take about 50 million. Whether or not justice requires the United States to accept so many displaced people, it clearly is not going to do so. What happens to the displaced people then? Nobody knows, except that they are unlikely to be welcomed in other countries (although surely some will cross borders), and they will surely not be provided with the resources they need to care for themselves.

As the displaced seek new places to live and try to rebuild their lives, everyone will be affected. Think again about Bangladesh. This is one of the most densely populated countries in the world—far more densely populated than any other country with a population of more than 10 million. In Bangladesh, there are about 1,100 people per square kilometer. Compare that with the second most densely populated large country, South Korea (population 48 million), which has about 482 people per square kilometer. The Netherlands, which people in Europe and North America rightly think of as having a high population density, has about 385 people per square kilometer. The United States has 33 people per square kilometer.

Now, imagine what happens when Bangladesh loses almost a fifth of its land. Where will 20 million displaced people go? We can start with the morbid reality that some number of these people will not go anywhere because they will die in storms, floods, and their aftermaths. But this will still leave many millions looking for homes. The number will not be limited to those who are literally driven off their land by rising seas. It will also include those who can no longer coax enough food from the ground to survive and those whose homes become so exposed to seasonal flooding and storms that they are forced to move.

There are so many ways that a disaster of this magnitude can make Bangladesh worse off that it is impossible to catalog every one. By way of illustration, consider how it will affect food production and consumption. Although the exact impact is hard to predict, a 30 percent decline in crop yields is entirely possible.[30] This is particularly significant because agriculture makes up almost one-fifth of Bangladesh's GDP.[31] The decline in food production is certain to exacerbate hunger, which is already a serious problem. Almost half of the people living in Bangladesh do not consume the minimum recommended number of calories.[32] "Nearly half of under-5 children are moderately to severely underweight and 36 percent suffer from moderate to severe stunting (chronic malnutrition)."[33] Whether or not an individual Bangladeshi is displaced, there is an excellent chance that he or she will go hungry, very possibly to the point of starvation.

It is not so much that we do not know where these people will go as it is that we do not like the answer. The affected people will go where populations always go when they are pushed off their land: they will go to cities hoping to find a way to survive. Of course, the cities of Bangladesh may be less than enthusiastic to receive so many people seeking shelter, food, and other services. As more people stream into cities that are already at the bursting point, quality of life will be reduced for everyone. The meager public services that exist will be overtaxed, congestion will get worse, and the challenge of finding work or even enough food to eat will grow.

If they cannot find room in Bangladeshi cities (or if they encounter so much hostility that they must flee the cities) and if they are prevented from moving (at least in large numbers) to other countries, the displaced people in Bangladesh may have no choice but to live in refugee camps. The country will also be dealing with unprecedented loss of land and economic activity along with the displacement of millions. In other words, as poor as it is now, it will be in much worse shape when it comes time to respond to this large-scale displacement. Like everything else, camps for displaced people cost money, and someone has to pay for them. It is a safe bet that any camps will be crowded, unpleasant, unsanitary, and without adequate services such as sewers, water, and food. The unfortunate people who live in them will likely face daily indignities, a constant threat of violence (including sexual violence) from one another and from those who work in the camps, and hopelessness.

No doubt, some people will conclude that they have no choice but to leave the country. A few will flee by sea or air, but the vast majority will cross into neighboring countries. Refugees crossing the border on foot (or in a vehicle) will end up in India or Myanmar, Bangladesh's only two neighbors. How will these countries react to streams of climate refugees trying to cross into their countries?

India is the more likely refugee destination. It is larger, richer, and more open than Myanmar. Will India welcome a flood of Bangladeshis? Certainly not. First of all, there is already suspicion and resentment about Bangladeshis moving into India. The tension surrounding immigration is so high that India is building a fence on the border in an attempt to keep migrants from crossing.[34] Second, Bangladeshi refugees will be overwhelmingly Muslim. India is predominantly Hindu and has existing tensions between Hindus and Muslims. Third, India will be dealing with its own climate-change crisis. Remember, for example, that more than 4 million Indians live in the Indian Sundarbans. So when Bangladeshis arrive, they will be adding to a crisis already under way in India.

The sheer scale of the migration may be so large that India cannot effectively manage the border. Will it be prepared to use more aggressive and forceful tactics to keep climate refugees out? Put bluntly, if standard law-enforcement strategies are not enough to respond to the number of Bangladeshis trying to cross the border, will India adopt other, less palatable solutions? One hopes that humane solutions can be found, but history tells us that atrocities are possible. The potential for violence along the border is real. The combination of desperate refugees on one side and a country trying to prevent massive illegal immigration on the other is a recipe for conflict.

The modern world has seen plenty of examples of displaced populations seeking shelter, and these experiences offer a grim picture of what climate-change refugees should expect. Let's consider just one example, the Cambodians who fled to Thailand in the late 1970s and early 1980s.

In 1975, the Khmer Rouge, led by Pol Pot, seized power in Cambodia. Until 1979, its members terrorized Cambodia, which they renamed Kampuchea, with policies that included genocide, forced-labor camps, murder, torture, and starvation. The death toll was somewhere in the range of 20 percent of the country's population. Despite the suffering, the Khmer Rouge was sufficiently ruthless that they prevented large numbers of Cambodians from fleeing into neighboring Thailand.

This changed in 1979 as Vietnam waged a successful war against Kampuchea. The ensuing confusion allowed Cambodians to seek shelter in Thailand. The flow of refugees started small, and the Thai government did not immediately adopt a systematic policy in response. Some refugees were allowed to enter, while others were denied permission to do so. In 1979, however, the numbers seeking to cross the border swelled, and Thailand had little choice but to make decisions about how to respond. The initial responses were harsh and led to a great deal of suffering and death among the refugees. To cite just one example, in mid-1979, 43,000 refugees were forcibly transferred to the Cambodian border, where they were driven at gunpoint down a mountainside cluttered with landmines. Thousands were killed or injured.[35]

By late 1979, under international pressure, Thailand became somewhat more accommodating and granted "temporary asylum" to some Cambodian refugees. Holding centers were established with the intent that they would be temporary and that the United Nations High Commission for Refugees would provide supplies. Beyond these "holding centers" (a euphemism for "refugee camps"), many more refugees ended up in settlements straddling the border between Cambodia and Thailand. After Vietnam deposed the Khmer regime in 1979, refugees were exposed to violence between Vietnamese forces and Khmer guerrillas. Finally, in 1984–85, a major Vietnamese offensive drove more Cambodians into Thai camps. In 1987, there were 243,000 Cambodians in thirteen camps.

By this point, it had been close to ten years since the large-scale arrival of refugees. Thailand was not thrilled with the burden of supporting this group or the prospect of absorbing it into its own population. It denied refugee status to new arrivals and resisted attempts to have refugees move further into Thailand, where they would have greater protection from attacks by Vietnamese forces or spillover fighting in Cambodia. When camps had to be evacuated as a result of fighting, there was often a shortage of water, medicine, and food, and plans did not account well for the need to transport children, the elderly, pregnant women, or the injured. Sanitation and health care in the camps were terrible.

The threats to personal security did not come exclusively from warring factions. Other Cambodians, running smuggling and black-market operations, used violence, including beatings, rapes, and killings, as an intimidation tactic. Even some of those given the task of guarding the camps—known as rangers—took advantage of the helplessness of the refugees. Beatings, rapes, and thefts were perpetrated by these individuals. Refugees who violated the rules were disciplined in a manner that was often wildly out of step with the seriousness of their offenses. Trade between camp residents and Thai villagers, for example, was not permitted. Those who violated the rule risked a beating or worse. It was not until 1994—fifteen years after the number of displaced people exploded—that the United Nations took up the final round of resettlement efforts aimed at repatriating the last 370,000 Cambodians in refugee camps near the Thai border.

Climate-change refugees will, of course, face a different reality from that of the Cambodian refugees. They will normally not be fleeing violence or seeking protection from hostile forces. This may make their actual movement from one place to another less dangerous. On the other hand, for many climate-change refugees, a return to their old homes will be impossible. This fact will alter the concerns and the actions of receiving states. Accepting hundreds of thousands or even millions of refugees on a temporary basis may not be possible. Receiving states will know that refugees are likely to stay permanently, and so these states may be even more reluctant to permit people to cross their borders. They may also be less enthusiastic about providing resources to camps if they will have to do so indefinitely.

Once we start thinking about Bangladesh, the problems facing the island nations of the Maldives and Tuvalu seem downright quaint. There is no prospect of finding a new home for 20 million displaced Bangladeshis, and there is little hope that they will be able to rebuild their lives elsewhere within Bangladesh. At best, the lucky ones will find themselves in refugee camps for years or fighting to survive on the streets of the cities. Some will find their way into India and try to survive there, but there is no chance that India will welcome large numbers. To prevent a flood of climate refugees from spilling over the border, India will have no choice but to refuse entry to displaced Bangladeshis, and those who manage to get into India illegally will be met with hostility, resentment, discrimination, and possibly much worse. Some will find themselves at the mercy of predators, such as human traffickers, who will get them out of Bangladesh and to more prosperous countries, including the United States, but at the terrible price of being forced into slavery and prostitution.

As bad as things will be in Bangladesh, it will not be the only country attempting to deal with large populations displaced by climate change. Wherever people are displaced as a result of a warming world, there will be effects analogous to those described for Bangladesh. Those forced to leave their homes in search of new places to live will face the most obvious effects. But as these people search for ways to survive, they will influence how others live their lives. Cities will grow more crowded, public services will be burdened, and existing social and legal orders will be challenged.

There are already a lot of people who have been displaced by climate change. For example, Burundi has experienced increased droughts and desertification in the last fifteen years, forcing people from Kirundo province, once considered the nation's granary, to move internally or cross the border into neighboring Rwanda. In Somalia, droughts seem to have become a regular feature of life and have triggered ongoing movement. In the first six months of 2009, for instance, some 45,000 Somalis found their way to refugee camps in Kenya, swelling the population in those camps to 300,000.[36] In Mozambique, the problem has been more severe flooding on major rivers. In 2000, the worst floods in 150 years left millions homeless. In 2007, more than 100,000 were displaced by floods, and in 2008, there was more of the same, displacing 80,000. As you would expect, there has been extensive internal migration.[37]

What stands to change is the scale of the problem. It is quite likely that we will see more displacement than at any other point in human history. By way of comparison, at the end of World War II, there were about 40 million displaced people. Peace allowed many (though certainly not all) to return to their homes. Climate change threatens to displace five times that number.

As the numbers grow, so do the challenges of resettlement and preserving order. At some point—though nobody knows exactly when—important social structures may simply collapse under the weight of the crisis. Borders may cease to function as millions of refugees stream across them. Cities may stop working as police systems are overwhelmed, sanitation systems are unable to keep up with the increase in population, and communities are rattled by the arrival of many desperate people, often from different ethnic or linguistic groups, trying to survive. National resources will be stretched to the breaking point in countries with millions of displaced people in need of shelter and the most basic human services. Overall, the social fabric within countries and among countries will be strained and may ultimately tear.

E. Rich Countries Feel It, Too

By this point, I suspect you are convinced that rising oceans are going to be a disaster for Bangladesh and its citizens. Not only that, you can probably also see how this will create serious problems for Bangladesh's neighbors India and Myanmar. But if you are not from that part of the world, you might ask why you should care. After all, poor people die all the time in ways that could be prevented if the rich world were willing to expend resources to save them. Malaria kills close to 1 million people every year, yet little research money goes to a cure or a vaccine because it is a poor person's disease. Worse still, there are millions of deaths every year that could be prevented at low cost. For children younger than five, the most common causes of death are acute respiratory infections (19 percent), diarrhea (17 percent), prematurity (10 percent), neonatal sepsis (8 percent), and birth asphyxia (8 percent). Most of these problems can be prevented or treated quite cheaply, yet rich countries and rich people have not devoted the resources necessary to bring down the number of deaths.[38] Isn't the story of Bangladesh and sea rise just more of the same?

To some degree, it really is just more of the same. The problem is that it is *so much more* of the same. That being poor in the world is already terrible does not strike me as a good reason to be indifferent to the possibility that it will get even worse. So while Bangladesh may be far away and may seem easy to ignore, this is not just a small perturbation in existing suffering. It is instead a dramatic increase, with millions and millions more people facing deprivation, dislocation, and death. The current way the wealthiest on earth treat the poorest is no justification for a failure to do anything about the disaster that climate change will trigger.

But I want to make the point that those of us lucky enough to be economically well off and to live in rich countries should care about climate change in general and rising seas in particular for reasons beyond charity. It is a mistake to conclude that because I have focused on Bangladesh and small island states, those of us living in the richest parts of the world have nothing to worry about. Even someone living in a rich country and completely disinterested in the well-being of people in other countries should not think that the impacts of climate change can be ignored.

There is no doubt that poorer countries will suffer more than richer ones. They have the misfortune of being located (generally) closer to the equator, where the effects of climate change are likely to be more damaging, and they tend to depend more heavily on agriculture, which is likely to be hit particularly hard.

Wealth also gives developed states a greater ability to react to climate change through adaptation, making changes that reduce the damage from climate change. This might include, for example, better levees or seawalls, better strategies for relocating those who must be moved, and so on. Rich countries also benefit from the fact that their existing systems are more resilient. In places where storms and flooding have long been a risk, for example, developed countries already have systems in place to manage those hazards. Although nature is getting angrier over time, having such existing systems is far better than not having them.

So there is no denying that poor countries will face larger impacts than rich ones, and I certainly do not wish to claim otherwise. Yet every country, regardless of wealth, faces major challenges as a result of climate change. Here I want to point out the threats that are associated with rising seas. I leave one obvious and important issue for later in the chapter: the threat of violent storms. The devastation of New Orleans, Louisiana, caused by Hurricane Katrina was not so long ago, and that city, along with others, remains at risk from future storms. As Katrina demonstrated, there is no easy way for the United States to protect itself from a Mother Nature made angrier and more violent by climate change.

The news gets worse if you think about other ways in which rising seas can threaten the country. For example, about 2.6 million people in the United States live within a meter of sea level—slightly more than the population of Houston, Texas. In the Netherlands and Germany, 13 million people live in coastal floodplains that are vulnerable to a one-meter rise in sea levels.[39] Rising sea levels also increase the pace of erosion along coastlines. It is difficult to predict erosion rates with any precision, but a reasonable guess is that a one-foot rise in sea levels would cause a 100-to-200-foot swatch of the South Carolina coastline to erode and up to 1,000 feet in some areas of Florida.[40] As sea levels rise, salt water pushes into new areas. This can have a profound impact on ecosystems that rely on fresh water. Coastal wetlands—which are highly productive ecosystems—are particularly vulnerable. This is true of the Florida Everglades, for example, the most famous wetland in the United States. Much of the Everglades is just inches higher than today's sea level. A higher sea level will cause saltwater intrusion, upsetting its ecosystem.

Just as saltwater can intrude into wetlands, it can press into aquifers, reducing the quality and availability of drinking water. The Potomac-Raritan-Magothy aquifer system, for example, which supplies the greater Camden, New Jersey, area, relies on fresh water from the Delaware River estuary. A rise in sea levels could cause salt water to intrude into this system. We saw this happen during the drought of 1964, when low freshwater flow allowed salt water to intrude into the aquifer system. A single event of this sort is not the end of the world, as there are normally alternative sources of fresh water that can be tapped. Rising seas, however, will have this same effect in many places, and unlike a drought, it will not be a temporary phenomenon. To the extent that freshwater sources are lost, there will simply be less fresh water available in the country.

So even if the land you are on stays dry, rising waters will cause erosion patterns to change, allow salt water to get into freshwater supplies, ruin agricultural land and damage or destroy the structures we rely on. These impacts are less likely to involve a direct loss of life than those in Bangladesh or Tuvalu, and there is a much greater capacity to respond to crises and threats, but the dangers remain real and may have widespread impacts that disrupt millions of lives.

One of the problems in discussing these issues is that rising seas will generate a large number of threats that seem manageable when viewed one at a time but are much more daunting when taken together. To recognize the problems that will crop up often requires a fairly detailed knowledge of local systems, making it difficult even to get a handle on the size of the problem for a large country like the United States, let alone to present the problem in an easy-to-appreciate way.

With all of this in mind, I want to give just one fairly simple example of how higher seas will create serious problems in the United States. This is certainly not the only challenge we face as a nation, but it gives a flavor of the kinds of problems you can expect to crop up wherever land meets the sea.

My home state of California includes what is known as the Sacramento–San Joaquin Delta. This region was once marshland, but by draining the land and constructing levees to prevent flooding, a great deal of land has been made available for farming.[41] It now contains approximately 1,100 miles of levees and fifty-seven islands.[42] The delta is important both for its agricultural production and for its water, which is pumped to many other areas in California and used both for agricultural purposes and for drinking water.[43]

The delta's levees face a variety of risks, some of which have nothing to do with climate change. For example, subsidence of land and the potential for earthquake damage are concerns.[44] To these risks, we now must add the threat of rising seas. Some of the levees leave little allowance for water-level increases, so as seas rise, the salt water from the oceans will overcome the levees more frequently, threatening the state's freshwater supply.[45] According to geologist Jeffrey Mount, "The forces arrayed against those levees are inexorable.... [The levees] will inevitably go."[46] The California delta region has been compared to the Mississippi delta, which was devastated by Hurricane Katrina: "Both are bounded by fragile levees that protect land that has subsided below sea level."[47]

Failure of the levees poses a risk of flooding that could harm agriculture and infrastructure in addition to threatening the water supply, as fresh water

and salt water would no longer be separated.[48] A 2004 failure of just one levee
forced water pumps to be temporarily turned off to prevent the infiltration of
salt water from the bay into the freshwater supply as twelve thousand acres of
land were covered in water.[49]

If more levees fail, the results could be even worse. As seas rise and storms
grow in intensity, of course, the risk of a large-scale failure grows. How serious
could this be? Very. "In a worst-case scenario, levee failures during a storm
could cause many islands to collapse at once, and the delta could 'gulp' in
enough salt water to shut down freshwater supplies to 20 million Californians
for months."[50] This is not an abstract or distant concern for those of us who
live in California. To have more than half of the state's residents' water supply
disrupted is almost unimaginable, yet it could happen.

Perhaps the citizens of California will invest in upgrading the levees in
the delta or protecting themselves in some other way.[51] Fighting the ocean,
however, is not for the faint of heart. One wonders whether that project
will become enough of a political priority to generate the needed investments. If seas rise by a meter or more and if climate change brings more and
stronger storms, it seems likely that the most populous state in the country
will eventually lose a critical source of fresh water. Think about how the
country has responded to the aftermath of Hurricane Katrina. Years later,
the area remains badly affected. How much more serious would it be if the
number of affected people was multiplied by ten or more? Or if the disaster
itself lasted months rather than days? And we should not forget that this is
only one potential area of vulnerability in the United States. The point here
is that Americans (or residents of other wealthy countries) are mistaken
if they think that the dangers of climate change threaten only developing
countries. We are all exposed.

II. How High Will the Water Get?

Like most climate issues, sea rise is no longer just a matter of future concern. It
is already here. Several islands in the Sundarbans have disappeared in the last
twenty-five years, for example, leaving six thousand families homeless.[52] By
2020, it is expected that the largest island on the Sundarbans will have lost 15
percent of its habitable area.

Global sea levels have already risen about 17 centimeters since the year
1900.[53] This is a rapid rate of increase but smaller than what is happening
today and what will happen in the coming decades. Because the impacts of
our past activities have not fully worked their way into the climate system,
seas will rise regardless of what we do to curb greenhouse-gas emissions in

the future. The speed and magnitude of that rise, however, depend heavily on whether we succeed in reducing emissions.

When we consider the threat from rising seas, we would obviously like to know as much as possible about how high the water is likely to get. If there is any area in climate change that demonstrates how fast science is changing, it is sea-level rise. In its 2007 Fourth Assessment Report, the IPCC projected sea-level rise of 0.18 to 0.59 meters by the end of the twenty-first century. Today those estimates are widely considered overly conservative, and most recent work predicts the ocean level to increase by more than twice that amount. In other words, the one-meter rise hypothesized above for Bangladesh is likely, and greater increases are possible.

The good news is that scientists know a fair amount about how and why the seas will rise, which at least helps us come to grips with the most likely scenarios. To begin with, we have a sense of the extreme boundaries of sea levels over the earth's history. At various times, sea levels have been up to 120 meters lower than today and up to 70 meters higher. But of course, nothing humans are doing at the present threatens to push us all the way to these extremes.

There are three important contributors to rising seas that are of interest to us. (There are others, including tectonic shifts, but these operate on time scales that are not relevant to current concerns about climate change.) Examining them and the role of icebergs, the melting of which does not affect sea level, helps to explain not only what may happen but also why public debate surrounding this issue seems so confused.

A. Icebergs

Suppose you were to fill your kitchen sink with water, leaving several inches of space at the top. This represents the ocean. Add several large chunks of ice. These represent icebergs floating in the sea (rather than resting on land). Now, imagine that the temperature of the water increases by a couple of degrees. One effect will be a melting of the "icebergs" that are floating in the sink. This melting will not, however, change the height of the water. When ice floats, it displaces the same amount of water as it does after it melts. So the melting of icebergs that are already in the water has no impact on sea levels.

There are a lot of icebergs in the Arctic, and they are melting much like the chunks of ice in the sink. Indeed, they are melting quickly enough that current projections suggest that the Arctic Ocean will be ice-free by 2040. If the recently observed acceleration of ice loss continues, that date moves up to 2030.[54]

Dramatic milestones of Arctic melting are not limited to the future, however. At least one has already taken place. In 2008, it became possible, for the first time in at least 125,000 years, to circumnavigate the North Pole. Until the summer of 2008, there had always been a barrier of ice preventing ships from traveling around the pole. Both the Northwest Passage and the Northeast Passage are now open during the summer.[55]

This is one of those bits of evidence about climate change that leave me baffled about how someone could, in good faith, deny that the earth is warming. We know that the ice has changed, because ships now make the voyage from the Atlantic to the Pacific (above either North America or Europe and Asia) that would have been impossible to accomplish less than ten years ago.

Although the melting of icebergs does not contribute to sea-level rise, it does pose a different problem. Because the ice melts earlier each year, the ocean warms more quickly and reaches a warmer temperature. The energy needed to melt ice that is already at the freezing/melting point of 0° C is about eighty times that required to raise the same amount of liquid water from 0° C to 1° C. This is why ice melts slowly even when the temperature is slightly above freezing. Today a great deal of energy is consumed by the melting of icebergs. Once all of the ice has melted, that energy turns to heating the water itself. In other words, icebergs serve to moderate temperature increases. When they melt, it will be like turning off one of the air conditioners the world uses to keep cool.

Loss of Arctic ice will also affect future warming in another way. If you have ever stepped outside on a bright winter day with lots of freshly fallen snow around, you know that snow and ice reflect a lot of sunlight. This also reflects some of the heat from the sun and is known as the albedo effect. The same effect is why people often wear white on hot days and why houses in hot climates are often painted white or some other light color. If the melting of icebergs works like an air conditioner for the world, the albedo effect works like a coat of white paint on a house: it reflects sunlight and heat. This, too, reduces the pace of warming. When ice melts, the effect is the same as replacing the house's white paint with dark paint. When the ice is gone, sunlight hits the dark ocean surface, and more of the heat from that sunlight is absorbed into the ocean.

B. Thermal Expansion

As high school physics teachers everywhere can tell you, liquids expand when they get warmer. So if you filled your sink with water as suggested above, the water level will rise slightly as the water warms. Oceans work the same way. As they warm, the water expands and contributes to rising seas. So one factor in rising seas is simply the warming of the water, a phenomenon referred to as thermal expansion. This law of physics means that a warming of the oceans contributes to a rise in sea levels even if no extra water is added.

The present and future role of thermal expansion is pretty well understood. Scientists know how much water is in the oceans, and they know how much water expands for a given increase in temperature. If CO_2 levels were to peak at 450 ppm, which is an extremely optimistic scenario, thermal expansion would cause the seas to rise by about 20 centimeters by the end of the twenty-first century, with further rise afterward. On the other hand, if CO_2 levels were to rise to 1,200 ppm, a catastrophic scenario, thermal expansion would cause a sea-level rise of 50 centimeters by the year 2100.[56]

C. Melting Glaciers

Suppose that in addition to filling your sink and adding ice to the water, you also scatter large pieces of ice around the sink. These chunks of ice are resting on "dry land" rather than floating in the water. As long as the temperature is cold enough, the ice will not melt and will sit happily next to the sink. If the temperature gets too warm, however, the ice will melt, and the meltwater will flow into the sink. When the ice is on land, as opposed to when it is already in the water, melting contributes to a rise in the seas, because it causes new water to find its way into the oceans.

These pieces of ice represent the glaciers and ice caps sprinkled throughout the world. The glaciers are melting, and the water is finding its way to the sea. The Gangotri glacier in the Himalayas, for example, is an important source of water for the Ganges River.[57] The glacier is approximately 30 kilometers long, but it is quickly diminishing in size.[58] Another example is the Bering glacier in Alaska. It measures 204 kilometers and is the longest glacier in North America.[59] Since 1996, this glacier has retreated by about 5 kilometers and thinned by more than 60 meters.

We have a pretty good understanding of what is going on with glaciers and ice caps and how they contribute to sea-level rise. If these glaciers and ice caps continue to melt as they are doing now, they will add another 10 to 20 centimeters to the sea level by 2100.[60] This is a significant increase in the level of the oceans, but there is good news here. There is only so much water contained in these sources, so even if they were to melt completely, they would cause the ocean to rise by only about 33 centimeters. When the pieces of ice placed around your sink melt, they add to the water in the sink but only until they are completely melted.

So while the melting of glaciers is contributing to the problem of rising seas, the threat posed by glaciers and ice caps is limited. The same can be said of thermal expansion. These influences are important contributors to sea-level rise, but at least we know the limit of their impacts, and at least those impacts are not on the order of many meters. Figure 3.1 is a table showing that even under pessimistic assumptions, these sources are unlikely to lead to rising sea levels of more than 83 centimeters. This would be a substantial increase and one that would cause a lot of damage around the world, but it represents only a piece—and not the most important piece—of the puzzle. The table also helps us to understand some of the confusion around rising seas. The two sources included in the table are the ones we understand best. For this reason, it makes sense to ask what effect they will have. This allows us to speak with some precision about at least a part of the problem. It also allows us to identify a lower boundary. It is unlikely, for example, that we will escape with less than a 30-to-40-centimeter increase in sea levels, and 83 centimeters is likely the upper limit of what could happen this century from these two sources.

To summarize what we have so far, seawater expands as it warms, but this cannot generate more than about a half-meter increase in sea levels by 2100. There is also some increase in sea level as glaciers melt into the ocean, but this is not enough water to cause a massive rise.

Source	Low Estimate	High Estimate
Thermal Expansion	20 cm	50 cm
Glaciers & Ice Caps	10–20 cm	33 cm
TOTAL	**30–40 cm**	**83 cm**

Figure 3.1 Sea-level rise attributable to thermal expansion and glaciers. Source: Anil Ananthaswamy, "Sea Level Rise: It's Worse Than We Thought," *New Scientist*, July 1, 2009. Data from Golam Mahabub Sarwar and Mamunal H. Kahn, "Sea Level Rise: A Threat to the Coast of Bangladesh," *Arnold Bergstraesser Institut* (2007): 375–397.

D. It's the Ice Sheets, Stupid

In the run-up to the 1992 presidential elections in the United States, it appeared that President George H. W. Bush would be reelected easily on the basis of good foreign-policy news, including the end of the Cold War and success in the Persian Gulf War. The campaign of candidate Bill Clinton recognized the situation and concluded that it needed to turn attention from foreign policy to the domestic economy, which was not doing well. In an effort to keep campaign workers on message, campaign strategist James Carville hung a sign at campaign headquarters that read, "The economy, stupid."

With Clinton's victory, the phrase "It's the economy, stupid," came to symbolize the importance of identifying and focusing on the single most important issue at hand while avoiding the distractions of secondary issues—even when those secondary issues are themselves important. In the presidential campaign, it was the economy that motivated voters. In the context of climate change and sea-level rise, it's the ice sheets, stupid.

Let's return to thinking about the sink full of water, with chunks of ice around it. So far, we have a pretty good sense of what is going on and the potential impacts of climate change on the level of the water. There is, of course, some uncertainty about how warm things will get and therefore how much the water will expand, and we cannot be sure just how fast the pieces of ice next to the sink will melt, but overall, we have a fairly good sense of the situation.

The only way the oceans can rise beyond the amount already discussed is if a lot of water is added to the sea. It happens that there are only two places on earth that have enough water to make a difference: Greenland and Antarctica. That is the good news.

The bad news is that there is a *lot* of water in these places. In both, vast expanses of ice—known as ice sheets—sit on the land. Because they are on the land, sea levels will be affected if this ice or its meltwater finds its way into the oceans. In terms of the water in your sink, imagine placing two enormous blocks of ice, one on each side of the sink. These represent the Greenland and Antarctica ice sheets.

It is important to understand just how big these sheets of ice are. One way to get your mind around the sheer size of the ice sheets is to compare them with places you know well. The Antarctic ice sheets cover 98 percent of Antarctica's 14 million square kilometers (5.4 million square miles). This is an area equivalent to almost 60 percent of the United States. The ice in the ice sheet is, on average, about one mile thick. The Greenland ice sheet is much smaller (656,000 square miles) but still covers an area larger than Texas, California, Florida, New York, Pennsylvania, Ohio, and Virginia combined. It averages almost one and a half miles in thickness.

If all of the water found in those ice sheets were put into the ocean or if the ice itself were to slide into the ocean, the sea level would rise perhaps 80 meters (the Antarctic ice sheets would account for more than 90 percent of this sea rise). The table in figure 3.2 shows just how much water is in these ice sheets and what would happen if all of that water were to find its way into the oceans.

Needless to say, a sea-level rise of this magnitude is unimaginable. Fortunately, there is no evidence that such a dramatic change is happening.

Location	Volume (km^3)	Potential Sea-Level Rise (m)
East Antarctic ice sheet	26,000,000	64.8
West Antarctic ice sheet	3,300,000	8.1
Antarctic Peninsula	200,000	0.5
Greenland	2,600,000	6.6
All other ice caps, ice fields, and valley glaciers	180,000	0.5
Total	**32,280,000**	**80.5**

Figure 3.2 Potential contributors to sea-level rise. Source: United States Geological Survey.

Although a lot of melting is taking place and huge amounts of water and ice are indeed flowing into the sea, these represent only a small fraction of the ice that is contained in these two formations.

This means that when you hear discussions of truly massive rises in sea levels—increases of anywhere from a few meters to 20 or more meters—it is all about the ice sheets. If things go very badly with the ice sheets, the world faces an unimaginable disaster. If they go well, we face "only" a major crisis.

The distant past has something to tell us about GHGs and the ice sheets. The last time CO_2 levels were where they are now was 14 million to 16 million years ago. At that time, CO_2 levels were between 350 and 450 ppm, about the same as the 2009 level of 397 ppm. There were no large ice sheets on Antarctica or Greenland, sea levels were 25 to 40 meters higher than they are today, and temperatures were 3° to 6° C warmer.[61]

You might wonder how it can be that climate change is being created by GHGs and yet we remain so much cooler than the last time GHGs were at their current levels. The unfortunate explanation is that this is just a reflection of how quickly humans have increased the concentration of GHGs. The climate we are experiencing today is still warming. If we were to maintain the current level of GHGs in the atmosphere, we could expect additional warming that might well put us in the range of 3° to 6° C warmer than today. It is also the case that the present climate could very well eventually lead to a disappearance of the ice sheets and a rise of many meters in sea levels. These are not especially controversial facts. The real question is one of time. The record from 15 million years ago does not tell us how fast the ice sheets will shrink and, therefore, how fast the oceans will rise. If the relevant time scale is thousands or even tens of thousands of years, there is little reason for alarm.

This explains some of the things that are said about extreme sea-level rise. Those who fear a large rise in sea level are really making the claim that some substantial amount of water or ice from the ice sheets will find its way into the oceans over a time period that we should worry about. Those who discount the possibility of much higher seas are assuming that the ice sheets will mostly stay as they are—frozen and on land—for a long time to come.

This makes it clear why scientific inquiry into the behavior of the ice sheets is critical. To predict future sea-level rise, we need to predict ice-sheet behavior. In its 2007 report, the IPCC recognized this problem, but because the dynamics of the ice sheets are so complicated, there was no straightforward way for the IPCC to take potential future contributions from these sheets into account. What they did, then, was simply to assume that the rate at which these sheets have lost mass (meaning the rate at which they have added water to the oceans) would be the same in the future as it was from 1993 to 2003. This is perhaps understandable as a scientific matter—they did not have a good estimate of what the ice sheets would do. The problem is that there are reasons—seemingly more every day—to think that the contributions of the ice sheets are increasing with time and that the future will be very different from the 1993–2003 period. As a consequence, the IPCC FAR estimate (18 to 59 centimeters by 2100) is best viewed as a lower limit on sea-level rise rather than a "best guess." Since 2007, there has been important progress in our understanding of what is going on in Greenland and Antarctica. Precise predictions are still elusive, but there is ever more evidence that the ice sheets will, indeed, be important contributors to sea-level rise during this century.

There is no serious doubt that the ice sheets are melting. It is even possible to observe what seem like enormous quantities of water pouring off these sheets into the ocean, and large pieces of ice have broken off and slid into the sea. It is tempting to conclude that the ice sheets are shrinking and therefore are threatened. But this might only be half right. It turns out that while they are shrinking, the amount of water and ice that is finding its way into the ocean is, at least at present, small enough that it would take a very long time for the ice sheets to disappear or shrink to the point where the seas would rise by many meters.

The problem with predicting sea-level changes is that these large ice sheets interact in complicated ways with their surroundings. Let's go back to your sink full of water. Suppose you put a fan in the kitchen, near the sink. If the fan blows over the large blocks of ice that represent the ice sheets, that ice will melt more quickly. For the real ice sheets, the same holds true. We know that changes in wind patterns affect the speed of melting. We also know that climate change affects wind patterns. What we do not know is just how climate change and wind patterns interact. We cannot say with confidence whether the effect will be to increase or decrease the rate of melting. Add to this a host of other factors that influence the rate of melting (including the rate at which the surrounding water warms, which, as I explained above, is influenced by the presence of icebergs), and you can see why it is hard to make precise forecasts.

Another complication is generated by formations known as ice shelves. These are peninsulas of ice that stick out into the ocean and are often grounded on the ocean floor. As these melt, the pace at which the ice sheets melt will accelerate. Just as flying buttresses on cathedrals hold the walls of the building in place, these ice shelves help to hold the ice sheets in place. Once they are melted, the weight of the ice sheets causes the ice to move more rapidly toward the water, and streams of meltwater find their way to the ocean more easily. In short, the melting of the ice shelves will remove one more impediment to the rapid discharge of ice and water from the ice sheets into the ocean.

To make it all still more complicated, the melting of the ice sheets is not the only concern. When ice on the surface of the sheets melts, it can run into existing crevices, making them wider and deeper over time, eventually creating a crack that runs all the way to the ground. Now, instead of a large block of ice sitting on land, there is a series of tall and thin structures that are much less stable and that can tip over and push one another into the sea like dominoes, raising sea levels.

The most recent efforts to study the behavior of the ice sheets have involved the use of satellite imagery. Eric Rignot, a professor at the University of California, Irvine, found that Greenland is now losing enough ice each year to raise sea levels by 0.83 millimeters. Antarctica, meanwhile, is losing enough to raise sea levels by 0.55 millimeters. Taken together, these two sources are contributing 1.38 millimeters a year. Even this rate of loss is not too alarming—it would only lead to a sea rise of some 12 centimeters by the end of the century. The real danger comes from the fact that the rate of loss is increasing, and nobody knows just how fast that is happening. Rignot's best guess is that the rate of ice loss will accelerate enough to cause an increase in sea level of a meter by 2100, in addition to the effects of thermal expansion and melting glaciers, leading to a total of about 1.5 meters.[62]

Estimates of sea-level rise remain very rough. Tad Pfeffer and his colleagues in environmental engineering at the University of Colorado, Boulder, have tried to estimate some limits to what is likely. On the low end, they have concluded that even with very conservative assumptions, sea-level rise is likely to be about 80 centimeters by 2100. At the other end of the spectrum, the greatest sea rise they think plausible is in the range of two meters.[63]

I should repeat yet again that these are all very rough estimates. There is a lot we do not know about how things will develop. It appears that everything is speeding up, but we do not know how fast that is happening or whether it will continue indefinitely. A recent analysis of ice loss in the two large ice sheets, for example, has found that the rate of ice-mass loss doubled for both Greenland and Antarctica. This translates to a 5-percent acceleration in sea-level rise.[64]

There does appear to be a broad consensus among scientists, however, that the IPCC estimates from just a few years ago are too conservative. Robert Bindschadler works for the NASA Goddard Space Flight Center in Maryland (which, despite its name, studies all manner of changes to the earth's environment), and he sums up the current view: "Most of my community is comfortable expecting at least a meter by the end of the century."[65] And while this book is focused on the period between now and 2100, it is worth keeping in mind that nobody thinks the seas will be done rising at that time. Indeed, there is every reason to think that their rise will continue to accelerate for a long time to come after that.

The bottom line is that the evidence about melting is quite clear. Not only are the ice sheets melting, but they are doing so faster and faster as time passes.

To give one example, scientists are able to determine the area of the Greenland ice sheet that has been at the melting point or higher for at least one day during the summer. From 1979 to 2008, that area increased in size by 50 percent.[66]

Although there are many estimates, using many different methods, done at different times, it is fair to say that predicting a sea rise of one meter or more by 2100 is a good bet.[67] If anything, this prediction is likely to understate what the world will experience. In this chapter, I have that one-meter rise in mind, but it is important not to forget that there is potential for much higher levels. There is concern among glaciologists that the ice sheets might start to change very quickly and dramatically increase their impact on sea levels. This could take the form of much faster melting or massive parts of the ice sheets simply sliding or tumbling into the ocean. It is important to understand that nobody is making confident predictions that this is likely to happen on a scale that would lead to a sea rise of many meters over a period of time measured in decades. The worry is more speculative than that; there is concern that it *might* happen. Even if the likelihood of a bad event is small, however, it is worth acting to prevent it if the potential harm is large enough. If your home had a furnace that presented a 5-percent chance of causing a fire and burning down the house, you would probably replace the furnace. With respect to the ice sheets, the potential harm from a rise in sea levels of several meters (or something similar) is almost unimaginable.

I should add that while everybody agrees that the behavior of the ice sheets is not well enough understood to make predictions with certainty, there are serious voices expressing fear of much larger increases in sea levels within the next century. James Hansen, director of the NASA Goddard Institute for Space Studies and a well-known advocate on the subject of climate change, handicaps things this way: "For the moment, the best estimate I can make of when large sea level change [on the order of several meters per century] will begin is during the lifetime of my grandchildren—or perhaps your children."[68] Hansen is in his seventies, and his grandchildren are roughly the same age as the new millennium, so his prediction suggests devastating sea-level changes during this century. How realistic is this assessment? It is very hard to know. Certainly, it is possible—the earth has seen very rapid sea-level rise in the past. About fourteen thousand years ago, for example, seas rose four to five meters per century for a period of several centuries. About one hundred twenty thousand years ago, the evidence indicates that a two-to-three-meter rise in sea levels took place over a period of fifty years or less. Such rapid changes suggest a collapse of ice sheets.[69] Anything approaching that rate of change would devastate humanity.

All of this leaves us with one important question: How will warming temperatures change the behavior of the ice sheets? Current research suggests that the effect will be to increase sea levels by at least one meter and possibly more.

If predictions of how fast the world will heat up turn out to underestimate the pace of warming, then we can expect the ice sheets to shrink and sea levels to rise less quickly. If existing predictions are about right, we are going to experience sea-level rise that causes catastrophe on a scale rarely, if ever, seen before. If the reality is worse than predicted, perhaps because the ice sheets become destabilized more quickly than expected, we can expect larger sea-level changes and even greater damage.

III. If You Thought Katrina Was Bad…

The threat of a major natural disaster is often a distant and abstract concern, but in late August 2005 it became real for everyone living in the United States. The nation watched in horror as Hurricane Katrina struck Florida, Mississippi, and Louisiana. We had become accustomed to watching news reports of hurricanes approaching, of people boarding up windows, and then the aftermath of the storms, which never seemed to amount to much beyond isolated damage. Before Katrina hit the coast, the news reports were somewhat more alarming than normal as the potential threat to New Orleans started to materialize, but we were no more prepared for what happened than were the levees designed to protect the city.

When Katrina first made landfall in Florida, it was barely strong enough to be classified as a hurricane. As it passed over southern Florida, it weakened to a tropical storm but regained hurricane strength soon after entering the Gulf of Mexico. It strengthened quickly to a Category Five hurricane—the most powerful type—before mercifully backing off to a Category Three by the time it hit the Gulf Coast. As terrible as Katrina was, it would have been worse if the storm had not weakened when it did.

What happened next is familiar to the millions of us who watched on television as a major American city was flooded. The levees protecting the city were breached, and the city's pump stations were not even close to being up to the task. Eighty percent of the city was flooded. In some areas, there was fifteen feet of water. More than two hundred thousand homes were destroyed. Katrina was the costliest U.S. hurricane on record, with damage in the New Orleans area and along the Mississippi coast estimated at $75 billion. Katrina was also the deadliest hurricane to hit the United States since 1928, with casualties numbering approximately eighteen hundred people.

A new system of levees is being built, but there is already criticism that it is insufficient. The levees are "one-hundred-year" levees. This means that each year, there is a 1-percent chance of a storm that is too strong for the levees. Whether this is the right balance between risk and expense is an open question, but as the seas rise and storms get more severe, that 1-percent chance will increase. If you were to buy a house in New Orleans today and finance it with a thirty-year mortgage, you'd have about a 26-percent chance that there would be a storm strong enough to breach the levees before you paid off the mortgage. If the seas are higher and the storms stronger, that risk gets bigger. If storms that happen every hundred years happen instead every fifty years, for example, you would have a 45-percent chance of being flooded before paying the mortgage, and if such a storm happened on average every thirty-three years, it would be a 60-percent chance.

Hurricane Katrina should be seen as foreshadowing what is coming in a warmer world. Storms like Katrina will be more frequent and more powerful as the climate changes. We will see other cities flooded, including ones like New Orleans that are located in wealthy countries. In some places, the rescue and relief efforts will be even less effective, and the harms will be greater.

A. Did Climate Change Cause Katrina?

Did climate change cause Katrina? The answer is that we do not know. With respect to individual storms, there is no good system to predict when a hurricane will form or where it will go once it is formed. At the level of a single storm, it is extremely difficult to say anything definitive. This is why events like Hurricane Katrina, although they are sometimes offered as evidence of climate change, do not form the centerpiece of sensible attempts to demonstrate that climate change is affecting us.

But we should not confuse our inability to identify the relationship between an individual storm and climate change with the relationship between climate change and storms generally. As the world warms, there is no doubt that we will experience more storms and that those storms will tend to be stronger. This is true even if it is not possible to specify that any particular storm is a result of climate change.

Imagine participating in the following experiment along with a lot of other people. In round one of the experiment, each person is given a small bag containing a hundred marbles. The marbles are either black or white, and you know that all of the bags are the same, but you do not know how many of the marbles in each bag are white and how many are black. You reach into your bag and pull out ten marbles. Everyone else does the same, and each person records the number of white and black marbles he or she has pulled out.

You play a second round that is the same as the first, except that the organizers tell you that they may or may not have increased the number of white marbles in each bag. Once again, everyone draws ten marbles and records the results.

If there are enough participants, you will be able to tell with considerable accuracy whether the number of white marbles in the bag increased in the second round. If the average number of white marbles drawn increases, it is likely that the second round had a higher percentage of white marbles in the bags. The more participants there are, the more reliable this conclusion will be.

Suppose that there are, say, a thousand participants, and the average number of white marbles drawn jumps from four in the first round to six in the second. This is extremely convincing evidence that the proportion of white marbles increased in the second round. Based on the increase in the average number of white marbles drawn, you can conclude that every bag, including your own, had more white marbles in the second round. More than that, you can come up with a fairly accurate estimate of just how much the proportion of white marbles increased. This experiment takes advantage of what is called the law of large numbers. The idea is that when the same experiment is done many times, the average results provide an excellent estimate. In this case, having more people yields a better estimate of the number of white marbles.

Now, suppose I point to a specific white marble that you drew from your bag in the second round and ask, "Did you draw this marble as a result of the increase in the percentage of white marbles, or would you have drawn it regardless?"

There is no way for you to answer this question with any confidence. Even if nothing had changed between the first and second rounds, you would have probably drawn some white marbles in the second round. Because the proportion of white marbles increased, it is likely that you drew more marbles in the second round than you otherwise would have (although even that is not guaranteed). But there is no way to know whether a particular white marble was drawn only because there were more white marbles in the second round.

Extreme weather events work something like the white marbles. As the climate changes, the number of extreme storms increases. You can think of this as drawing marbles from the bag, except that now the white marbles say "storm" on them and represent an extreme weather event that will take place during the next year. We cannot, however, say with confidence that any specific storm took place because of climate change. Any individual storm might have happened even without climate change. Nevertheless, we know that without a changing climate, we would have fewer severe storms.

This explains why Hurricane Katrina is used as an example of how climate change increases the threat of extreme weather despite the fact that we cannot say with certainty that the storm was caused by climate change. What we do know is that the likelihood of "another Katrina" or of a storm that is even more damaging is significantly higher. This is why it makes sense to think of Katrina as a warning sign, even if we do not know that this specific storm was caused by climate change.

As global average temperatures increase, the oceans warm along with the rest of the world. Heat from the oceans is fuel for major storms, so as the oceans warm, there is more fuel available. This means that the strongest hurricanes will have more fuel to draw on, making them even stronger than they would otherwise be. This is both what scientists predict and what has already been observed.[70]

In the North Atlantic and eastern Pacific, we use the word *hurricane* to describe tropical storms of sufficient strength. In the Indian Ocean, those storms are referred to as *cyclones*, and in the western Pacific, they are known as *typhoons*. When I talk about hurricanes, I am also referring to storms known as cyclones and typhoons. Between 1975 and 1989, there were 171 storms classified as Category Four or Five—the strongest and most destructive. During the next fifteen-year period, from 1990 to 2004, there were 269 such storms. This is more than a 50-percent increase in the most violent of storms.[71] In the North Atlantic, the change has been especially large—a tripling of the number of Category Five hurricanes.[72]

B. Why So Worried about a Little Rain?

The experience of Hurricane Katrina is enough to convince most people that Mother Nature can deliver powerful, costly, and deadly weather. Even if one considers only the economic threat from hurricanes, it is easy to understand why they are taken so seriously. In 2003, for example, losses from hurricanes in the United States alone totaled about $42 billion. In 2005, the year of Katrina, the total was in the hundreds of billions.

Like so many other impacts from climate change, the threat in the United States is real, but the danger elsewhere in the world is even greater. In many places, communities are much less prepared to deal with extreme weather, because buildings are not designed to withstand severe storms; emergency services are weak or nonexistent; violent storms are more common, more violent, or both; and the populations in threatened areas are much larger.

Cyclone Nargis struck Myanmar on May 2, 2008, reaching winds of 240 kilometers per hour and bringing storm surges up to twelve meters high.[73] More than 140,000 people were killed. In addition, between 450,000 and 700,000 homes were destroyed, and 2.4 million people were left homeless. The storm swept through the Irrawaddy delta region and Myanmar's capital, Yangon (Rangoon). Damage was most severe in the delta region: high storm surges compounded extreme winds to destroy an estimated 95 percent of housing. Nargis hit Yangon directly, downing power and communication lines and damaging buildings. Flooding or debris blocked roads entering and leaving Yangon and roads into the delta region. In the delta region, where most transportation is conducted by waterway, severe damage to water-transport infrastructure diminished accessibility to the devastated area. More than half of the schools and nearly three-quarters of the health facilities in the delta region and the capital were greatly damaged or destroyed.[74]

The four states occupying the Irrawaddy delta region and the adjacent coastline suffered the worst devastation from the cyclone. These states also produce nearly 60 percent of the country's total rice crop. Storm surges inundated vast areas of farmland, flooding rice paddies. It is estimated that Myanmar's production of rice was down 7 percent in the 2008–2009 growing season compared with the previous year. The land area available for rice cultivation was down 4 percent.[75] In a World Food Programme report released in January 2009, the organization stated that rice production in the Irrawaddy and Yangon areas was projected to be 50 percent of the previous year's yield.[76]

Eighteen months after Cyclone Nargis made landfall in Myanmar, hundreds of thousands of people were still living in makeshift homes. Significant controversy surrounded the Myanmar government's response to the cyclone, which met with emphatic condemnation from the global community. As a result of either ignorance or denial, the generals of Myanmar's junta failed to grant permission to French and U.S. naval ships carrying supplies to deliver much-needed aid to the public soon after the cyclone stuck. The government also rebuffed many other offers of aid.

As is true of Hurricane Katrina, there is no way to know if global warming caused Cyclone Nargis or made it stronger and more damaging or if the cyclone would have happened even without climate change. What we do know is that we will see more storms like this, and likely some worse storms, in the future. It is worth noting the size of the impact. When dealing with thousands of deaths and tens of thousands of people displaced, it is difficult to maintain a sense of scale. The death toll from Nargis was seventy-five to eighty times that of Katrina. To say that warming will bring about more storms like Nargis is just another way of saying that there will be hundred of thousands, and perhaps millions, more people killed.

C. The Aftermath of Storms and Floods

The most frequent of all natural disasters are floods. From before the story of Noah and his ark, floods have been a constant part of human existence. Because humans have always tended to live near water, we have always faced the risk of flooding. I have already talked about how rising seas and the flooding they will create are almost certain to displace many millions of people and consume large amounts of land. Although the modern world (at least, the wealthy parts of it) has found ways to insulate itself against flooding, it has by no means tamed this particular corner of nature. From 1990 to 2009, for example, more than 2.2 billion people were affected by floods.[77] This does not just mean that these people observed flooding or had their property flooded. To be "affected" by flooding enough to be included in this category, a person must require immediate assistance during a period of emergency. This includes, for example, people who are injured and those who are displaced or evacuated. That is about one out of every three people on the planet. Put another way, the number of people affected by flooding was larger than the populations of China, the United States, and the European Union combined. The one piece of good news about floods is that they are not as deadly as you might think. During the same 1990–2009 period, only about 160,000 were killed by floods. Now, 160,000 is a lot of people, but considering the frequency and severity of floods and the number of people who are affected by flooding, it could be a lot worse.

The larger problem with flooding is not the death toll it causes—or at least, not the death toll it causes directly. The problem is the aftermath of major floods. Surviving a flood is often only a first step for those who are affected. The relatively modest number of deaths caused by flooding is misleading, because while the actual flooding usually does not kill in large numbers, it creates conditions that can kill very many more. In the aftermath of a serious flood, people suffer from injuries and diseases that come about because they are displaced from their homes and often living in dangerous and unsanitary conditions. The loss of livelihood that accompanies displacement can also lead to malnutrition or outright starvation. As a result, death often does not so much arrive with the flood as swoop in just as the waters recede.

In early 1931, China endured one of the worst floods in history. Rainfall was unusually heavy, swelling the Yellow River, which runs thirty-four hundred miles from western China across much of the country and into the Bohai Sea, not far from Beijing. Making things worse, the region suffered through a harsh monsoon season, including seven cyclones in the month of July alone.[78]

The Yellow River has never been a quiet river, and there had been earlier efforts to build structures to prevent flooding. In 1931, however, there was just too much water. Dams and levees failed, and there was extensive flooding.[79] For good measure, other major rivers, including the Yangtze and the Huai, also flooded.[80] The results were nothing short of catastrophic. It is estimated that 70,000 square miles were affected (about the size of the state of Oklahoma). The greatest tragedy was the death toll: 3.7 million people lost their lives.

Although the flooding was certainly responsible for these deaths, the floodwaters themselves killed "only" about 130,000 people, a small fraction of the total.[81] The rest were killed by other causes, including starvation and disease, triggered by the devastation left behind by floodwaters. Food production and distribution systems were crippled, disease-breeding standing water was everywhere, people were forced into cramped and filthy living quarters, and sanitation systems were destroyed. Engraved invitations had been delivered to malnutrition, starvation, and disease.

It was not long before the invitees appeared. At one point, nearly 17 percent of the affected population was estimated to be sick as a consequence of the flood.[82] Think about what it means for a population already in grave distress resulting from the physical damage caused by flooding to have to deal with illness affecting almost one in five people. If finding adequate food is already a major challenge, are the sick left uncared for all day while others try to find something to eat? When people are living in tiny spaces, with others all around them, what do they do with the bodies of the dead? At what point do you stop giving precious food and water to the sick who are going to die anyway so that you can give a little more to a child or an adult who needs the energy to find tomorrow's food?

The Chinese government attempted to respond to the crisis. It set up the National Flood Relief Commission in August 1931. The commission sought to provide basic necessities for flood victims, repair broken dikes, and protect the population from outbreaks of disease.[83] The commission's Department of Hygiene and Sanitation was created to provide medical aid and to combat disease through vaccinations, distribution of health information, and improved sanitation.[84] These were important steps, but the scale of the disaster was simply too large for relief efforts.

Most of the victims died without being recorded or receiving serious medical treatment, but a few found their way to the limited medical facilities that existed. This allowed the National Flood Relief Commission to collect information on 157,000 patients between September 1931 and March 1932. These records provide a glimpse of the deadly stew of diseases that were circulating following the flood. Dysentery and other gastrointestinal diseases, malaria, smallpox, measles, typhoid, cholera, and skin diseases (scabies, impetigo, fungal infections) were all found among the victims.[85]

There is no mystery about why this flood was so deadly. The magnitude of the flooding and its location forced 14 million people out of their homes. The flood simply overwhelmed the capacity of the government to respond effectively, devastated food and water supplies, and left the large affected population almost no resources with which to survive.

Although Hurricane Katrina in 2005 created a terrible flood in New Orleans, the death toll was kept relatively low because, for all of its failures, the relief effort succeeded in preventing widespread disease or famine, and affected individuals were able to find sanitary places to live in the aftermath of the flood. Hurricane shelters were established at which people could get access to food, water, and medical attention, and resources were made available to help victims find places to go. In the longer term, people were able to find shelter, even if only in a Federal Emergency Management Agency (FEMA) trailer. All of this was possible because the flood happened in one of the richest countries in the world; because the damages affected only a very small portion of the country, making it possible for the rest of the country to respond at a relatively small cost; and because it was not accompanied by similar disasters elsewhere in the country.

I teach at Berkeley Law School at the University of California, Berkeley. Despite the distance between Berkeley and New Orleans, the community in which I lived was shocked by the impact of Katrina, as were communities across the country. People were ready to dip into their own pockets to help with the relief effort. Beyond giving money, we all wanted to *do* something. Students from my school traveled to New Orleans during their school breaks to assist in reconstruction, for example. Within twenty-four hours of the hurricane, the idea emerged to invite law students from the affected area to continue their studies at our school. There were plenty of people suffering more than the law students we would welcome, but as a law school, we could at least reach out to a few people from New Orleans and help in some small way. When my faculty discussed taking action, we did not realize that we were not the only academic institution with this idea. We soon learned that schools across the country were offering to host displaced students and faculty, offering them places to continue their work and studies.

I was the person at Berkeley Law School charged with coordinating our effort, and it was amazing to watch my institution, often known (with good reason) for its bureaucratic nature, open its doors so easily and enthusiastically. Law schools guard the seats in their classrooms jealously. There are always many more people who want to be admitted than we can accommodate. Yet when it was suggested that we invite twenty-five students from Tulane Law School (and from Loyola New Orleans Law School, although no Loyola students ended up coming), the faculty enthusiastically endorsed the idea. When we needed to find space for these students in classes that were already full, faculty relaxed limits on class size. When the Tulane students needed to go to interviews for jobs at law firms, our students pulled business suits out of their closets to lend.

We were proud of our response at my law school, but what we were doing was in no way unique. Tulane students who chose to do so were generally able to find a space in a law-school classroom and did not have to lose a year of their education while their own law school was closed. Like many others, my law school did what we could to make a small difference and help a few people. Our modest effort was only possible because we had the resources necessary to carry it out. We could accommodate these students in our classes, we could devote time and energy to getting them settled, and we could spend money to ease their transition. In many countries, such resources would not have been available.

Our effort was tiny compared with what many others did and what was needed. But in a large and prosperous country, tiny efforts add up. Across the United States, people and groups contributed, often in small ways, to what became a major relief effort. The pressure on government relief efforts was reduced as a result of many private actions. Displaced people found places to settle, and many victims managed to continue with their lives with only modest disruption.

One of the most important examples of outside assistance came from the city of Houston. It took in more than 250,000 evacuees from along the Gulf Coast, with thousands more arriving three weeks later in the wake of Hurricane Rita. FEMA, although it responded slowly and in many ways ineffectively, provided temporary housing to 144,000 households. There is much to criticize about FEMA trailers, including, for example, "potentially hazardous levels of toxic formaldehyde gas," but they are a better option than having hundreds of thousands of people living on the streets.[86]

In 1931, China had no hope of providing similar help, and so the victims of the flooding were left with very little outside assistance. Think about the example of Bangladesh. A flood that displaces a large share of the Bangladeshi population, decimates the domestic food supply, compromises water supplies, and destroys sewage and other systems will look a lot more like the 1931 flooding in China than the 2005 Hurricane Katrina. Bangladesh is currently unable to respond to widespread and crushing poverty within its borders. There simply are not enough resources available to allow for an effective response to future disasters.

Why is the aftermath of a flood so dangerous? One important reason is that floodwaters have a way of disabling a variety of human and natural structures and institutions that we rely on every day, often without even noticing them. Food production is reduced, water systems are contaminated, transportation and communications systems are disrupted, and sanitation systems are ruined. When these systems do not function, people's health is endangered. Economic systems also fail, denying people the economic means to meet their basic needs or rebuild their lives.

With their ability to grow their own food severely hampered, victims of the 1931 flood were reliant on outside help from the government and other relief organizations.[87] Displaced persons gathered in camps, some of which were government-controlled, some of which were not. As of August 1931, months into the crisis, some camps provided meager, though regular, distribution of food.[88] In other camps, in particular those that were not government-run, such distributions were nonexistent.[89] One account of food delivery at a refugee camp described the desperation felt by the flood victims, who "ravenously devoured" the food provided, which amounted to the "bare minimum necessary to sustain life."[90] It is no surprise that by 1932, famine had become a serious problem.[91]

Beyond the unusual nature of the flooding, the ingredients of this famine were not especially remarkable. Large-scale flooding can be expected to destroy crops, perhaps for more than one season. This will be true as rising seas and stronger storms cause flooding, with the additional threat of salt water contaminating freshwater supplies and damaging fields. When food production falls, people still need to eat. If there is less food available, the two possible solutions are to import food or export people. For small-scale flooding, both of these solutions can be effective. Some people depart, reducing the local need for food and allowing local production, combined with relief supplies or simply increased purchases of food from farther away, to meet the needs of those who remain.

These solutions, however, break down when the flooding is sufficiently serious. In Bangladesh, there will be severe disruption of food production. How will that country feed itself? The option of importing food is not promising. Bangladesh is already one of the world's poorest countries. If it had the resources to import enough food for its people, it would already be doing so. With no other options, people will crowd into cities or camps. Why would we not expect a replay of China 1931?

In addition to the threat of sickness and death directly caused by starvation, hunger and malnutrition generally reduce one's ability to fight disease.[92] Following a flood, the water does not recede completely. Any dip in the land, any basement, or any other space that can capture water is filled. The water has nowhere to go, so it just sits there. This standing water presents a number of risks. If it becomes contaminated, contact between an exposed wound and the water may cause infection.[93] Floodwater can also contaminate well water, which may cause disease if consumed or used for other purposes, such as bathing.[94] Standing water is also a favorite of mosquitoes, which use it for breeding and whose population can increase as a result.[95] This raises the risk of mosquito-borne diseases such as malaria.[96]

Following the 1931 flood in China, it took six months for the water to recede.[97] Not surprisingly, disease was a serious problem, including the sorts of diseases exacerbated by the presence of standing water following a flood. The incidence of malaria was very likely increased by an increase in the mosquito population, contaminated drinking water contributed to the spread of gastrointestinal disease, and contact with contaminated floodwater contributed to the spread of skin and other infections.

Floods also force people from their homes, often until long after the water has receded. Despite the wealth of the United States and the relief efforts made following Hurricane Katrina, many of the displaced never returned home, including some who were still in FEMA trailers years after the hurricane struck. In the case of Katrina, the displaced were at least able to find shelter. This is not always the case.

The 1931 flood in China forced an estimated 40 percent of the people out of their homes.[98] As I already mentioned, some displaced people found temporary shelter of a sort in camps, which came in a wide variety of forms. The camps were often located in buildings such as schools and churches. Others consisted of huts, sometimes constructed by the families themselves.[99] Some housed thousands under one roof. Some had divisions for privacy (e.g., providing some separation between men and women), and others did not.[100]

These camps and other shelters had the features one would expect. They were extremely crowded, they had poor sanitary conditions, and they often did not have adequate clean water or sewage. What came next was also what one would expect. The combination of crowded conditions and unsanitary conditions made the spread of contagious disease much more likely.[101] It is no surprise that sickness such as dysentery, colds, and measles were all reported following the flood.

The headline of one report in the *New York Times* conveys a sense of just how bad things were: "Conditions in Refugee Camps of Flooded District Almost Beggar Description."[102] The story described conditions at one of the camps, known as Black Hill, in September 1931:

> These [shelters] afford no protection against the wind and rain, and the 20,000 people, fully half of whom are sick, have no place to sleep except upon the soggy ground. Flies are almost as thick as swarming bees. Most of the sick people are suffering from dysentery, and there is no water to drink except what can be dipped from the river, and this is stagnant and foul.[103]

Although 1931 may seem like a long time ago, climate change promises to bring with it the same headlines for future floods and storms. The Yellow River flood killed several million. Climate change promises flooding and storms that lead to much more catastrophic death tolls.

IV. How High Should We Make the Oceans?

We have already committed ourselves to a significant increase in sea levels. It takes time for the effects of our GHG emissions to work their way through the global climate system and influence the height of the oceans. Temperatures do not go up immediately, and ice does not melt instantly, so thermal expansion, melting glaciers, and melting ice sheets all influence the ocean with some delay. If we knew exactly what was coming, we might be better able to prepare for it. We might, for example, have a better sense of which communities have to be relocated and what forms of infrastructural changes will best reduce the cost of rising seas. Even in this scenario, however, higher seas would extract an enormous toll. Unfortunately, we cannot predict with certainty what is coming. We do not know exactly how violent storms will become, and we do not know exactly how high the seas will rise. This uncertainty makes it more difficult to plan and more difficult to respond appropriately.

We do know that we are continuing to release more GHGs into the atmosphere. We know that doing so will further aggravate the effect of climate change. Global average temperatures will increase more quickly and will not stabilize until they reach a high level. Ice sheets will melt more quickly, raising ocean levels higher and doing so more quickly, making it even more difficult to respond. Hurricanes and other forms of extreme weather will become stronger, cause more damage, and lead to more tragedy.

Think of the many cities and countries that have been built based on current sea levels or that are vulnerable to an increase in the violence of hurricanes and other extreme weather. New Orleans, Miami, the Netherlands, Bangladesh, the Maldives, and many other places would make this list. The damage caused by higher oceans will be great enough that the impacts will spread beyond those who are displaced and will affect us all.

There is a lot we do not know about how climate change will affect the oceans, but we know that by triggering changes in our oceans, we have dug ourselves a sizable hole. Getting out of the hole will take at least decades of adjustment and crisis management as higher seas impose their will on humanity. Along the way, it will be important to do everything we can to adapt to the reality of rising seas. This may mean helping people to find new homes, building levees and dikes, rebuilding freshwater systems to protect them from saltwater intrusion, and much more. These sorts of strategies are necessary, but they will not get us out of the hole.

The first rule of holes is that when you find yourself in one, you should stop digging. We need to stop digging. As long as we continue to increase the level of GHGs in the atmosphere, the earth will continue to warm, the challenges we face will get larger, the consequences for human beings will become more severe, and the hole will get deeper. The events described in this chapter have been based on fairly modest assumptions about the pace and extent of climate change. I have focused on a sea-level rise of one meter, which is a realistic and, indeed, conservative projection if average global temperatures increase by 2° C. By continuing on our current path of ever more GHG emissions, we will drive the seas ever higher. Keep in mind how much ice is in the ice sheets. The faster we push temperatures upward, the faster the ice sheets will melt or fall into the ocean. It is time to decide how high we want the oceans to be.

4

A Thirsty World

"When the well's dry, we know the worth of water."
—Benjamin Franklin, 1746

A healthy person, under normal conditions, should drink about two liters of water (roughly 8.5 cups) each day. Taking in too little water, even if the shortfall is small, can cause fatigue, weakness, and headaches and impair mental performance. More severe dehydration can cause serious and permanent damage to the kidneys, liver, and brain. Without water, a human being can survive for about three days. With the exception of oxygen, nothing is more important.

Countries, which, after all, consist of a collection of people, also need water. At the top of the list of reasons water is needed is, of course, drinking. Not far behind this is the need to grow the food necessary to feed a population. Beyond this, water is needed to operate sanitation systems, to generate power, for ecosystems to survive, and for almost everything else people do.

There is a ruthless and inescapable arithmetic to water distribution. In any region, there is a finite supply of fresh water provided by precipitation, rivers, lakes, aquifers, and so on. Although some modest addition to this supply is possible through desalinization, that process is much more expensive than most other sources. However much water is available, it must serve the countries of the region. If one country gets more, another must get less. If water supplies are interrupted or reduced, people and countries must make do with less if they are to survive. If water supplies fall too much, however, neither individuals nor countries can exist for long.

In many countries, including almost every developed country, we take access to water for granted. Most of us do not think about it beyond the act of turning on our faucets. We certainly do not spend much time considering how much water it takes for an entire city—let alone a country—to get through each day or how that quantity is supplied. This complacency reflects the success of our water-distribution systems. Fresh water is delivered to where it is needed at low cost and without interruption. Our water systems have seemingly secured this most basic of human needs.

These systems, which we have come to rely on, are threatened by climate change. The source of the danger is surprisingly simple. Water-distribution systems do just what their name implies: they distribute water. They take water from where it is found to where it is needed. When this is done reliably and on a large enough scale, and when there is a large enough supply of water to start with, all is well. But if the supply of water disappears, there is nothing to distribute. The infrastructure left behind, as impressive, expensive, and reliable as it is, can't do what it was made to do, because there is no water.

Think of the water-distribution system in the most simplistic terms; imagine it as a pipe that runs from a water source, such as a lake, to a destination, such as a farm, where it is used for irrigation. Although actual water-distribution systems are more complex in many ways, their basic function is not so different from this imagined pipe. As long as there is water available at the source, the pipe can deliver it. Add a valve that the farmer can open and close, and the farm gets as much water as it needs and no more. The system works.

Each day, the farm uses water from the lake to irrigate its crops, for drinking, and for bathing. Back at the lake, meanwhile, fresh water arrives from rivers or streams that feed the lake and from precipitation. The rivers and streams, in turn, are created by falling rain and, perhaps, meltwater from glaciers. As long as the flow of water into the lake is at least as large as the volume of water taken out of the lake by the farm, the water-distribution system is sustainable. It can last indefinitely, and the farmer can sleep comfortably knowing that a secure and inexpensive source of water exists.

Now, imagine that climate change alters precipitation patterns so that the lake and its surrounding area receive less rainfall. Climate change is also likely to affect the farm, of course. If it is close enough to the lake, it is likely to experience a similar decline in rainfall, which means that it will rely even more heavily on the water it gets from the lake. If it is farther away from the lake, it may get more rain, less rain, or about the same amount. To keep things simple, let's assume it continues to need the same amount from the lake as it did before the climate changed.

So less water is flowing into the lake, and the farm continues to use the same amount as before. If the system was previously in balance, this change means that the farm is withdrawing water more quickly than the lake is being replenished. Over time, the water level in the lake will fall. This can go on for a while, but eventually, the arithmetic of water will cause the lake to run dry. Water will still come through the distribution system, but it will be reduced to (at most) the rate at which water is arriving in the lake. The farm's yield will be reduced, because it will not have access to as much water as it needs. If the shortage is severe, there may be a large fall-off in production and, perhaps, the farm will go out of business.

Notice that throughout this story, nothing has happened to the water-distribution system. The pipe remains in place, ready to deliver as much water as the farm needs. There is nothing wrong with the engineering of the pipe. The problem is more fundamental. The problem is that there is less water available.

The image of a single pipe flowing to a single farm is, of course, silly. The basic lesson is the same, however, if we imagine a more realistic water-distribution system. Picture, for example, a community of many farms, households, and businesses using water delivered from a freshwater source through a sophisticated and modern system. You can think of this as a town, a city, a state, or a country—the point is the same for any of them. This water system might have thousands of miles of pipes, pumping stations, valves, treatment plants, storage tanks, and more, all managed and monitored by both humans and computers. All of these components are important to make efficient use of the water, and although the systems are expensive to build and maintain, they provide far more reliable access to water. No matter how sophisticated the system is, however, it cannot avoid the fundamental arithmetic of water that is illustrated by the example of a single pipe serving a single farm. If the demand for water is larger than the available supply, there will be a shortage.

It requires only a small step of the imagination to see how this discussion applies directly to water issues in every corner of the world. In my own state of California, for example, the local population uses far more water than can be obtained from within the state. California solves this problem by importing water. Even within the state, nature has put the water in places other than where it is most needed. California has responded with a complex water system that transports the water from its source to its destination.

That system relies on many different water sources and many different infrastructures to move the water. Like a single pipe connecting a lake to a farm, however, it cannot escape the arithmetic of water. As effective as the system is today, it has been built on the assumption that water supplies will remain more or less fixed over time. If climate change alters the availability of fresh water, California's sophisticated water system will face the same problem as the single pipe in my illustration: it will not be able to deliver water that is not there.

I pick up the story of California later in this chapter, so I will not go into further details here. For now, it is enough to make the point that when climate change disrupts existing water supplies in the United States and around the world (as it will; more on this point below), many people will have less water than they have now. When I say many people, I mean billions of people.

In discussing the impact of climate change on water availability, it is important to keep in mind that climate change will, of course, not actually change the amount of water on the planet (although it may cause some fresh-water systems to be contaminated by salt water). The problem is not that there will be less fresh water but, rather, that it will be in different places. Human beings have made critical decisions about population centers, land-use pat-terns, and infrastructural development based on existing water patterns. If those patterns change, our water-distribution systems will be no more effec-tive than the single pipe in my original example. As temperatures increase, we will also see glaciers shrink and eventually vanish. These glaciers, along with snowpacks, play a critical water-storage role. As they melt, they will trigger vio-lent flooding during some periods and harsh droughts at other times of year.

As climate change transforms water patterns, then, it will disrupt both nat-ural and man-made water-distribution systems. The consequence for humans will be a reduction in access to water where it is most needed. This will have an obvious impact on farming and food production, meaning that we will see not only water shortages but also food shortages and famine.

I. A Lesson from Hundreds of Years Ago

From the ninth to the fifteenth centuries, the Khmer kingdom thrived in what is now Cambodia. At its peak, the kingdom's capital city of Angkor was home to 750,000 people and is thought to have been the largest city of its time."[1] Angkor featured, as one might expect from a thriving civilization, impressive palaces and temples. Of interest to us, however, is the fact that the Khmer also built an elaborate and sophisticated system of reservoirs and canals to control the flow of water.[2] The infrastructure included hundreds of miles of canals and dikes that diverted water from the local rivers to large man-made reservoirs. The largest part of the water system was a reservoir measuring five miles in length and one and a half miles across and capable of holding 1.8 billion cubic feet of water.[3]

This system served the city's needs in the same way that today's water sys-tems serve their populations: by providing water storage and distribution. Angkor faced two major water challenges, and this system addressed them both. First, the local climate featured dramatic swings in rainfall between the rainy and the dry seasons, but the city needed water all year round. Second, the city needed the water to be delivered both to farms for irrigation and to households for personal use. Angkor's system of canals and reservoirs pre-vented flooding during the wet season. That water was then available for both irrigation and household use during the dry season.[4]

The water-management system was an enormous success. Its most important impact was to increase rice yields. More productive agriculture allowed Angkor to grow and bolstered the king's power.[5] The system was an important factor in the kingdom's success from the ninth to the fifteenth centuries. Over the course of roughly a century, however, the kingdom declined and all but vanished.[6] Many theories have been advanced to explain the kingdom's collapse, including changing religious practices,[7] economic changes,[8] and foreign invaders.[9] Recent research, however, including excavations in and around Angkor, has suggested another answer: a failure of its water system.

During the fourteenth and fifteenth centuries, there were two extended periods of drought in the region: 1362–1392 and 1415–1440. These droughts, perhaps combined with preexisting water-management problems that are thought to have existed but are not understood, may have spelled the end of the Khmer Kingdom's heyday. For all of its sophistication, the Angkor water-management system relied on annual monsoons to deliver water. Everything was built on the assumption that the rains would come every year. When precipitation patterns changed, there was nothing the water-distribution system could do. Like the water pipe described above, the system relied on water arriving in the same place and with the same volume as it had in the past. Without enough water, the system could not serve the population.

People living in the south of Angkor were probably spared the worst of the effects of drought, because they relied on the Mekong River, which, in turn, was fed by the Tibetan glacier fields. The meltwater from these fields would not have been significantly affected by drought, so agriculture production could be maintained. In the north, however, the monsoons were critical to food production. As clever as the Khmer engineers were, they had no way to move water from the low-lying Mekong River to the higher-elevation northern region. Throughout the system, they relied on gravity to move the water, and in this instance, it worked against them.

This tale of a failing water system feeds into the other likely explanations of collapse. A smaller rice crop would have weakened the power of the king, and northern starvation would have added internal strife and unrest. All of this would have left Angkor vulnerable to foreign incursions. Toward the end of the second major drought (1431), records from the kingdom of Ayutthaya indicate that it captured Angkor. This military defeat, however, was not the end of Angkor. The ruler of Ayutthaya put his son on the throne, so there was clearly an intent to allow Angkor to prosper under its new ruler. The defeat does show, however, that Angkor had lost its earlier might and that its best days were in the past. The droughts had overwhelmed the water system that was the keystone of the civilization. There would be no return to glory for Angkor.

Are there lessons to be drawn from this ancient civilization? Should we really worry that we will face a similar fate? Our world is certainly very different from that of the Khmer Kingdom, as are our technologies. The arithmetic of water, however, has not changed. Like the Khmer, we are able to move water from one place to another, and we have made major infrastructural investments to do so. Like them, we have built our system on the assumption that water will continue to be available from the same places and largely in the same way as it has been for millennia. The problem for Angkor was that the water supply changed. Long periods of drought reduced the amount of water available, a problem that the impressive distribution system could not fix. We face the same problem. As climate change alters our water sources, our water-distribution systems will be unable to deliver enough water when and where it is needed. The world will experience a modern version of Angkor's crisis.

The greatest threat to the world's water comes from the mountains and their disappearing glaciers. Scattered throughout the world are glaciers and ice caps that are melting as temperatures rise. It is already clear that these formations are shrinking, and a 2° C increase in average global temperatures will be more than enough to cause them to melt. By 2050 (if not sooner), most of them will be gone.[10]

Why should anyone care? Because we all need the glaciers. Hundreds of millions of people in the United States, Europe, China, and elsewhere rely on the runoff from mountain glaciers and snowmelt for agricultural and personal use. Think of them as massive water-storage devices: They hold rainwater that falls during rainy seasons and dispense it in the form of meltwater during dry seasons. When a glacier disappears, rain cascades down the mountain, creating floods. During the dry season, the lack of glacier runoff creates droughts.

Here again, humans have built systems based on an assumption that climate does not change rapidly. Glaciers and snow have provided a cheap and convenient way to manage the water supply that we have counted on for at least hundreds of years. This has helped humanity prosper. In simple terms, an enormous amount of the world's water use and food production relies on the water storage that glaciers provide. When the glaciers are gone, the water will not be there when it is needed, too much will be there at other times of year, and entire agricultural systems will be threatened.

With this perspective, the relevance of the experience in Angkor is clear. The Khmer built a thriving society based on an agricultural and irrigation system. When that system failed, so did the civilization. We have built a global system that relies on the water storage provided by glaciers, and now those glaciers are disappearing.

An optimist might point out that humans are clever and innovative and may find ways to cope with the disappearance of the glaciers. This is certainly imaginable, but I would feel better about it if we had at least some viable strategy to do so. We don't. The quantities of water involved are enormous, and the kind of physical structures that could replicate even a fraction of what glaciers do would be unimaginably complex and expensive to build. More to the point, replacing what the world's glaciers do for our water supply is not currently possible. Counting on some future technological fix is ultimately an appeal to luck and providence to ensure that the world's water system continues to work. If luck and providence do not come through, we face widespread shortages of both food and water and a death toll that could easily be in the tens of millions, perhaps much more.

If you have ever gone shopping in the United States on the day after Thanksgiving, also known as "Black Friday," you have a sense of what happens when everyone wants a scarce resource. On Black Friday, stores offer attractive discounts on many products in an attempt to lure customers into the store. In the rush to get low-priced items, people push, pull, and sometimes kick their neighbors, all while running full-tilt toward the sought-after product. Customers compete with one another because, while it is easy to know what items are on sale, there is no easy way to know which customers will get to buy them at the low sales price. If one hundred flat-screen TVs are on sale, it is easy to predict that one hundred customers will walk out with a great deal. Until the doors are opened, however, it is hard to know who will get the TVs and who will not.

Knowing that there will be food and water shortages is a little like knowing that there will not be enough TVs for everybody. We know there will not be enough, but we do not know who will get it. When the shortages arrive, people will behave like Black Friday shoppers: they will do whatever they can to get a share of the available food. This means that rich and powerful countries will almost certainly be less affected than poor ones. In countries such as the United States, we can expect higher food prices, for example, creating hardship for many who already have trouble making ends meet. In poor countries, it will be much worse. If, indeed, the rich countries manage to feed themselves, there will be less available for the large majority of the world that is not wealthy.

Of course, those who cannot get enough food may not sit quietly while they and their children starve. Black Friday shoppers seeking scarce merchandise can be described as desperate, and they sometimes act in ways that are violent, selfish, and unkind. People trying to feed themselves, their families, and their countries will be desperate in a much more serious sense. They, too, will sometimes act in violent, selfish, and unkind ways. The difference is that in a food crisis, the stakes and the actions are far more extreme. In regions where tensions are already high and shortages are severe, there is every reason to anticipate great violence. That is the subject of chapter 5.

II. Our Melting Water Towers

A. Bolivia: Thirsty

The story of Angkor emphasizes how dependent humans are on reliable access to water. When that access is disrupted, our social structures are compromised, and everything from economic growth to health to food production suffers. This was true at the time of the Khmer civilization, and it is true today. We do not know the specifics of the decline of Angkor and the Khmer civilization. We do know, however, some of the ways in which climate change will affect our own water-supply systems. In some places, we can already watch water systems struggling under the strain of climate change.

In most of the developed world, including the United States, we have not really begun to focus on the effects of climate change in our daily lives. It is not so much that the United States remains unaffected as it is that the country has not paid attention. Warmer and more severe weather in recent years, for example, has not been enough to draw the attention of the public.[11] We notice when there is a severe storm or a particularly dry summer, but it is difficult to know what causes these changes. Even experts who study weather and climate cannot normally connect specific events to climate change. We can attribute a general increase in major weather events to the warming of the globe, but we cannot say that any individual event is the result of climate change.[12]

In many other parts of the world, climate change is harder to ignore. When changes are visible, represent a stark departure from the past, and threaten a community's way of life, the role of climate change is more easily recognized and acknowledged. There are lots of places where the consequences of climate change have this effect. Examples come up throughout this book, including the Maldives and Bangladesh in chapter 3, sub-Saharan Africa in this chapter, and Pakistan, the Middle East, and others in later chapters. Many more could be included—so many that to discuss them all would more than fill up the rest of this book. As an illustration of how climate change is already interfering with water supplies and as a preview of what is to come in many other places, I focus on Bolivia.

The Uru Chipaya are an indigenous people who have lived in Bolivia since long before that country was created. They have been living in the same area for some four thousand years. They are thought to be the oldest living culture in the Andes and had already been around for a long time when the Incan Empire arose. They witnessed the arrival of Spanish colonists in the New World and the birth of the modern Bolivian state. Throughout their long history, the Uru

Chipaya have relied on the same source of water: the Lauca River. Today, that source is failing and may be taking their society with it.

The problem facing this population, who in a bit of dark irony are known in local mythology as "water beings," is that their river and their water supply rely on glaciers in the Andes mountains.[13] For thousands of years, this has proven a reliable system. Without glaciers, however, the system does not work. The glaciers, like those everywhere else in the world, are disappearing.

Climate change is the culprit in this matter: "Rising temperatures have caused retreat of Andean glaciers throughout Bolivia, Colombia, Ecuador and Peru." The word "retreat" in this statement is a euphemism for "shrink."[14] The tribe, which does not have alternative water sources (and why should they—this one has been reliable since long before year one of the modern calendar), has noticed the change. The Lauca River, which once flowed powerfully and reliably through the region, has been reduced to a trickle. One older tribe member explained bluntly, "We are at risk of extinction.... The Chipaya could cease to exist within the next 50 years. The most important thing is water. If there is no water the Chipaya have no life."[15] Other elders remember when water and life flourished in areas that are now dry and desolate.[16] Within their lifetimes, climate change has pulled the rug out from under their world. These are not simply modest changes or seasonal variations. The Uru Chipaya have been living in the region for a long time and recognize the differences. These are fundamental and long-term changes for which they are entirely unequipped.

To understand the Uru Chipaya's problem—a problem that actually affects all of Bolivia—we have to look to the source of the water. A lot of water comes from small, tropical glaciers. They absorb and store water that falls as precipitation during wet periods and release it in a relatively steady fashion during dry periods. This is an essential function for farmers, because agriculture needs a fairly steady supply of water. Indeed, it is important to every human being for the same reason.[17]

Once the glaciers are gone, the water-storage service they provide will also be gone. This is bad for farming, bad for people, and bad for energy. Hydroelectric power represents about 50 percent of Bolivia's electricity, and much of it relies on water flowing from the glaciers.[18] Put simply, glaciers are vital to the everyday survival of many Bolivians.

Bolivian glaciers are in retreat, and they have lots of company. Glaciers throughout the world have been fighting a losing battle with warming temperatures for a long time. They started a slow retreat toward the end of the nineteenth century, started melting faster in the 1940s, and sped up considerably (sometimes by a factor of four) starting in the 1980s.[19] This long-term trend has left the world's glaciers in a sorry state, and the pace of melting is only expected to increase and will not stop until the glaciers are gone. Bolivia's glaciers represent just one example. A similar story can be told about glaciers all over the world.

When will glaciers disappear? In Bolivia's case, soon. The precise date is not known, but in 2007, the IPCC predicted that warming temperatures could destroy all of Bolivia's (and Latin America's) glaciers within fifteen years.[20] As I write this, only ten years are left on this projection. Some estimates are slightly more optimistic, but everyone agrees that the glaciers are in their final years. Even if the IPCC is wrong about the speed of their disappearance, it is unlikely that they will last more than a few more decades. For example, the last remnants of the eighteen-thousand-year-old Chacaltaya glacier, once home to the world's highest ski runs, melted away in 2010.[21] Glaciers are not living creatures, of course, but if it is possible to speak of the death of a glacier, Chacaltaya is dead. Scientists even held special ceremonies to commemorate its passing.[22] The remaining glaciers will likely be gone within a generation.[23]

The Uru Chipaya people live on isolated, rural lands, so the loss of their main source of water presents great challenges to maintaining their agricultural and pastoral way of life. Isolation, however, is not really the cause of the problem. Larger population centers face the same challenges. The village of Khapi, which is near La Paz, Bolivia's capital and second-largest city, is similarly dependent on runoff from glaciers. The lower edge of the glacier it depends on has been advancing up the mountain, while the flow of runoff has decreased and is sometimes so dirty that it is unusable.[24] The cause of these problems is not lost on the local population. One activist, Alivio Aruquipa, declares that Western countries, responsible for the lion's share of past GHG emissions, should compensate his community for the resulting harm.[25]

Moving from the village to the big city reveals more of the same. Bolivia's high-elevation urban areas such as La Paz, El Alto, and Cochabama are nestled in the valleys of the Andes and are nurtured by a steady flow of water from glaciers. In all of these areas, the impact of national water stress is already visible. The water-storage function of disappearing glaciers has already started to break down. With little to stop it, precipitation causes water to rush down the mountains as it falls, creating flooding. When the dry weather comes, not enough water comes down from the smaller glaciers, and there is drought. Flooding, drought, and landslides have all increased in the last fifteen years.

Until recently, the reliable supply of meltwater has meant that small dams and wells have been enough to generate water for farming, household use, and electricity. Like so many others in the developing world, Bolivian cities have seen rapid population growth that has put pressure on available resources. Climate change represents an additional and growing problem. The melting of the glaciers threatens the water supply needed to keep these cities functioning.

The situation is desperate enough that there is even talk of moving people to other places within Bolivia.[26] It is not quite the same problem as in Tuvalu or the Maldives, which may disappear altogether, but it has the same feel.

Glaciers supply 30 to 40 percent of potable water to La Paz and El Alto, two of Bolivia's three largest cities. During the dry season, glaciers are sometimes the only source of water.[27] Although problems are being felt today, future challenges will be much more severe. As glaciers melt, there is actually an increase in total runoff relative to what occurs when the glacier is maintaining its size from one year to the next. In other words, as the glaciers melt, there is some additional water available during the dry season. Once they are gone, however, that flow disappears. Even today, while there is some extra water flowing, many people in the cities do not have ready access to water.[28] The increased flow, which might seem beneficial in the short term, also causes more destructive flooding. As one farmer observed, "It's completely useless" for agriculture.[29]

For many Bolivians, then, retreating glaciers are not an abstract problem. It is comparable to Americans being told that the lakes or reservoirs they rely on are disappearing—wiping their key water-storage systems off the map.[30] Without adequate water at the right times of the year, crops do not grow, and rural communities cannot survive. Without water, businesses cannot operate, and people cannot go about their everyday lives, so cities fail. In the end, it comes down to the simple fact that humans need water all year round, and without glaciers, Bolivia will not have a consistent supply of it.[31]

If glaciers are failing and causing major disruptions in the water supply, it is natural to look for alternatives. The bad news for much of Bolivia is that geography is working against it. The most obvious alternative, irrigation, will not work in this mountainous terrain, where moving water any significant distance requires getting it to flow uphill. This explains why only about 10 percent of Bolivia's cultivated land uses irrigation. The rest relies on precipitation, underground aquifers, and water from glaciers.[32] Other human solutions, such as man-made reservoirs, dams, and projects to shore up entire mountainsides, would be technologically demanding anywhere, all the more so in Bolivia's mountains. Perhaps more importantly, they would also be prohibitively expensive and produce uncertain environmental impacts of their own.

Humans are good at adapting to different and changing environments. This skill has allowed us, as a species, to live and thrive in almost every part of the world, including inhospitable and mountainous parts of Bolivia. But when change comes too fast, our ability to adapt is overwhelmed. This is part of the story of climate change. Climates are always changing, but those changes are measured in very long periods of time. Human activity is causing the climate to change much more quickly. The Uru Chipaya have adapted over the centuries to changes in their environment, in their neighbors, and in technology.

For millennia, they have been up to the task, but they appear to have met their match with climate change.

As melting glaciers create water crises in much of Bolivia, they will also be creating a larger food crisis in the country. Bolivia has never been well suited to agriculture and can hardly afford the kind of blow to its agricultural production that climate change and melting glaciers are going to provide. A little less than 3 percent of the country's land is arable, and only 0.2 percent contains permanent crops.[33] Yet almost half of the population is involved in farming the land, mostly on small-scale subsistence farms. As water shortages make it increasingly difficult to scratch a living from the soil, farmers will have no choice but to move to the cities in search of alternative ways to survive. Doing so will add to the burden on urban infrastructures that are already straining. Looking globally, similar scenes will be playing out in many parts of the world. As melting glaciers, drought, floods, saltwater intrusion, and other factors disrupt food production, food prices will rise. If its own production falls off and global food prices rise, it is hard to escape the conclusion that Bolivia, already one of the poorest countries in Latin America, will simply have less food to eat.

The harsh impact of climate change on Bolivia is all the more tragic because Bolivia has played virtually no role in creating the problem. The country remains poor and has never had a large industrial economy of a sort that emits large quantities of GHGs. In 2004, for example, Bolivia contributed less then one-third of 1 percent of global GHG emissions.[34] Although no country deserves the kind of water crisis that Bolivia is facing, the disconnection between those who have caused the earth to warm and those who are suffering most is striking.

B. California: Unquenchable

One of the reasons Bolivia's water problems are serious is that the country lacks the financial muscle to respond effectively. The United States is in a different situation. As one of the richest countries on earth, it has much more flexibility in how it deals with the effects of climate change. This makes a big difference in how climate change is likely to affect the country, but it would be a mistake to think that money is enough to protect us fully.

Despite the dramatic difference in wealth (Bolivia's per capita GDP is about $1,200 per year, compared with the United States' $37,000),[35] the United States can expect a water crisis that, in many ways, resembles Bolivia's. The specific water issues I would like to discuss are centered in California, the country's richest state. For fifty years, California has been the largest agricultural producer in the country.[36] In John Steinbeck's novel

The Grapes of Wrath, the state is portrayed, with some reason, as a land of agricultural opportunity: "All of California quickens with produce, and the fruit grows heavy."[37] If the Golden State's output were removed from grocery stores in the United States, more than half of all domestic produce would be gone.[38] In some bins—for example, those holding almonds, dates, figs, olives, and artichokes—virtually all of it would disappear.[39]

California's agriculture is a far cry from Bolivia's subsistence farms. Production takes place on a massive scale, using the most modern technologies to increase yields and employing sophisticated marketing strategies. But no technology or business practice has been able to change the basic fact that producing food requires water. We have found ways to use water more efficiently so that less water can make more food, but the need for H_2O remains. The bottom line is that, like Bolivia, California uses all the water it can get, and climate change will disrupt that supply. California's system, for all of its sophistication, is still not very different from the single pipe we imagined earlier.

California has a long history of worrying about water. Access to water has always been a priority for agriculture in the state, in part because so much of the farming takes place far from the largest sources of fresh water. Of the top ten producing counties in the state, seven are in the drier areas of California (the lower middle to the far south), and none is located north of San Francisco, where much of the water can be found: "75 percent of the state's water demand originates south of Sacramento, although 75 percent of water supply in the state comes from north of the capital city."[40] The solution has been to move the water. Even relocating the water found within the state is not enough, however, and so California imports a great deal of water, much of it from the Sierra Nevada mountains. Without these efforts, crops would be desiccated in the beautiful California sunshine, and pastures would not yield enough food to sustain their livestock.

Water is needed for much more than just agriculture, of course. The lush green lawns in much of the state, for example, could not survive if they had to rely on the water that falls from the sky. To stay green, those lawns need to be watered. More generally, the people of California have the same water needs as everybody else—they need water for operating businesses, cooking, drinking, bathing, sewage systems, and so on. They are also American, and Americans love to use water. We use more water per capita than almost any other people on the planet.[41] That is fine as long as the water is available, but as the globe warms, it is likely that there will simply not be enough water—or enough water at the right times of year—to meet the demands of Californians.

Any serious water shortages will affect everybody in the state. There is no way to predict how political wrangling over water use will play out, and so it is hard to say with confidence which groups will fare better or worse, but it is a good bet that there will be plenty of pain to go around. We have already seen such shortages on a small scale. In 2008, for example, officials informed farmers in the Westlands Water District that water allocations would be cut by 60 percent. This is a district that produces $1 billion in farm revenue each year. There is no way to adapt to a cut of that size. When the announcement was made, the district's general manager, Tom Birmingham, said bluntly, "Half the people in this room are going to go broke."[42]

It is no secret that water supply is a constant problem for California. This reality is played out, among other places, in the halls of power. Farmers, environmentalists, cities, and businesses all fight with one another over access. This political jockeying is important to those involved, and to the state, but it can sometimes obscure the more important underlying issue. The political battles are about how the existing supply of water is to be distributed. One group may be able to do better if it is more successful in these battles, but that victory is at the expense of some other group. Giving more to farmers, for example, means giving less to others. As climate change makes water a larger problem, these fights will get more intense, and each group will invest more energy in trying to secure what it can, but none of these efforts will address the real problem, which is an overall shortage. The analogy to Black Friday shoppers applies here: the political battles determine who gets what but does not add any water to the system.

California's water challenges come about for slightly different reasons from Bolivia's, but the end result is the same. Like Bolivia, California relies on ice and snow in the mountains as its water-storage devices. Like Bolivia, California will have to deal with climatic changes that disrupts this system. In California's case, it is the Sierra snowpack that provides the water-storage and water-distribution services. As much as 65 percent of the state's water supply comes from the snowpack.[43] As is true with Bolivia's glaciers, the snowpack collects snow and water during the wet winter months and then dispenses it as meltwater during the dry spring and summer months.[44]

Having seen the challenges facing Bolivia, you will not be surprised by California's story. Rising temperatures have two main effects on the snowpack. First, a larger share of the annual precipitation falls as rain rather than snow, and so more water flows immediately toward the ocean during the wet season rather than being stored until the dry season. In other words, less snow is accumulated during the winter months. By 2050, for example, it is expected that the snowpack will have shrunk by at least 25 to 40 percent.[45]

Second, warming will cause an earlier spring runoff. By 2050, warmer weather will cause the runoff from the snowpack to happen about a month earlier than it does now.[46] This may not sound like a big deal, but it makes a large difference to the state's water management. Simply put, an earlier runoff is less useful than a later runoff. The problem is that an earlier runoff delivers more water early in the year than can be used or stored, which creates shortages later in the year. As water flows down from the snowpack, the fields, for example, do not need it as much as they will later in the year. Some of the water will flow into reservoirs and be available during the dry summer, but once these are full, there is nowhere for the additional water to be stored. Rather than being captured, then, much of the fresh water running down from the mountains will simply drain into the ocean.[47] That water will be lost, leaving less for human use.

Imagine eating a spicy dinner at a restaurant. When you first arrive, the waiter gives you a glass of water and places a pitcher of water on the table. Let's suppose that the pitcher holds the equivalent of three glasses, and this is all the water available for the meal. Whenever your glass is empty, the waiter refills it from the pitcher. Because the meal is spicy, the water is important to your enjoyment. Finally, let's assume that the four glasses of water you are given (one glass and a pitcher with the equivalent of three glasses) is just about the right amount of water for your dinner—meaning that this situation works well. The pitcher of water in this parable represents the water storage provided by the snowpack. The water in your glass represents the water that California receives during the wet season and either consumes immediately or stores in reservoirs. If you do not get enough water in a restaurant, you do not enjoy your meal. If the state does not get enough, it produces less food, suffers economically, and individuals' access to water is disrupted.

Now, think about how the impact of climate change fits in. Just as before, you are given a glass of water and a pitcher. This time, however, the pitcher is only two-thirds full. The missing water is provided to you, but rather than putting it into your pitcher, the waiter immediately tries to pour it into your glass. The glass was already full when you received it, so this extra water overflows, spills onto the table, and cascades down onto the floor. Although you were, in a certain sense, provided with the same amount of water, some of it is lost to you.

The water that is poured into your already-full glass as soon as you sit down is like the winter precipitation that falls in the Sierras as rain rather than snow and that immediately runs down toward the sea. The state may be able to use some of this water, much as your glass may be able to hold some of what the waiter pours, but much of it cannot be used when it arrives, and so it flows into the ocean and is lost, just as the water in the restaurant story falls onto the floor.

Next, imagine that as you begin to eat, the waiter arrives to refill your glass sooner than he did in the original version of the story. In fact, he picks up the pitcher and pours the equivalent of a full glass of water while your glass is still half full. You are not especially thirsty so early in the meal, so even if you knew that he was going to return so quickly, you would not want to gulp down a full glass of water in that time. The water he pours is useful in that it fills your glass, but he does not stop at that point, and enough water to fill half a glass spills onto the table and falls uselessly onto the floor. Once again, water is wasted. This time, it is because it was delivered from the storage device (the pitcher) before you were ready for it. This is what an earlier melting of the snowpack will do for California. The water will be delivered to the state, but it will leave the storage device (the snowpack) before we are ready for it. Although we will be able to capture some of it, some will be lost into the ocean.

As you can see, water is wasted in two different ways. First, the waiter pours too much into your glass to start with, leaving less in the pitcher, and then he pours from the pitcher into your glass too soon in the meal, causing the glass to overflow. At first, this wasted water is not a problem, because you still have enough in your glass. As the meal progresses, however, if you drink at your normal pace, you will run out of water. The water that was poured onto the floor is lost, and you will miss it. Making matters worse, when the water spills, you may not be thrilled to have it spilling onto the table or running off it, possibly into your lap. Too much water is its own problem.

California will have essentially the same problem. Too much will come during the wet season, and less will be stored in the snowpack, leading to a loss of water. When the spring comes, water will pour down from the mountains too early, once again causing some to be lost. This does not create an immediate shortage, because the reservoirs are full and the wet season has barely ended. A few months later, however, the dry season will be upon us, reservoirs will be running out, and we will miss that water. Just as you dislike water spilling onto the table or into your lap, the extra water early in the year is itself bad for California. An increase in water flow when it is not needed will increase the risk of flooding and the severity of floods.

If you know that there is less water available for your meal, you may opt to drink what you have more slowly. In the same way, California may try to conserve water more effectively. Even so, you will enjoy your dinner less, because you will spend the whole time wishing you could drink more water to offset the spicy food. For California, conservation is even harder. The political decision to conserve will require denying some users the water they are accustomed to. Something has to give if there is less water.

As with most climate-change projections, there is no way to know exactly how significant these effects will be, but it is fairly clear that they will be both large and negative. Using our conservative estimate of a temperature increase of about 2° C by 2100, the total annual flow of water from the Sierras is expected to fall off, although there is some possibility that it will actually increase. This is determined primarily by annual precipitation, which is very difficult to predict. What matters most, however, are the seasonal flows. For the April-to-June period, when dry weather increases the need for water, every projection anticipates a reduction in flow. An optimistic projection would be a falloff of about 11 percent during this period, while a pessimistic projection puts that figure at 20 percent.[48] If we assume a faster increase in temperatures, the loss of water will be even greater, of course.

Despite the irreplaceable role of the snowpack, the harmful impact of climate change would be smaller if precipitation patterns in California changed in favorable ways. If climate change makes it rain more within the state, and especially if it makes it rain more in the summer, this will provide at least some modest help. The scientific projections, however, do not offer good news. There are two main precipitation concerns. First, the total annual rainfall matters. More rainfall each year would help fill reservoirs and reduce the hardship during dry years (a below-average year is less serious if the average year is wetter). Second, and at least as important, is the distribution of precipitation during the year. Summer rainfall is especially valuable in California, so any shift in the timing of rain can make a big difference.

With respect to overall precipitation, the most likely scenario is a modest decrease as the world warms. These precise results depend on the particular model that is used, but overall, the message is that by 2050, we can expect a fall in precipitation.[49] If nothing else were changing, this would probably not be large enough to cause great anxiety, although estimates for the end of this century show larger reductions that might prompt more concern. Seasonal estimates are the same; they tend to show small reductions in precipitation in both summer and winter, but these changes are not dramatic. I don't want to focus too much on these precipitation changes, however, as they are somewhat more speculative than the snowpack effects. The more important point, I think, is that there is no reason to think that precipitation will increase enough to offset—even partially—the loss of water from the melting snowpack.

Once in a while, the state will get lucky, and a year (or even several years in a row) of better-than-average precipitation will come along, relieving some of the pressure. This will help with the water shortages, to be sure. Even these good years will not be entirely benign, because more precipitation will lead to more water flowing through the state during the wet season and more flooding.

Think again about the story of the spicy food. A year of above-average precipitation would correspond to a dinner in which you are allotted more water. This is good news, because late in the meal, when you most want a drink, it is more likely that you will have some water left. It also means, however, that more will be spilled onto the table both at the very start of the meal and soon thereafter when the waiter tries to refill your glass. This represents additional flooding in the state.

The flip side to these years of above-average precipitation will be years with less rainfall than normal. Drought has always been a fact of life in

California, and that is not going to change. Even if the water available in an average year is enough to meet the needs of California, that is not good enough. It is necessary to meet those needs in both good years and bad years. Remember that climate change will not only reduce the water available during summers, but it will also increase weather variability.

Returning one more time to the spicy-food story, it is easy to see what a drought means. Rather than starting the meal with the equivalent of four glasses of water, the restaurant gives you only three glasses. The waiter still pours too much to start the meal, and he still refills your glass too soon, so there is still some water loss. With less water to use, you will run out sooner and enjoy the spicy meal less. This is essentially what California will have to do. There will be years—and periods of several years—when there is less water than usual. There will be more frequent, and more severe, droughts.

Somehow, simply saying that there will be droughts does not convey the seriousness of the problem. One way to get a sense of how severe water issues will be is to compare what we can expect with the worst we have ever seen. The worst drought in the more than one-hundred-fifty-year history of California was the Great Western Drought of 1977. Based on research carried out by the California Department of Water Resources, we can expect water shortages worse than the 1977 drought in one out of every six to eight years by 2050, and one out of three to four years by the end of the century.[50] The most severe drought in one hundred fifty years will be replayed with the same frequency as the Summer Olympics.

To summarize, a shrinking snowpack, earlier runoff, and more frequent and severe droughts are all conspiring to undermine the state's water security. California will have no choice but to make do with less water, even without considering other problems such as a larger population, greater water demand as a result of higher temperatures, and so on.

Less water use will, of course, have an economic effect. Less food production in California means higher food prices everywhere. We can also expect, among other things, water rationing, more expensive water bills, more frequent fires (as a consequence of warmer, dryer summers and more droughts), changes in wildlife and natural vegetation composition, and an overall reordering of how we access food and water.

C. What We Have to Lose: Egypt and the Aswan Dam

It is difficult to get a sense of how catastrophic it will be to lose the world's permanent glaciers and other, similar, natural water storage devices because they have been with us since the dawn of civilization. Humans have always treated them as a fact of life, and we have adapted our existence to them. Once they are gone, we will have to adapt again. One way to get at least a glimpse of what such adaptation will entail is to examine an instance in which humans created a water-storage system that fulfills the function that glaciers have performed for many thousands of years. The benefits of this human effort give a sense of how much nature has provided with its glaciers and snowpack and how much we stand to lose.

In 1971, after twenty years of planning and work, Egypt completed the Aswan High Dam on the Nile River. The massive structure is more than two miles wide and higher than a football field is long. The dam created the Lake Nasser reservoir, which covers more than twenty-five hundred square miles of land in Egypt and Sudan.

Egypt built the Aswan High Dam to control the flow of the Nile. The river, which originates outside of Egypt's boundaries, has been the country's lifeblood for as long as humans have lived there. The Nile, however, has a mean streak. Prior to the construction of the dam, it flooded regularly. Years with heavy flooding could destroy farms and villages. Years with unusually low flooding brought drought. The Nile does not benefit from the moderating influence of glaciers on water flow. With the completion of the Aswan High Dam, however, Egypt was able to protect itself against the cycle of floods and droughts that the Nile had imposed for thousands of years. In other words, Egypt built a massive dam that served some of the same functions as the world's glaciers.

By controlling the flow of the Nile, Egypt was able to increase cultivated land by 20 percent and use existing farmland more intensively. This was a boon to food production, which supported rapid population growth in the country. More important, perhaps, the dam provided protection against droughts and floods. From the late 1970s into the 1980s, the region suffered through a devastating drought and famine that may have killed as many as a million Ethiopians and several hundred thousand Sudanese. The famine drew widespread international attention, and a major relief effort was launched. If you are old enough, you probably remember the song "Do They Know It's Christmas?" released in 1984 by a collection of well-known British and Irish musicians who called themselves "Band Aid." The song was created and sold to raise money for famine victims in Ethiopia. American musicians soon followed suit with a similar effort and a song called "We Are the World."

As the drought persisted, Egypt relied on the water stored in Lake Nasser to maintain its growth. The flow of the Nile was far below what Egypt needed to sustain itself. By the time the rains came in 1988 (and later years), even the reserves in the lake were perilously low. Without the dam and the water reserves it provided, Egypt would have faced its own version of the drought and famine that plagued its neighbors.

For many parts of the world that are losing glaciers, the story of Egypt and the Aswan High Dam will be told in reverse. Nature has provided glaciers that store water and moderate the effects of floods and droughts. When those glaciers are gone, countries and people will no longer be able to rely on them. Irrigation will be less reliable and effective, water flows will be less predictable, and droughts and floods will be more common. Food production will suffer in general, and during times of drought, there will be no water reserve to call upon. Egypt avoided the impact of the drought of the 1980s, while Ethiopia and Sudan did not. As the glaciers disappear, affected countries will lose the kind of protection that the Aswan High Dam provides for Egypt and instead be exposed in the same way that Ethiopia and Sudan were.

D. Half the World's People

The challenges facing the glaciers in Bolivia and the snowpack in the Sierras are not unique to those two places or contexts. In fact, just the opposite is true: they are replicated all over the world. There are glaciers sprinkled around the globe, and rising temperatures are melting them. Many glaciers will disappear before the end of this century, some long before then. More than one out of every two people on the planet live in watersheds of major rivers that originate with glaciers and snow in mountains.[51] This means that more than half the world's people will be directly affected by the loss of our natural water towers.

Melting glaciers tend to have a common set of features. As illustrated by the Bolivia case, as glaciers melt, there is an increase in both flooding and droughts and the disruption of water-supply systems that have sustained human populations for centuries or millennia. I discussed the Bolivian example because it shows so clearly how melting glaciers are bringing tremendous hardship to those who rely on glaciers for their water. It also illustrates that this reality will get worse as the earth continues to warm.

To appreciate the scale of this problem, however, we have to step back and look at glaciers around the world. It is, or at least it should be, terrifying to realize how many billions of people around the world are dependent on the role glaciers play as natural water towers. We know that climate change is causing glaciers to fail and that many will cease serving humanity over the next few decades. When they stop protecting us from floods, storing our water during wet seasons, and delivering it during dry seasons, we will have lost a water-management system that has been used by humans for millennia. Nobody knows how we will manage without it.

The dynamics of glaciers are quite complicated, and nobody knows exactly how fast they will melt. The timing depends, among other things, on the level of GHG emissions and the rate at which temperatures increase. Even if we make assumptions about temperature changes, the best estimates remain quite uncertain. We have to work with the information we have, though, and these estimates are better than nothing, as they give us some sense of how quickly things are changing. According to one serious and plausible attempt to predict future outcomes, a warming of 2° C by the end of the century—the working assumption of this book—will cause a loss of almost half of the world's glacier volume. For a temperature rise of 4° C, only 10 to 30 percent of glaciers are likely to remain.[52] In reading these predictions, it is important to keep in mind that major problems will arise long before the glaciers are completely gone. Most obviously, a smaller glacier stores less water during the wet season, triggering more floods, and then has less water to dispense in the dry season, prompting droughts. So a 50-percent loss of glacier volume will mean an enormous reduction in water security for many parts of the world.

I do not want to provide a detailed discussion of each of the world's important glaciers. That would do little to help explain why the melting of these natural structures is a threat. I do, however, want to mention a few of the most important glaciers. My goal here is to illustrate how many people and places in the world rely on glaciers and snow. When we talk about melting glaciers, we are talking about the dismantling of a central component in the world's water and food system.

The most affected part of the world, at least when measured by the size of the affected population, will be in Asia. This is hardly surprising, given that Asia is home to something like 60 percent of the world's population and the world's largest and highest mountain range. Among the river basins that are most dependent on glaciers and snow for their water flow, the Indus river basin in India serves a population of 178 million people, the Syr Darya and Amu Darya river basins in central Asia serve an additional 41 million, and the Tarim river basin in China serves 8 million. Other river basins that are highly dependent on glaciers and snow include the Ganges in India (407 million people), the Yangtze in China (369 million), the Huang He or Yellow River in China (147 million), and the Brahmaputra, which flows through Tibet, India, and Bangladesh (119 million). As climate change destroys the water-storage function that these regions depend on, floods and droughts will become more common, and access to water will be compromised in ways that resemble what is happening in Bolivia. In Asia alone, then, well more than a billion people face the risk of severe water shortages. For the key mountain ranges in Asia (the Himalayas-Hindu Kush, Kunlun Shan, Pamir, and Tien Shan), a reasonable estimate is that for temperature changes ranging from 1° C to 6° C, the current coverage of glaciers will decline by 43 to 81 percent.[53]

It is impossible to discuss glaciers in Asia without addressing a controversy surrounding the Himalayan glaciers that came along after the IPCC's 2007 assessment report. The IPCC stated that the likelihood of these glaciers "disappearing by the year 2035 and perhaps sooner is very high if the Earth keeps warming at the current rate."[54] Having read about the importance of glaciers, you can understand why this prediction was alarming—or, perhaps more accurately, panic-inducing. Fortunately, the prediction was wrong. In 2010, the IPCC itself conceded that it had made a mistake and that the 2035 date was not supported by reliable evidence.[55]

Needless to say, this was embarrassing to the IPCC, led to a series of blame-shifting efforts, and, most regrettably, provided fodder for deniers who sought to use this mistake to impeach the entire IPCC report. Putting aside the impact of the mistake, it is important to be clear that 2035 is not a meaningful prediction. Those who study Himalayan glaciers point out that there are, in fact, many such glaciers, and they are not all behaving the same way. Although most are retreating, a small minority of glaciers are actually advancing as a result of changing precipitation patterns.[56]

Despite the 2035 confusion, it remains the case that Himalayan glaciers are, by and large, shrinking. If the glaciers were, indeed, to vanish by 2035, we would face a humanitarian crisis of unprecedented scale within the next twenty-five years. In reality, we face a less apocalyptic but still critical crisis in the most populous region of the world. We do not know just when the glaciers will be gone, even if we assume warming at current rates. We do know, however, that there will be severe impacts long before the last glacier melts.

The discussion of Bolivia demonstrates that the Andes are also affected by glacier melt. Beyond Bolivia, other states in the region are affected, including Peru, Ecuador, and Chile. In Peru, for example, mountain ice fields have shrunk by more than 20 percent over the last thirty-five years.[57] Glaciers in the tropical Andes have been diminishing, particularly in regions at higher altitudes.[58] The pace of this decline has been increasing.[59] Diminished water supply caused by the melting of glaciers in the tropical Andes will affect about 80 million people.[60]

The glaciers in the Alps are also melting quickly. From 1950 to 1980, the Alps lost a third of their area and half of their mass. Since the 1970s, they have lost 20 percent of their size.[61] Since 2000, the volume of these glaciers has been falling by 2 to 3 percent per year.[62] At this pace and given likely climate scenarios, most glaciers in the Alps will be gone by 2100, with some scientists predicting an even earlier demise by 2050.[63] The Alps are the water tower of Europe, providing water to major rivers such as the Rhine and the Rhone.[64] As glaciers melt, it is expected to decrease the summer flow in major European rivers by as much as 50 percent in central Europe and 80 percent in some rivers in southern Europe.[65]

The above list—Himalayas, Andes, and Alps—captures the most significant glaciers in the world but certainly not all of them. Additional glaciers can be found in North America (especially in Canada and Alaska), Norway, Russia, central Asia, the Tibetan plateau, and even Africa. Not all of the glaciers in these places are central to human water-management systems, but many are. Virtually all of them are shrinking.

III. Drought Days

California's coming water crisis is a serious problem that will affect the lives of millions of people. When compared with Bolivia, however, the state has the enormous advantage of being wealthy, and while money cannot make the problem go away, it can limit the damage. Money, for example, makes it easier to build structures—canals, reservoirs, or dams—to manage the flow of melt-water. Money also makes it easier to import additional water or to deal with dislocations caused by water shortages. Although California is likely to be hit hard, it seems quite unlikely, for example, that California will suffer wide-spread starvation or famine.

Despite its wealth, California's agricultural system is at risk and is likely to be less productive. This is just one example of global food production under strain. Similar problems will exist in many parts of the world as climate change upsets farming practices. A rise in food prices is the obvious consequence of a reduction in food production (especially when coupled with a growing global population). If Californians are still able to get enough to eat, there will be other people—perhaps a lot of people—who will not be getting enough. A fall in global production has to show up in the form of less food on somebody's dinner plate. The losers in this game will be the world's poor.

More bluntly put, a reduction in global food production presents the risk of famine in many parts of the world. Although there is certainly poverty and hunger in every country, it has been a very long time since the Western, industrialized world, including the United States, has faced wide-spread starvation and famine. The rest of the world has not been so lucky. In the twentieth century alone, famines are blamed for more than 70 million deaths.[66]

For the sake of clarity, let's make sure the terminology is understood. The word "starvation" is used to describe an extreme form of hunger and malnutrition. People suffer from starvation when they do not take in enough vitamins, nutrients, and energy. Starvation and its gentler cousin, hunger, are rampant in the world. They are so widespread and cruel that the elimination of hunger is one of the eight "Millennium Development Goals" established by the United Nations at the dawn of the new millennium as part of a campaign to fight global poverty. Unfortunately, more than a decade later, progress has been slow. In 2000, about 14 percent of the world's population lived with hunger. By 2010, the number was 13.5 percent.[67]

It is possible for an individual person to suffer from starvation. *Famine*, in contrast, is distinguished from "normal starvation" by its scale.[68] Famine is starvation-plus. If there is famine, there must be starvation, but the opposite is not necessarily true. The 70 million killed by famine, then, represent just a small fraction of those killed by hunger and starvation. Both famine and starvation will increase as the world warms, but famine is somewhat easier to think about because it is triggered by large societal factors that we can try to identify. Starvation affects one person at a time and can be caused by any number of things.

There is no single cause of famine. Politics, economics, war, population growth, natural disasters, and more can all contribute to, or even produce, a famine. Climate change will affect some of these factors (e.g., chapter 5 of this book discusses war), but the greatest threat from a warming world comes from another common cause of famine: drought.

Examining specific regions is a useful way to learn about drought and, in particular, its impacts on people. We will do this below when we consider the Sahel region. It is also helpful, though, to get a sense of the big picture. Since the 1970s, when climate change was just starting to be noticed, the share of the planet's land area suffering from serious drought has more than doubled.[69] This one piece of information speaks volumes about the problem. When drought hits, human suffering is not far behind. Although not every drought leads to famine, more droughts means more famine.

The connection between drought and famine is so obvious that it hardly needs explaining. Shortages of rainfall and other sources of water make it difficult or impossible to grow crops. Harvests shrink, and there is not enough food to go around. Somebody has to go without. To be sure, there are often other influences: corrupt or incompetent leaders may prevent solutions from being found, or economic systems may price the poor out of the food market. These kinds of man-made problems can create famine even without a collapse of production. That said, there is no denying that less food production makes famine more likely. When drought affects harvests, it can trigger hunger, starvation, and, ultimately, famine.

Every parent has, at some point, sought to teach his or her child that the world is not always fair. "Life is not fair" is sometimes used to justify arbitrary outcomes ("Yes, your brother got a larger piece of cake—life is not fair") and sometimes to inculcate a greater sense of resilience ("Yes, the referee made a bad call on that play—life is not always fair—you have to deal with it and play hard anyway"). If one wants to see just how unfair the world can be, though, it would be hard to outdo the impact of climate change on Africa.

If you had to pick one place in the world that is likely to suffer the most from climate change, Africa would be the obvious choice. This is so for three main reasons. First, the continent is desperately poor and lacks the resources to respond to climate change. It cannot easily build seawalls to protect its coasts, develop irrigation systems to sustain agriculture, or provide assistance to individuals who are affected by climate change. Poverty also means that many people are already living on the edge and may not be able to survive bad events. Africa's social safety net is already in tatters and has no hope of responding effectively to growing demands and dwindling resources. Governmental institutions in Africa, which will be charged with managing a response to the changing climate, are often weak and ineffective and may not be up to this challenge. The continent's physical infrastructure (roads, water systems, etc.) is already in bad shape, and there is little money to adapt it to the needs of a different climate. The same is true of its health-care systems, police and security systems, and governmental institutions. All of these will be strained by climate change, often beyond their capacities.[70]

Second, the economy in Africa is heavily reliant on agriculture, which will be hit particularly hard as the climate changes. Reductions in agricultural yield will hurt the continent in two ways. It will reduce the amount of food available in a part of the world where there is already plenty of malnutrition and even starvation. According to one estimate, for every 1° C increase in temperature, grain production in Africa will decrease by 10 percent.[71] This is food that Africa cannot afford to go without. Less food will mean more hunger, worse health, and fewer productive citizens. In addition, the many people working in agriculture (in sub-Saharan Africa, this is 60 percent of the economically active population) will find it difficult to survive as their fields dry up.[72] The already-mentioned infrastructural weaknesses (both physical infrastructure and governmental capacity) will be especially acute here, because potential solutions such as improved irrigation are much less likely to be present or to be created.

The third reason for Africa's particular vulnerability is its location in the lower latitudes and—the issue I want to focus on—its vulnerability to more severe droughts. An IPCC report concluded with "very high confidence" that climate change will increase the frequency and intensity of water stress in Africa.[73] The amount of land considered semiarid or arid is expected to increase by 5 to 8 percent by the 2080s, for example.[74] One-third of the population of Africa already lives in drought-prone areas.[75] In part for this reason, an increase in the frequency or severity of droughts means something different in Africa from what it means in most other parts of the world. The region is already exposed to drought, so a further increase in that risk is extraordinarily harmful. If we think of Africa as a person, it is already suffering from malnutrition and dehydration. Climate change threatens to reduce further both the water and the food that it receives. A person in this situation, already clinging to life, may not survive. A continent cannot die, but more droughts in Africa will kill many people and will challenge the ability of individual countries to operate effectively.

To look at the prospects for and impacts of drought in Africa, I focus on two specific examples. Recent history has delivered plenty of other case studies that I could use. By one count, there were eighteen distinct famines on the continent in the twentieth century, eleven of them with death tolls of more than 100,000.[76] The two famines I have chosen teach different lessons. The Sahelian famine of the early 1970s highlights the catastrophic effects that climate conditions can have across a huge expanse of land. The Ethiopian famine of 1984, perhaps the best known of the African famines, gives us a chance to look at some of the local details that contributed to the disaster. These two experiences illustrate the tragedy that drought and famine can cause. Looking forward, there is no sign that famines are restricted to Africa's past. There remain food shortages in much of the continent, especially in sub-Saharan Africa, where one in three people still suffer from hunger.[77] As the planet warms, the future will bring more instances of drought and death.

A. Rescue Us: The Sahelian Famine

World War I came to be known as the "Great War" because its impact on the world (or at least Europe) was unprecedented. It was "great" in comparison with all prior European conflicts because so much of Europe was embroiled in war, because it led to so many casualties, and because entire societies, and not just militaries, were a part of the war effort. The "Cold War" earned its name because it was not a "hot war"—it did not involve direct military conflict among the superpowers. It did, however, involve the buildup of arms, proxy wars, and ideological conflict. The "Black Death" was named for the black spots it produced on the skin of the infected. In each of these cases, a major historical event was given a name that reflected reality. The name carried with it the emotion and importance of the situation.

In the early 1970s, the Sahel endured a harsh famine. Like the above-mentioned events, this one was given a name by those affected. The name reflects how people felt as they suffered through the darkest days of the crisis. Those affected called it ifza'una, which translates to, simply, "rescue us."[78]

The Sahel, whose name means "shore" in Arabic, stretches across the entire continent of Africa, directly south of the Sahara desert. Parts of Eritrea, Ethiopia, Sudan, Chad, Nigeria, Niger, Algeria, Burkina Faso, Mali, Mauritania, and Senegal are included (see figure 4.1).

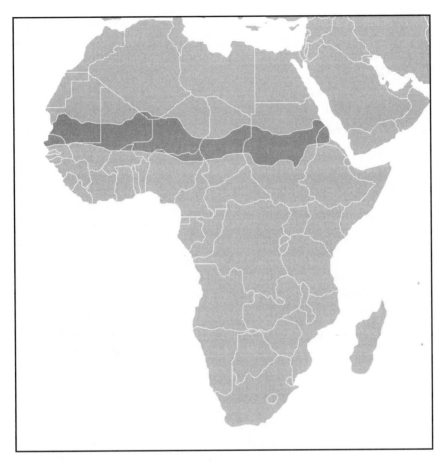

Figure 4.1 The Sahel. Source: http://mapsof.net/uploads/static-maps/map_sahel.jpg.

Starting in 1968 and continuing in subsequent years, rainfall began to decline in frequency and strength, especially in the northern regions of the Sahel. At the same time, there was also a shift in rain patterns that had a severe and negative effect on the agricultural economy.[79] These changes all translated to less water for the people of the Sahel, for their plants, and for their livestock. Without enough water, there was not enough food; crops withered, and animals died. This, of course, triggered a food crisis for the human population. At the time (and, indeed, still today), much of the region was isolated from major population centers and had poor ground transportation. These facts, combined with the poverty of the region's inhabitants, meant that when local food sources failed, no good alternatives were available. In normal times, residents relied on what they could grow themselves. When the crops did not grow, there was nothing else.

As this short summary suggests, the story of the Sahelian famine is in large part a story of drought. But it needs to be recognized that famine does not happen in isolation. Political and social structures, in addition to the actions of human beings, are always relevant to the question of how much food is available and who gets it. I certainly do not wish to suggest that policies in place in the Sahel were ideal or that human decisions were irrelevant. That said, while these man-made influences mattered to the Sahelian famine, nobody disputes the fact that drought provided the trigger.[80]

By 1973, the peak of the famine, the Sahel had endured five years of declining rainfall and a corresponding falloff in food production. About 100,000 people died from malnutrition in that year alone.[81] From 1968 to 1973, drought is estimated to have killed 250,000. As tragic as this figure is, it understates the damage done. Malnutrition is the obvious way in which famine kills, but it is not the only one. A lack of food weakens the human body in every way, leaving it more vulnerable to whatever challenges come along. When the region's refugee populations were examined, they were found to be infected by a laundry list of serious health problems: measles, cholera, cerebrospinal meningitis, whooping cough, viral hepatitis, tuberculosis, pertussis, and others, were common.[82]

Even the absolute number of dead fails to convey the devastation caused by the famine. Niger was one of the hardest-hit countries. Its mortality rate— the proportion of people in the population who died during the period—was 7 percent.[83] This translates to about 330,000 deaths in a country with a population of 4.8 million. If the United States faced the same mortality rate, 21.5 million people would die in just one year. Niger is a poor country, and some of these people would have died even without the famine, of course. But even taking this into account, the impact of the famine is staggering. Pakistan, for example, had a mortality rate of 1.5 percent in the same year. In the United States, the figure in 1973 was 0.94 percent.[84] Today, Niger's mortality rate is 1.4 percent.[85] The highest rate in the world is only 2.3 percent (Angola).

So, while we cannot attribute all of the deaths in Niger in 1973 to the famine, its death rate that year was off the charts. Even those who survived the famine and its effects often had to leave their homes and homelands to move to new countries, where they were at best tolerated and where national governments were poorly equipped to deal with a burgeoning refugee population.[86]

Countless details could be added to this simple story of drought, but they would not change the main message. When the rains do not come, especially when this happens year after year, millions of people who rely on agricultural production are vulnerable. For many people in the region, crops and animals are both a supply of food and the main source of income. Drought and famine ruin both.

There is no doubt that we could see a repeat of the Sahelian famine. Climate change makes this more likely, of course. Even without accounting for drought, the warming globe will produce a permanent decrease in food production sufficient to replicate the consequences of a famine. The IPCC estimates, for example, that the crop yields in Africa could fall by as much as 50 percent in some countries by 2020, less than a decade away.[87] If we add the effect of periodic droughts (and remember, the frequency of droughts will be higher), the prospects for the continent are, indeed, grim.

B. Ethiopia: Band Aid

The Sahelian famine of the 1970s was just one of several examples of drought and disaster in the region. A second, better-known famine occurred in Ethiopia in 1984. This example is worth looking at because it makes the point that catastrophic droughts are somewhat regular events in the Sahel and also because it allows us to look more carefully at how drought and famine played out in a single country.

Ethiopia is in eastern Africa and has an area of about 435,000 square miles, a little more than one and a half times the size of Texas (see figure 4.2). It did not escape the Sahelian famine of the early 1970s; 500,000 Ethiopians are thought to have died as a result of that catastrophe.[88] Just ten years later, another, even more deadly famine came along.

In 1983, just before the worst of the famine, the country's population was a little more than 40 million. The famine affected the entire country but was especially deadly in the northern and central regions.[89] The precise number of people killed is difficult to determine. The United Nations put the figure at 1 million,[90] but some observers claim that this number is too speculative to be taken seriously. Another estimate, based on surveys of survivors, estimates the deaths caused by the famine at 700,000.[91] Whatever figure one uses, it is a staggering death toll.

The drought in Ethiopia took place against the backdrop of a repressive and corrupt government led by Mengistu Haile Mariam. In 1991, an Ethiopian court sentenced him, in absentia, to death for genocide.[92] During his reign, it is estimated that he was responsible for killing between 500,000 and 1.5 million Ethiopians. Mengistu's political acts of repression and cruelty were disastrous. They included totalitarian rule, purges of political enemies, widespread killings, and the forcible relocation of hundreds of thousands. His general management of the country's economic and social systems was no better. When the drought arrived, the country was exposed and virtually defenseless.

Ethiopia's overall economic condition provided the ideal environment for a devastating famine. The country was (and is) heavily reliant on agriculture, and subsistence farming in particular sustains a large share of the population.

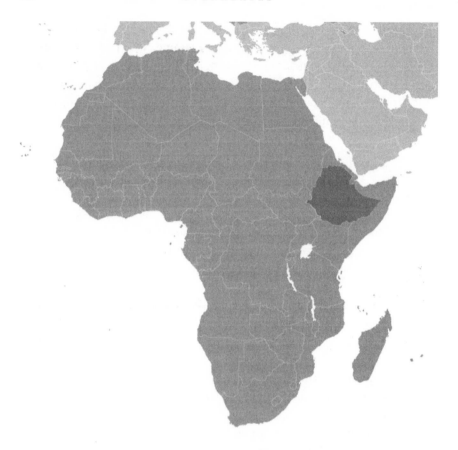

Figure 4.2 Ethiopia. Source: CIA World Factbook, 2012, https://www.cia.gov/library/
publications/the-world factbook/maps/et_largelocator_template.html.

This is at least in part because the arid conditions in the country lead to low
agricultural yields. Irrigation technology would help but was largely absent in
the early 1980s. In 1984, only 3 percent of irrigable land had actually been fit-
ted with irrigation systems. This left the large majority of Ethiopia's farmers
reliant on rain as the primary source of water for their crops.

As was the case with the Sahelian famine, this one began with a drought. The
country endured several consecutive years of low rainfall prior to 1983. Especially
poor precipitation in the second half of 1983, including a rainy season that ended
a month earlier than usual, delivered the critical blow. The consequence for food
production was catastrophic. Crop production fell by almost 2 million tons—
enough to feed between 6 million and 8 million people. In a country already
racked by poverty, there was no safety net and few alternative sources of food.

The Ethiopian government was aware of the problem long before 1984.
As early as May 1981, before the worst of the drought, it sought international

assistance. For the most part, these requests failed to mobilize the international community. In the middle of 1984, Ethiopia adopted a new strategy. It invited journalists and television crews into the country to see the ongoing suffering. The power of the media worked. When the food crisis was broadcast around the world, aid started to pour in. With the help of foreign aid, the famine ended in 1985. By that time, hundreds of thousands were dead, and countless more had suffered malnutrition and starvation. By early 1986, almost 6 million people were dependent on relief food;[93] without food aid, the scale of the tragedy would have been several times worse.

The Ethiopian famine offers an important lesson for the study of climate change and its future impacts. This experience shows in vivid detail, and at a price of hundreds of thousands of lives, the ease with which a drought can trigger famine and a massive death toll. This is especially true in a country that is already poor. A few years with less-than-usual rainfall can generate a social catastrophe. In 1984 in Ethiopia, the catastrophe took the form of 700,000 deaths. Looking forward, it remains the case that Africa, especially sub-Saharan Africa, is the poster child for drought and famine. It is more vulnerable than any other part of the world and is among the most likely to be hit hard by drought.

But it is a mistake to think that this is the only place affected. In the discussion of California, I mentioned that state's recently ended drought. Central America was hit by drought in 2001, during which 1.5 million were unable to feed themselves.[94] China, with its massive population, is also prone to droughts, as is the arid Middle East. As climate change increases the variability in weather patterns, we will see more periods of drought (and flooding, for that matter), more hunger, and more famine. In richer countries, there are more protections in place, a healthier population to start with, and greater financial resources to dull the impact of a drought. All of this means that we are not likely to see famine in the United States or Europe that resembles what we saw in Africa in the 1970s and 1980s. We are likely, however, to see agricultural crises, reduced production, economic losses, and displaced people. Less access to water means less food, and less food means that somebody in our already hungry world gets less to eat.

IV. When Climate Change Helps

The discussion until this point has presented a great deal of evidence that global warming is going to present many challenges to agriculture and, therefore, many challenges to ensuring that all people have enough to eat. Not everything written about climate change agrees with this assessment. Some observers even argue that climate change will be a net positive for food production, at least in some areas. For example, it is sometimes argued that Canada and Russia might benefit from higher temperatures and become more agriculturally productive.

There is something to these arguments. Specifically, there are places where agricultural conditions will improve. On the other hand, there is not much reason to think that the total worldwide effect will be positive, and there is plenty of evidence suggesting the opposite. The easiest way to understand this discussion is to walk through the key points made by those who suggest that there will be a positive effect.

There are two reasons it is sometimes said that climate change will increase agricultural yields. The first relates to the increase in carbon dioxide in the atmosphere. The basic idea is simple and relies on the fact that plants absorb CO_2 as they photosynthesize. If CO_2 "feeds" plants, then perhaps more CO_2 will allow them to grow faster and larger. The theory is that increased atmospheric CO_2 can act as an extra source of nutrients and help feed crops, something known as carbon fertilization.[95] If one were extremely charitable, carbon fertilization might be what Lord Monckton was talking about when he said, as mentioned in chapter 2, that reducing carbon emissions would be taking plant food out of the atmosphere.

Before leaping to the conclusion that increased emissions will create a bonanza for agriculture, however, it is important to look at what scientists know about the relationship between CO_2 and plant growth. The bottom line is that the purported advantages of carbon fertilization are mostly speculative, and we certainly do not have enough evidence to count on them.[96]

The idea that higher concentrations of carbon dioxide will promote plant growth is correct, but it comes with a lot of caveats. To start with, even if carbon fertilization works, it only works with some crops. It does not help, for example, with what are known as C4 crops (including corn, sorghum, sugar cane, and millet), which account for a quarter of all crops.[97] For crops that might benefit from increased CO_2, there is evidence that increases in yields as a result of carbon fertilization are accompanied by a decrease in nutritional value, so even if increased CO_2 benefits crops, it may not be good for humans.[98] Much more could be said here, but the point is that the effect of higher concentrations of CO_2 on plant growth is highly uncertain and may be so close to zero as to be insignificant. We may learn more with future scientific research, but for now, clear evidence that we will benefit from a burst of increased plant growth is hard to find.

The second way that global warming might help agriculture is related to the change in temperature itself. This is where our instincts about Canada, Russia, and other cold climates come into play. A modest warming in these places, without any other changes, is quite likely to increase agricultural output, by, for example, lengthening growing seasons.

When we step back to consider the worldwide effect, though, the story is not nearly as happy. In warmer parts of the world, higher temperatures slow plant growth by increasing the rate at which moisture evaporates from the soil and the rate at which plants lose moisture from their leaves (transpiration). On a global scale, this increase in evaporation is related to an expected increase in precipitation. There is a race, then, between evaporation/transpiration ("evapotranspiration") and precipitation. The winner in any particular place depends on local factors, but worldwide it appears that evapotranspiration will win, meaning slower growth.[99]

What we ideally want is a reliable model of agricultural output that takes all of these things (and many more) into account. Unfortunately, such a model does not exist. The system is too complex, and there is too much uncertainty to generate anything so comprehensive and precise. All is not lost, however. We do have reasonably good models that provide some guidance, and we have some sense of what they do and do not take into account.

The results from these models are sensitive to the assumptions made, but it is fair to say that overall, they do not offer a great deal of optimism about global agricultural output. First, the good news, or at least the less bad news: if we adopt optimistic assumptions about carbon fertilization and assume only modest temperature increases, and if we ignore a range of harmful effects that I will discuss below, the effect of climate change on agriculture is a fall in output of about 3 percent by 2080. The less good news is that if we abandon the highly optimistic assumption about carbon fertilization, food output falls by a more alarming 16 percent.[100]

We already live in a world with too much hunger, so any fall in food production is a bad thing. An honest assessment, however, forces us to acknowledge that the models almost certainly understate the losses we will face.

The problem is that the models ignore much of what is changing in the world. The basic strategy in these studies is to look at how changes in temperature and precipitation have influenced agricultural productivity in the past. Once the relationship is calculated, projected future temperatures and precipitation are plugged in to estimate future impacts. The results, then, represent estimates of future output assuming that nothing changes other than temperature and precipitation. There is a reason, however, that I have not emphasized the role of temperature on agriculture. I have focused instead on how climate change would undermine water-distribution systems and how increased weather variability would affect production. These effects are likely to be larger than the impact of temperature or annual precipitation levels by themselves.

Where does that leave us? Discussions of the potential for climate change to increase crop yields tend to focus only on temperature and precipitation. Looking only at these effects generates an unrealistically positive prediction of food production in the future. If we also make highly optimistic assumptions about carbon fertilization, the effect of climate change on agriculture is a small loss of output. If, instead, we acknowledge that the effect of carbon fertilization is largely unknown, the prediction is for a 16-percent loss of output. These losses are in addition to the losses already discussed. The disruption of water supplies and the increased variability of weather will do their own damage to food production. To illustrate, the price of wheat almost doubled between the summer of 2010 and early 2011. The main cause of higher prices was a fall in world production, explained in large part by reduced output in the former Soviet Union. This is a region that many people expect to benefit from higher average temperatures. In 2010–11, however, it was extreme weather that made the main difference: a record heat wave and drought caused a collapse in production.

All of this puts the argument that climate change will have some positive effects on agriculture into perspective. The argument is not wrong, because some countries (again, think of Canada) may, indeed, benefit from higher temperatures. Some of those places will also be well positioned to take advantage of the higher temperatures, because they will have access to fresh water, will have or will be able to build appropriate infrastructure, and will not be heavily affected by the increased variability of weather. Many other places, however, will see food output fall off dramatically as temperatures rise. Even where that is not the case, many of the places where the world's food is currently grown will experience water crises in the face of which it will be impossible to maintain current output levels.

V. Conclusion

To end this chapter, I return to Angkor, the capital of the Khmer Kingdom a thousand years ago. At its height, the collapse of the Khmer civilization must have seemed inconceivable. It had thrived for centuries and was (by the standards of the day) prosperous and technologically advanced. Yet it all came crashing down in a relatively short period of time, perhaps a hundred years. Although the exact details are not known, it appears that an important factor in the decline was a failure of the kingdom's water system.

Having read something about the water system used in the modern world, the parallel to the Khmer Kingdom should be clear. Our world has relied on the water storage provided by mountain glaciers and snow for many thousands of years. As these natural water towers shrink, year after year, our water system is being compromised. Little by little, we are losing access to water. Although more than half of the people alive today rely on these natural systems, we have no feasible plan to replace them. Within my lifetime or, if we are lucky, within the lifetime of my children, there will be acute water shortages affecting hundreds of millions, or perhaps billions, of people. Without enough to drink or to grow crops, we face the prospect of widespread famine.

Even places that do not rely on meltwater will face challenges. Africa, which depends on mountain snow and glaciers less than most places, will face severe water shortages of its own. Already poor and short of water, Africa will face an increase in the frequency and severity of droughts caused by climate change. The continent, already too familiar with the enormous toll that drought can take, will have little choice but to endure more dry periods, with scorched crops and mass starvation.

Looking globally, then, I fear that the future will be dry and hungry. Food prices will rise beyond the reach of many, famine will become commonplace, and entire communities—perhaps entire countries—will simply not be able to function. The changing climate will create a world of people dying of thirst and hunger.

|| 5 ||

Climate Wars: A Shower of Sparks

"There would be a nuclear war on the water dispute."

—*Nation*, Pakistan[1]

I. Sparks on Dry Hay

The summer of 1871 was unusually dry in Chicago. Hardly any rain fell in the weeks leading up to what would become the famous Great Chicago Fire. Winds blew in from the southwest, bringing heat from the plains and drying whatever moisture remained in Chicago's wooden buildings. Nobody could fail to notice the risk of fire. The city was like a pile of dry hay, waiting for a spark.

Even with the parched conditions and even with an urban landscape full of wooden buildings, fire was not inevitable. Everything was ready to burn, but the city hoped to avoid a fire long enough to make it through the dry spell. There was no way to eliminate the dangerous situation; Chicago simply had to hold on until rain reduced the risk of fire. It had to hope that conditions changed before some event, some ignition, caused the city to burn. Unfortunately, luck was not with Chicago that summer.

On Sunday, October 8, a fire started in the barn of Patrick and Catherine O'Leary. By the time it was put out on October 10, 1871, the fire had burned several square miles of the city, killed several hundred, and left 100,000 homeless.

To this day, the cause of the fire remains a mystery. One theory is that a man named Daniel "Peg Leg" Sullivan started it. Some cannot resist speculating that perhaps his wooden leg slipped on the floor, causing him to drop a match, a pipe, or a lantern. Another account centers on an eighteen-year-old named Louis Cohn, who was in the barn gambling with friends, including one of the O'Learys' sons. Mrs. O'Leary chased the gang from the barn, and it is thought that perhaps Cohn started the fire by accidentally knocking over a lantern as he fled.

The most colorful and best known of the stories, however, pins the blame on Mrs. O'Leary's cow. On October 9, 1871, the *Chicago Evening Journal* reported that the fire was caused by "a cow kicking over a lamp in a stable in which a woman was milking."[2] Poor Mrs. O'Leary and her cow were soon infamous, so much so that a song about the incident became popular:

> Late last night, while we were all in bed,
>
> Old lady Leary lit a lantern in the shed,
>
> And when the cow kicked it over, she winked her eye and said,
>
> "There'll be a hot time in the old town tonight."

History has come to the conclusion that Mrs. O'Leary was, in fact, not responsible, and there must have been some other cause. More than twenty years after the fire, the reporter who first printed the story blaming Mrs. O'Leary and her cow admitted that he had made it up.[3]

Whatever the truth, *something* started the fire. Without a spark, the hay would not have ignited, and the city of Chicago would not have burned. The story of the cow is so well known and colorful that it has lived on, so I'll refer to the cow as a stand-in for whatever really started the fire.

Even if the story of Mrs. O'Leary's cow were correct, the dangerous conditions created by the hot, dry environment make it ridiculous to say that the cow was the only reason for the fire. If the lantern had been extinguished when it was kicked, if it had fallen on a wet floor, if someone had immediately put out the flames, if it had been raining, if the event happened in winter, or if the fire department had responded more quickly, the city might not have burned. From this perspective, one might say that Mrs. O'Leary's cow did not "cause" the Great Chicago Fire.

The relationship between climate change and violent conflict is like the relationship between Mrs. O'Leary's cow and the Chicago fire. It would be an overstatement to say that the cow was solely responsible for the fire, but it is fair to say that the cow triggered the blaze. If the animal had never knocked over the lantern, the fire would not have started, or at least, it would have required some other triggering event.

Just as the Chicago fire required both the right physical conditions and something to cause ignition, warfare and other forms of violent conflict require both a background set of conditions and a triggering event. For many areas of the world in which there are high tensions, climate change could turn out to be that triggering event. It could cause war in the same way that something in the O'Leary's barn caused the Chicago fire: by providing the spark that turns a dangerous situation into a violent one.

When violence breaks out, it is always the result of multiple factors. Even when egomaniacal dictators use military force in an attempt to grab territory from neighbors, there is no single cause. The August 1990 Iraqi invasion of Kuwait, for example, is fairly described as an attempt by Saddam Hussein to expand Iraq and seize control of Kuwait's oil resources. But a whole series of other influences were also relevant to the decision.

Iran and Iraq fought a vicious war between 1980 and 1988. When the conflict finally ended, Iraq faced economic and political instability. It had a large and burdensome debt, repayment of which would be difficult in the face of inflation and unemployment. The government weathered several coup attempts and an assassination plot against Hussein. To explain the country's economic woes, Hussein asserted that Kuwait was producing and selling too much oil, thereby depressing prices. There were also allegations that Kuwait was "slant drilling," a practice by which oil wells on the Kuwait side of the border would be drilled at an angle so that they could reach oil on the Iraq side.

All of this explains why Iraq may have been interested in invading. Even so, had the United States reacted differently, Hussein might have been dissuaded from attacking. When Iraqi troops assembled on the border between Iraq and Kuwait, the United States failed to issue sufficiently strong warnings or credibly to threaten a military response to an Iraqi invasion.

So while it is reasonable to describe the invasion as an Iraqi grab for land and power, there were many factors at play. If Iran and Iraq had not gone to war, if that war had been less costly for Iraq, if other economic solutions had been available, if the United States had reacted differently to the possibility of an attack by Iraq, or if Iraq had more accurately predicted the response of the United States and other countries, the attack might never have taken place. Without the 1990–91 Persian Gulf War, of course, the American invasion of Iraq in 2003 also might not have happened.

More generally, ethnic tensions, historical animosities, poor governance, communication failures, and many other factors can push people to the edge of violent conflict. Climate change will introduce environmental stress to these situations. Groups that are already suspicious and mistrustful of one another will have to find new ways to share scarce resources such as food, water, and land. Climate change will not create war out of nothing; it is unlikely, for example, that France and Belgium will find themselves at war. Instead, climate change will amplify existing problems and in some cases push disputes from peaceful negotiations to violent confrontations.

Fire requires oxygen, fuel, and heat in order to burn. The city of Chicago provided plenty of oxygen and fuel. According to the legend, Mrs. O'Leary's cow provided the heat. Many different circumstances can create conditions ripe for warfare, but all of them require some sort of triggering event. Climate change will generate a competition for resources that could well be that triggering event in many places, leading to warfare, death, and suffering that might have been avoided in the absence of climate change. It will be the spark.

II. The First Climate-Change War?

During the first decade of this millennium, Darfur, in Sudan (see figure 5.1), endured the latest instance of humanity's greatest evil: genocide. (What was Sudan during the time period at issue is now divided into Sudan and South Sudan.) The region suffered through violence from 2004 to 2009. As a result of these years of fighting, 300,000 people died, and 2.7 million fled their homes. The Janjaweed, a militia of Sudanese Arabs alleged to have ties to the Sudanese government, systematically targeted black African ethnic groups—the Fur, Zaghawa, and Masalit. Acts of staggering cruelty and violence were perpetrated. In one town, for example, the Janjaweed killed at least sixty-seven people, abducted sixteen schoolgirls, and raped ninety-three others, some in front of their families. As if the rapes themselves were not barbaric enough, the hands of rape victims were branded as an eternal reminder of the assault and as a tool to ensure the victims' ostracism from the community.[4]

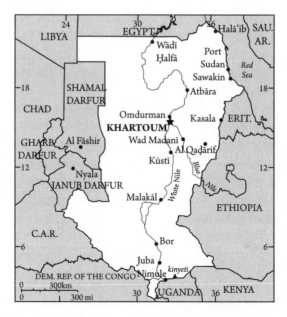

Figure 5.1 Sudan, including Darfur. Source: http://mapsof.net/uploads/static-maps/darfur_map.png.

The loss of life and displacement of people in Darfur would have been bad enough on its own, but genocide—the attempt to destroy an ethnic group— is its own brand of evil. The use of genocide put this conflict on the small yet chilling list that has become synonymous with the darkest faces of humanity: the Holocaust, Rwanda, Cambodia, Armenia, and now Darfur.

Perhaps because the West acted slowly in response to the 1994 genocide in Rwanda, Darfur received considerable media attention. There were, for example, calls for military intervention to stop the killing. Even the secretary-general of the United Nations suggested that a military response would likely prove necessary. No such action took place, however, and the violence continued. Nearly thirty resolutions on the conflict were adopted by the United Nations Security Council between 2004 and 2009, but they were mostly ignored by the Sudanese government. In 2007, the United Nations African Mission in Darfur was established to provide protection to civilians. By 2009, the conflict had mostly quieted, although occasional attacks and isolated violence remain.

As already mentioned, wars are rarely caused by a single, discrete act. It is sometimes said, for example, that World War I was caused by the assassination of Austrian Archduke Franz Ferdinand on June 28, 1914. There is a good deal of truth to that statement, because the assassination triggered a series of events that led to war. Gavrilo Princip, a member of the Serbian nationalist society known as the Black Hand, assassinated Ferdinand. Austria-Hungary responded with a severe ultimatum to Serbia, and when Serbia did not accept the entirety of the ultimatum, Austria-Hungary declared war on Serbia. This declaration led to others, and, like dominoes falling, all of Europe was soon involved in what started as a regional conflict. Russia was allied with Serbia and declared that it would mobilize its army. Germany, allied with Austria-Hungary, then joined the fray by declaring war on Russia. France was drawn into the conflict based on a treaty with Russia. When Germany invaded Belgium on August 4, 1914, Britain entered the war based on a treaty with Belgium.

So while the assassination can fairly be called a cause of the war, much more than the assassination was necessary to bring Europe into conflict. Among other important factors, a series of rigid alliances and a failure of efforts to find peaceful solutions were also critical. If the background conditions in Europe had been different, the assassination of Ferdinand would have led to no more than a small-scale conflict, and children today would not learn about it in school. But with things as they were, Princip's actions triggered one of the greatest slaughters in human history.

In Darfur, climate change may have played the role of Gavrilo Princip. It may have pushed an already fragile situation over the edge and into open conflict, just as it is likely to do in other parts of the world as the earth warms. Darfur provides a cautionary tale in this regard. Millions of people paid dearly while this story unfolded. That tragedy will be compounded if we allow climate change to trigger future conflicts.

To understand the Darfur conflict, it is necessary to understand the situation that existed before violence broke out. Many residents of northern Darfur were nomadic Arab groups who herded camels. These groups had no tribal lands, and so they used wells and pasture lands belonging to sedentary farmers to raise their livestock.[5] Nearly all of those who owned land were farmers of non-Arab descent. Prior to the drought of the mid-1980s, the two groups coexisted. Farmers allowed nomads passing through to use their wells and to feed livestock on the remainders from the harvest. Relations between the groups had always featured a certain degree of animosity, but disputes were resolved by tribal leaders, and those decisions were accepted in the Sudanese capital, Khartoum.[6]

This coexistence was disrupted by a drought that started in 1984, but the water shortages had been brewing for a long time. Average levels of rainfall fell by almost 7 percent from the 1960s to the 1970s and an additional 18 percent from the 1970s to the 1980s. Among other effects, this caused the growing season to contract; it used to run from May through September and is now June through August.[7]

When the drought took hold, things developed as you might expect. With water in short supply, farmers were less eager to share. They fenced off their land to protect it from the livestock of the nomadic herdsmen. The nomads had two options: go elsewhere in search of land, or resist the effort to keep them off land they had been using for many years.

When the drought worsened in the late 1980s, the nomadic tribes who had decided to stay stepped up their efforts to gain control of land owned by black farmers. In 1987, Arabs published a manifesto proclaiming the racial superiority of Arabs over the Fur, Darfur's largest tribe of farmers (the word *Darfur* means "land of the Fur"). Publication of the document sparked violence that left 3,000 people dead, mostly Fur. A peace agreement was reached in 1989, but fighting resumed and continued throughout the 1990s, by which time hostilities between Arab nomads and various tribes of African farmers (Fur, Zaghawa, and Masalit) had solidified.

An important player in the conflict in Darfur was the Sudanese government. Throughout the 1980s and 1990s, the government, dominated by Arabs, provided political and material support for fellow Arabs in Darfur.

In 2003, African farmers rebelled against what they described as the government's "neglect and political marginalization" of Darfur. Two rebel groups representing black African Muslims—the Sudan Liberation Movement and the Justice and Equality Movement—attacked government forces in Darfur, initially targeting military bases and airports, where they killed hundreds of soldiers. The government launched a counterinsurgency from Khartoum and supplied the Janjaweed with weapons, equipment, military intelligence, and air bombings. The Janjaweed response was merciless, targeting militants and civilians alike, killing 200,000, displacing millions, and destroying entire communities in Darfur.[8]

The participants in the conflict chose sides along ethnic lines. Arabs supported the government (although some Arabs who held land tried to remain neutral), while Africans opposed the government.[9] This division along ethnic lines, however, was as much coincidence as anything else. The source of the conflict is more appropriately identified as struggles over land and water, rather than ethnic tensions, although the latter were obviously relevant.

Among those who survived the conflict are many whose suffering continues. Of the more than 1 million people displaced by the fighting, some 200,000 Sudanese live in refugee camps in neighboring Chad, and many more live in the more than two hundred camps in Sudan. Some refugees have benefited from the fact that both they and the Chadians near the border belong to the Masalit ethnic group. The shared ethnic identity helped them to secure a friendlier welcome. As the years have passed, however, Chad's patience is wearing thin.

Chad is already a poor country and has experienced its own civil unrest, with its own displaced people. Among its problems have been accusations from the Sudanese government that Chad provided support to rebels in Darfur. Allowing Sudanese refugees to stay in Chad only increased the tension between Chad and Sudan.

Chad's poverty is relevant because the Sudanese refugees are almost entirely dependent on aid. Although some foreign assistance has been provided, these refugees also consume Chad's scarce resources. They forage for firewood and straw, for example, making it harder for locals to find those same resources. Even when assisting the refugees does not take anything from the local Chadian population, it can create friction. Chadians "watch as the refugees benefit from schools where children sit under canopies, adult literacy programs, health education and...food, all managed by the Red Cross." The reaction from nearby Chadians is predictable: "We don't have anyone who will give us food. We have nothing. Everyone is suffering."[10]

As I discussed in chapter 3 on rising seas, the refugees hardly have it easy. Despite policing by United Nations peacekeepers and the Chadian army (another commitment of Chadian resources), there are plenty of examples of violence against the refugee population. One source of violence was the Janjaweed militia, who would cross the border from Sudan to attack refugees. Women are particularly vulnerable and face an ever-present threat of violence and rape.[11]

Nobody could credibly argue that the crisis in Darfur was caused by environmental factors alone. It required a toxic combination of historical circumstances, long-standing ethnic tensions, environmental factors, conflict-management failures, and human decisions (sometimes cruel and ruthless). The drought of the 1980s and the environmental decline in Darfur were not the sole causes of the violent conflict, but they did play a central role in bringing existing tensions to a head.

Of course, the world has witnessed droughts throughout human history (and before, for that matter). You might be thinking that while you can accept that drought contributed to the suffering and atrocities in Darfur, climate change might have had nothing to do with it. Even if this were the case, the conflict in Darfur would be an important warning sign. It demonstrates how environmental problems in general, and drought in particular, can aggravate stress among humans, leading to violence. The cause of the environmental stress (e.g., natural climatic cycles versus climate change) is not of much consequence to those murdered in Darfur. They are equally dead either way. The lesson, then, is that drought can trigger conflict. Because climate change will increase the frequency and intensity of drought in many parts of the world, we can also expect an increase in violent conflict as a result of climate change.

All of that said, it is worth making the point that the drought probably was a product of climate change. We cannot pinpoint with complete certainty the origins of a particular drought, even though we know that climate change will increase the frequency of droughts. Nevertheless, the most likely cause of the reduction in rainfall in Darfur since the early 1980s is, indeed, global climate change.[12]

The Darfur conflict is just one example, of course. By itself, it does not prove that climate stress triggers conflict or, assuming it does, that it would do so frequently. The only way to get a sense of the role of climate in conflicts is to look to past events. The difficulty is that climate change will dramatically increase climate stress in the future, so the past is a poor guide. The best we can do, then, is look back to see where things stand at the present. We know that the future will be worse, so this at least gives us a partial sense of what is to come. A recent study by researchers in Colombia examined more than two hundred conflicts from 1950 to 2004 and compared the pattern of conflicts with El Niño years, which happen about every five years and which tend to bring hotter, drier conditions, and La Niña years, which tend to be cooler.[13] Both El Niño and La Niña affect tropical countries most severely. The study found that the risk of conflict in tropical countries increased from 3 percent during La Niña years to 6 percent during El Niño years. In other words, these climatic swings doubled the risk of conflict. Needless to say, this is a frightening result. There is already plenty of conflict in the world, and the thought that changes to the climate could double the frequency of conflict (or worse) is staggering. In the sections that follow, I identify just a couple of places in the world where major conflicts could emerge. If climate change increases the threat in these areas as much as this study suggests, the case for combating climate change is very strong indeed.

III. The Middle East: Too Much Oil, Too Little Water

In many parts of the world, including the United States, access to water is so easy and affordable that we rarely pause to think about it. This is true even in my own state of California, whose water challenges are discussed in chapter 4. Government officials charged with managing the water supply worry about how to ensure that the state has a sufficient supply to sustain itself, but the rest of us rarely even consider the issue. In practical terms, the most severe constraint most of us face is that we are told not to water our lawns or wash our cars during certain periods.

In this environment, it is all too easy to lose sight of the obvious reality that every human being needs a certain amount of water to survive. We use water for drinking, bathing, cleaning, and growing our food, among other things. A true shortage of water—one in which people cannot meet their basic needs—is a serious crisis. It harms human health, reduces food production, and, as the story of Darfur illustrates, can cause friction and, ultimately, conflict.

Despite our frequent disregard for water issues, the conflicts they cause should not surprise us. Water is, after all, the single most important natural resource for human survival, and in many places, water demand continues to grow rapidly as populations swell. Viewed from this perspective, it is perhaps remarkable that water does not provoke more violence. If we add the fact that water supplies are going to be disrupted by climate change, it is easy to see that the world faces very real risks. What, for example, will Israel or Iran do if it cannot secure access to enough fresh water? What if water is available but is being used by a neighboring country? Thanks to climate change, we are likely to learn the answers to these kinds of questions.

Our general indifference to water scarcity is reflected in the way resource scarcity appears (or doesn't appear) in discussions of the Middle East (see figure 5.2). The security situation in the Middle East is at least superficially familiar to anyone who reads the newspaper. Most people in the West, however, never focus on the very serious water challenges in the region. Water management, after all, does not immediately grip the imagination or cause one's pulse to accelerate. When you think of conflict in the Middle East, you probably think of religion, territory, or ideology. It is unlikely that you think of water.

Figure 5.2 The Middle East. Source: http://www.worldatlas.com/webimage/countrys/me.html.

And although water is certainly not the only, or even the most immediate, reason for the problems in the Middle East, it is an important part of the equation, and it will become more so as the planet warms.

The specific water issues vary from place to place in the Middle East, but the general theme is always the same: everybody needs more water, and there is only so much (or so little) to go around. Downstream countries accuse upstream countries of not sharing the resource appropriately, countries believe their neighbors are using more than their fair share, and water projects to increase access in one country are viewed as threats to the water supply in another.

The Middle East has everything that makes a climate war likely. First, it is chronically short of water. Second, it has a history of conflict that stretches back thousands of years, continues unabated today, and features some of the oldest and most venomous religious and ethnic animosities. Third, the region is of enormous strategic importance because it is the source of much of the world's oil. These three factors by themselves make the region volatile and explain why the rest of world devotes so much attention to the area.

The Middle East has all of the ingredients in place for violent conflict or, more accurately, conflict that is even more violent than what is going on now. International efforts have sought to improve the situation and build a more sustainable peace. These efforts can be thought of as having two main goals. The short-term goal is to avoid an outbreak of violence, but the larger and longer-term goal is to improve overall conditions and to reduce the risk of an outbreak in the future.

Unfortunately, a permanent solution to tensions in the Middle East has been elusive. The background conditions have not improved much over time, and there is an ever-present risk that the region will be engulfed in violence. Unless and until that fact changes, we have no choice but to hope that nothing happens to trigger war. In particular, we have to hope that climate change does not play this role.

A. Dry Hay

The region known as the Middle East and North Africa is home to 4.4 percent of the world's population but only 1.1 percent of total renewable water resources.[14] This makes it one of the most water-poor parts of the world. Needless to say, it also makes water an important regional issue. In recent years, the problem has been getting worse rather than better. Population in the region continues to grow, increasing the demand for water. At present, the region's population is growing at about 2 percent per year, making it the second-fastest-growing region in the world (after sub-Saharan Africa). The combined population of Syria, Lebanon, Israel, Jordan, and the occupied Palestine territories, for example, is expected to increase from 42 million in 2008 to 71 million by 2050.

It is no surprise, then, that water withdrawal has increased by 29 percent in the last decade. You do not have to be a math whiz to realize that if you already have major water issues, increasing the rate at which water is used cannot be a good thing. The general water shortage is made more dangerous by the fact that natural sources of water are not distributed evenly among the countries of the region. Within the Middle East, 75 percent of the region's fresh water is located in just four countries: Iran, Iraq, Syria, and Turkey.[15] Only three countries—Egypt, Turkey, and Iran—can be said to have an abundant supply of fresh water today, and every single country in the region other than Turkey relies on water originating outside its borders.[16] A majority of these countries have per-capita water supplies far below the point at which countries are commonly considered to be "water-stressed."

The region has dealt with the water shortage in a variety of ways, including more intensive use of water (through recycling), desalinization efforts, and the importation of food, which reduces the water demands of local agriculture. Even with these efforts, however, the Middle East and North Africa region currently consumes 120 percent of renewable water supplies.[17] In other words, every year, they use more water than nature is able to replace.

Depleting water supplies faster than they are renewed is obviously not sustainable, and there are signs that the situation is getting worse. For example, water is expected to be a limiting factor in agricultural production in the coming years in Iraq, Jordan, and Syria. Iraq anticipates that increasing regional demand will result in water shortages in the Tigris and Euphrates rivers between 2020 and 2030, just ten years away. Syria estimates that the area equipped for irrigation currently exceeds the country's irrigation potential. There are only so many ways this situation can develop. States may find ways to reduce per-capita water use, although this is politically difficult. Desalinization can help increase water supplies, but it is extremely expensive. A third method is simply to continue withdrawing groundwater at unsustainable yields. This last approach leads, ultimately, to acute shortages and, very possibly, to conflict over water.[18]

The entire region is so chronically short of water that it is impossible to describe all of the potential sources of stress. With the exception of Turkey, every country in the region has reason to be concerned that one or more other countries will interfere with its access to water. Rather than attempting to list all of the ways in which water and climate change might generate tensions, I will focus on just two situations to give a sense of how complex and explosive the situation is. First, I discuss Turkey's role as the starting point for the Euphrates and Tigris rivers. Second, I examine Israel's use of the Jordan River.

B. Upstream, Downstream

Water ignores national borders. When water flows from one country into another, the upstream country has little incentive to worry about either the quantity or the quality of water that finds its way to the downstream country. The downstream country, on the other hand, cares passionately about the flow of water across its border. The upstream country can pollute, dam, or divert rivers or in some other way make the water less useful for the downstream country. In some circumstances, such actions threaten the very existence of the downstream country and generate strong reactions. This basic struggle between upstream and downstream countries lies at the heart of many water disputes around the world, including in the Middle East.

There is a single dominant upstream country in the Middle East: Turkey. Turkey occupies a privileged position at the head of the region's most important water source, the Tigris and Euphrates rivers. This fact of geography makes it a critical and powerful player in regional water politics.

The Euphrates and the Tigris start separately in eastern Turkey and wind their way southeast through Syria and Iraq until they join in southeast Iraq and then empty into the Persian Gulf (see figure 5.3). This river system provides a critical source of water in the Middle East.[19]

Like any country, Turkey wants to take advantage of its resources—including water. To do so, it launched an ambitious water program in the 1960s called the Southeast Anatolia Development Project (GAP). The project, which is still not complete, calls for twenty-two dams, nineteen hydropower projects, and irrigation of more than 6,500 square miles of land. The goal is to promote the development of the southern Anatolia region of Turkey, home to some 9 million people. Along the way, it is expected to more than double the irrigated cropland in the country, increase electrical output, and make Turkey a food exporter.[20] These are all laudable goals—it is hard to criticize efforts to grow more food and create more hydropower, at least if we look at it from Turkey's perspective.

Viewed through Syrian or Iraqi eyes, on the other hand, the GAP project is a disaster. The GAP is expected to reduce Syria's water supply from the

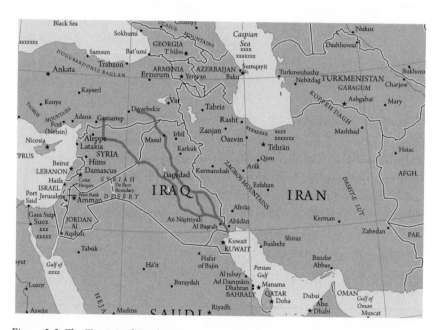

Figure 5.3 The Tigris and Euphrates rivers. Source: http://ehsworldstudiesjackoboice. wikispaces.com/Mesopotamia+-+Tigris-Euphrates+River+Valley+%28Current+Events%29.

Euphrates River by up to 40 percent and that of Iraq (which gets access to the water only after it flows through Syria) by 80 percent or more.[21] The volume of the Tigris River will be reduced by almost 50 percent.

Think about how you would react to Turkey's announcement if you were responsible for water management in either of these downstream countries. Predictably, Syria and Iraq have complained that the projects will reduce the water flow in the river and limit their own ability to use the water for energy or agricultural purposes. Things did not get any better when Turkey completed one of the dams (the Ataturk dam) and withheld the flow of the Euphrates for a month.

Consider Iraq's perspective on this change. It gets all of its water from these two rivers (40 percent from the Euphrates and 60 percent from the Tigris). It is facing a 54-percent reduction in its total water supply.[22] Could you cut the water use in your household by more than half without major disruptions? Think how difficult it would be for a country to do so. Now, think about how much harder it is to do in a country that is already unstable and already faces a shortage of water. If the expected extreme deprivation becomes a reality, you can be certain that Iraq will not simply accept it. The country will blame Turkey and Syria, its upstream neighbors. Iraq's accusations will no doubt include threats of action if the water flow is reduced so dramatically.

Recognizing the problem, Turkey and its downstream neighbors have made efforts to resolve the water tensions. In the early 1980s, the three countries formed a Joint Technical Committee for Regional Waters, but it never had much success and fell apart by 1994. In 1987, Turkey and Syria agreed that Turkey would guarantee Syria a minimum flow of at least 500 cubic meters per second from the Euphrates. Syria and Iraq have an unofficial agreement about the same river under which Syria has promised to provide Iraq with 52 percent of whatever water it receives from Turkey. There is no comparable agreement governing the flow of the Tigris. Even the agreements in place have not ensured a peaceful coexistence. Syria, for example, has accused Turkey of violating its commitment. Most recently, the three countries seem to have launched a renewed attempt to find ways to cooperate. Syria and Turkey are cooperating to build a dam along the Orontes River, for example.[23] Whether these ongoing efforts at cooperation will prove successful is difficult to predict. As water stress increases, there will be no way to avoid the reality of diminished supplies, which will test the resolve of everyone involved. When upstream countries such as Turkey find themselves with less water than they need, will they ignore this sort of agreement and simply use the rivers that flow through their countries to meet demand?

All things considered, the situation among Syria, Iraq, and Turkey is fairly peaceful. If and when the GAP is completed, however, it will have an enormous impact on all three countries and will greatly increase water shortages in Syria and Iraq. Faced with this kind of threat, downstream countries have few options. Syria and Iraq will have to confront Turkey and try to ensure the continued flow of water into their countries. From Turkey's perspective, the GAP is being built to provide more water for household use and to generate electricity. It would make no sense for Turkey to undertake this massive construction effort and then agree to leave water flows as they were.

The bottom line in this situation, as in many other water disputes, is that there is only so much water available. Turkey cannot consume more unless Syria and Iraq receive less. If there is to be peace, either Turkey must give up on some important and achievable development goals, or Syria and Iraq must make do with less water, even as their populations grow.

To these tensions will be added the stress of climate change. As the earth warms, the entire Middle East will become more arid. Climate change alone is expected to reduce the flow of the Euphrates by as much as 30 percent. This means that even without the GAP, existing tensions among Turkey, Syria, and Iraq will be magnified as each country tries to maintain its current level of water access. Even without the GAP, Syria and Iraq will be trying to persuade Turkey to reduce its water use, although doing so would be economically, politically, and socially painful for Turkey. With the GAP added to the mix, Syria and Iraq could face catastrophic shortages. Predicting what will happen is impossible, because we do not know how these countries will react. Will Turkey be willing to reduce its own water supply and share the pain? Even if it is, will Syria and Iraq accept the inevitably diminished supply? Keep in mind that for each country, the stakes are very high. The region is desperately short of water, and water is life.

When climate change reduces water supplies, the decisions that states make about access to water will be matters of life and death. If states treat the issue with the urgency it deserves, then they will be proactive in securing water for their own populations. These actions may make sense for each individual state, but they also make it difficult for the region to avoid bloodshed.

C. Heightened Conflict and the Golan Heights

As is so often true in discussions of the Middle East, we must pay particular attention to Israel. There is nothing especially unique about Israel's situation with respect to access to water or the expected impact of climate change, but the relationship between Israel and its neighbors is high on the world's list of potential flashpoints. So we can think of Israel as one of the driest and most combustible parts of Chicago before the Great Fire.

Like the rest of the Middle East, Israel already faces significant water stress, and the situation is only going to get worse as the climate changes. Israel's existing water supply faces at least two distinct threats that have nothing to do with climate change. First, overuse of some aquifers has led to their salinization and depletion, reducing the available water. Second, two-thirds of Israel's water currently comes from the Golan Heights and the mountain aquifer that straddles the West Bank and Israel. These are politically sensitive areas, and Israel's ability to maintain current water-use practices from these sources depends on how the politics of the Middle East play out. Israel's ability to increase its water use without provoking a backlash from others in the region is even more doubtful. The reverse is also true, by the way; the region's politics depend in important ways on the reality of the water situation.[24]

When Israel was created in 1948, there was enough fresh water in the Jordan river basin to support its population, in addition to the populations of other states in the region. During the 1950s, however, water needs grew with, among other things, a growing agricultural sector.[25] Since that time, pressure on water in the region has only increased.

Waterways have always made convenient borders. They offer a natural barrier to separate hostile groups, they provide a clear and (mostly) nonmanipulable boundary, and they can be agreed upon without painstaking surveys and endless squabbles over the exact location of a land boundary. This advantage comes at a price, however. A river or lake can be used to separate countries, but the water itself refuses to stay in place on a single side of the boundary. If one side removes water from a river, dams the flow into it, or pollutes the water, both sides are affected; thus, when rivers and lakes are on a boundary, they are an invitation to conflict. Each side has an incentive to use the water without regard to the needs of the other country. These problems are often addressed by agreement, of course. That is how Canada and the United States have managed to share a large border crossed by several rivers and the Great Lakes. In the Middle East (as in other regions), such agreements can be hard to negotiate. There is no natural or self-evident set of rules that should form the basis of a sharing arrangement, so almost every country can come up with reasons that it should be able to use more water rather than less. If the situation also involves suspicion and mistrust, resource-sharing efforts are even more likely to cause conflict.

Israel's most important source of water is the Jordan River, which runs between the Golan Heights and Jordan on one side and Israel and the West Bank on the other. It starts on the flanks of Mount Hermon in Lebanon and flows south to Lake Tiberias, also known as the Sea of Galilee. It flows southward from Lake Tiberias until it reaches the Dead Sea. The Jordan river basin includes parts of Jordan, Israel, Syria, the West Bank, and Lebanon, and for several of those places, it is the only significant source of surface water. The Golan Heights are located just to the east of the Upper Jordan River. Israel captured the territory during the Six-Day War in 1967 and has controlled it ever since.

Israel has always understood that its security is intimately connected with access to water. Just a few years after coming into existence, the country developed a plan for a major water project that would come to be known as the National Water Carrier (NWC) project. The goal was to divert water from the Upper Jordan River in the northeast of the country and deliver it to the cities and the arid south.

Surrounding Arab nations, already hostile to Israel, viewed this project as a threat to their own water supply. In 1960, leaders at an Arab League Summit decided that the Israeli program must be stopped. They devised a plan of their own to divert water from rivers in Syria and Lebanon before it reached the Upper Jordan River, rendering the NWC project useless. The stage was set for a confrontation. Israel's then-foreign minister, Golda Meir, did not mince her words. She warned that any attempt to divert the northern tributaries of the Jordan River would be "an outright attack on one of Israel's means of livelihood" and a "threat to peace."[26]

By the time the NWC was completed in 1964, the Arab project was under way. Israel responded with its own plan to divert water, which provoked a skirmish with Syrian soldiers. On January 1, 1965, the Palestine Liberation Organization tried and failed to attack the NWC system. There followed a series of military confrontations involving both soldiers and war planes. Sporadic fighting continued right up to the Six-Day War in 1967. Israel's occupation of the Golan Heights during and since that war ensured that the Arab water-diversion project would not be restarted.[27]

Tension over the NWC and the response from Israel's Arab neighbors led to military confrontations but did not, by itself, trigger a full-blown war. War did come to the region in 1967, though, and the water feud was a contributing factor.[28] Ariel Sharon, prime minister of Israel from 2001 to 2006, described the conflict as the trigger to the Six-Day War: "While the border disputes between Syria and ourselves were of great significance, the matter of water diversion was a stark issue of life and death."[29]

During the Six-Day War, Israel gained control of territory, including both shores of the Upper Jordan and about two-thirds of the Golan Heights. In 1973, Syria and Egypt launched an offensive, and fighting continued until March 1974, when an armistice was signed. In 1981, Israel annexed the Golan Heights (which it had controlled since 1967). That action was criticized internationally, including by the United Nations Security Council. Nevertheless, Israel continued to exercise control over the territory and does so to this day.

The Golan Heights are important for a variety of reasons, most obviously because they sit between Syrian, Lebanon, and Israel. They are also important to Israel because they supply that country with much of its water.[30] At present, Israel has full control of Lake Tiberias. If the pre-1967 boundaries were reestablished, as Syria sought during the 1999 negotiations hosted by the United States, the eastern shore of the lake would be controlled by Syria. From Israel's perspective, this would represent an important loss of water security.

This short history shows one critical reason Israel is reluctant to give up control of the Golan Heights. Giving up its control over Lake Tiberias and much of the Jordan river basin would be surrendering control of its national water faucet. On the other hand, Syria views Israeli control of the Golan Heights as an illegitimate occupation and as a breach of human rights based on the treatment of Syrians living in the region.[31]

D. Climate-Change Sparks

Up to this point, I have not said much about how climate change affects the water situation in the Middle East. Climate change and warfare interact most dangerously in areas where there is a large and preexisting risk of conflict. In those contexts, climate change threatens to magnify existing risks, perhaps making the difference between an uncomfortable peace and a shooting war.

I have focused on the non-climate-change problems in the Golan Heights to make the point that the risk of violent conflict is already high. In this sense, it is like the city of Chicago toward the end of the summer of 1871. Chicago was ready to burn, and all that was needed was a spark to ignite the blaze. Once the fire started, it grew and spread rapidly, causing enormous damage.

In the Middle East, tensions over water and other issues in the Golan Heights illustrate the fact that the region is primed for combustion. All that is needed for an explosion of violence is the right (or, more accurately, the wrong) spark. If war erupts in the region, it may spread just as the Chicago fire did, and the consequences for both the region and the world could be devastating.

I want to be clear that climate change is not the only thing that could ignite conflict in the region. There are plenty of ways that things could go badly in the Middle East, just as there were many places in Chicago where a fire could have started. What makes climate change special, and especially worrisome, is that it will destabilize the entire region. In national-security circles, climate change is often referred to as a "risk multiplier," meaning that while it is not likely to provoke large-scale violence all by itself, it can greatly increase the risk of war in places where that risk is already present. As climate change turns up the pressure on all countries in the region, that risk will be multiplied. Climate change threatens to be the spark that ignites the region.

This brings us to the question of how climate change will affect the area and, in particular, the Jordan and Euphrates rivers. The complexity of climate change and uncertainty about how humans will behave in the coming decades makes it impossible to identify future regional temperatures and precipitation with pinpoint accuracy. We can, however, find sensible estimates of what is likely. As with all such estimates, the reality may end up being better or worse. And, as is usually the case, the impacts of climate change grow much more quickly if reality is worse than expected than they shrink if reality is better than expected.

The IPCC FAR provides a relatively fine-grained set of estimates for temperature and precipitation changes over the rest of this century. Those estimates predict that the Middle East will see a reduction in precipitation of 20 to 30 percent and an increase in temperature of between 2° and 4° C, with slightly larger increases in summer than in winter.[32]

These estimates are based on an assumption that global average temperatures will increase by 2.8° C. Because I am making the more conservative assumption that global average temperatures will increase by only 2° C, we need to keep in mind that these predictions are worse than would be true under a global 2° C temperature increase. Even so, it is clear that there will be a dramatic reduction in precipitation. Suppose, for example, that precipitation falls by 20 percent—the low end of the above estimate—or even that it falls by only 15 percent. These are still enormous losses for a region that is already chronically short of water. Whatever the reduction, it will lead to shorter winters, dryer and hotter summers, and more frequent and extreme heat waves. All of this also increases evaporation of surface water, including from the key rivers in the region.

What does this mean for access to water? A reduction in rainfall obviously reduces the amount of water in rivers. Higher temperatures that increase the rate at which the surface water evaporates compound this problem. With both precipitation and temperature shrinking the volume of rivers, it is not surprising that experts expect reductions in the water flow.

In 2006, a team of researchers produced a projection of how climate change would affect twenty-four of the world's rivers, including the Euphrates, between now and the end of the century. The results of the study give us some insight into the challenges with which Turkey, Syria, and Iraq will have to contend. Once again, the news is not good. By examining precipitation patterns and evaporation rates, the study predicts a reduction in mean discharge from the Euphrates of 38 percent. In other words, more than a third of the water will simply no longer be in the river.[33]

It is easy to imagine that a loss of more than a third of the water will cause tensions between Turkey and its downstream neighbors to boil over. Their problems seem like a walk in the park, however, compared with the crisis likely to face Israel and the other states that rely on the Jordan River. It is expected that the flow of the Jordan River will fall by as much as 85 percent by the end of the century.[34] Israel's own Ministry of the Environment has warned that there may be a reduction in water supply of 60 percent from 2000 to 2100.[35] This is an almost unimaginable catastrophe. Even if both of these predictions are too pessimistic, a reduction of, say, 40 percent would still be disastrous.

These are not only future concerns. The early effects of climate change are already being felt around the world, and the Jordan River is no exception. Between the changing climate and the withdrawals of water from Lake Tiberias, the water in the lake has fallen by 14.5 feet since 1967, and the eastern bank of the lake has retreated anywhere from 120 to 300 meters in that same time. The lake is shrinking before our eyes.[36]

Measuring the flow of water in rivers is one way to evaluate the future water problems of the region. An alternative is to get a sense of how much the per-capita water supply will change over time. In the Middle East, it seems that every factor is pushing toward reductions in the per-capita water supply. When everything is taken into account, it is expected that per-capita supply of water will fall by 50 percent by 2050.[37]

One could say a lot more about water and climate in the Middle East, but the above is enough to make the point that existing tensions will be aggravated by extreme water shortages. Looking forward, the basic dynamic of water in the Middle East is actually quite simple. The region is rife with ethnic, political, and religious strife, it faces a rapidly growing population, and it already has less water than it needs. Climate change will reduce the available supply of water further. Large-scale violence is not inevitable, but climate change certainly makes it much more likely.

IV. Global Warming and Nuclear Warnings in South Asia

What are today's greatest threats to humanity? If you were asked to make a list of, say, the three most worrisome dangers we face as a species, what would you include?

You won't be shocked to know that climate change makes my list. A second entry would probably be global poverty, which condemns billions to live on less than two dollars a day.[38] Much of humanity struggles every day just to survive, endures deprivation and hunger, cannot properly provide for children, and ultimately dies at a much younger age than those of us fortunate enough to be among the wealthier on the planet. These two concerns—climate change and poverty—interact, mostly in harmful ways. Most important, those who are already so poor as to live on the edge of survival will bear more than their share of the burden from a changing climate.

As climate change and world poverty demonstrate, to make my list, a threat has to affect massive numbers of people. Most of the problems we focus on every day (e.g., elections, daily fluctuations in the business cycle, tensions with China) just aren't "big" enough to make the cut. But my list so far has only two entries, so I have to add one more. It seems to me that the next choice is easy and is something that many people would put in first place: the danger from nuclear weapons. From World War II until the end of the 1980s, we worried about the risk of a nuclear exchange between the United States and the Soviet Union. That concern receded with the end of the Cold War. It was replaced, however, with a different nuclear concern. By the late 1980s and early 1990s, the list of states with advanced nuclear-weapons programs (most of which were known to have nuclear weapons) included the United States, Russia, Britain, France, China, India, Pakistan, South Africa, and Israel.[39] Since that time, South Africa has dismantled its nuclear program, while North Korea and Iran have joined the club.

Nuclear weapons were first used by the United States during World War II. Nobody knows exactly how many people were killed in the attacks on Hiroshima and Nagasaki, Japan, but a reasonable estimate that includes the lingering effects from radioactive fallout is something in the range of 350,000. This is a large number by any measure, but it is even more shocking when you consider that the population of the two cities at the time of the bombing totaled only about 580,000. The bombs killed about 60 percent of the people in the cities that were targeted.

Fortunately, since 1945, human beings and the countries they govern have somehow managed to resist using nuclear weapons to attack one another. Whether we continue to avoid the almost unimaginable scenario of seeing these weapons actually used depends on the decisions made by the countries that control them. Two of those countries are India and Pakistan.

British rule over the Indian subcontinent (including India, Pakistan, and Bangladesh) came to an end in August 1947, when the Indian colony was divided into two nations. The larger of the two, India, was to be Hindu, and the smaller, Pakistan, was to be Muslim. For the first twenty-four years of its existence, Pakistan included two pieces of noncontiguous territory, one on each side of India, unimaginatively called West Pakistan and East Pakistan. When East Pakistan gained independence in 1971, it became Bangladesh.

Whatever the merits of dividing the former colony into two states along religious lines, the plan led to chaos. Millions of people found themselves in the "wrong" country and had to migrate to the "right" one. Hindu refugees traveled from Pakistan to India, and Muslim refugees moved in the opposite direction.

The princely state of Jammu and Kashmir lay between these two new countries. The problem was that it did not fit neatly into the plan to divide India and Pakistan along ethnic lines. Although the state's population was predominantly Muslim, a Hindu maharajah was in charge. The states (or, more accurately, their leaders) had the autonomy to join either Pakistan or India. The maharajah initially tried to avoid this catch-22 and took no position on accession to either India or Pakistan. Armed soldiers crossing into the territory from Pakistan quickly defeated his effort at neutrality. He responded with a promise to join India (he was Hindu, after all).[40] Pakistan refused to accept the legality of the accession, and the first war between India and Pakistan was triggered all of two months after their independence. The war lasted through 1948, and, while casualties were limited to fifteen hundred soldiers, it set the stage for tension and hostility that has remained in place ever since.

India and Pakistan have had a total of four outbreaks of violence in the six and a half decades since their independence. The second episode occurred in 1965, when Pakistan-controlled guerrillas crossed into India-controlled Kashmir. India launched a counterattack into Pakistan. The conflict was ended with the help of the UN Security Council, and the preconflict borders were restored, with both parties pledging to resolve their differences through diplomatic, rather than military, means.[41] However, these commitments to peace were short-lived, and the countries were at it again in 1971. This time, India successfully intervened on behalf of the independence movement in East Pakistan, leading to the creation of an independent Bangladesh.

In 1972, the countries entered an agreement called the Simla Accord, which clarified the border between them and relieved tensions, at least for a time. By 1984, however, a new flashpoint emerged: a dispute over the Siachen glacier. Ambiguity in the Simla Accord triggered a race for control of two strategically important mountain passes in the region. India managed to secure both passages, but the conflict is formally still going on today in what is the highest battleground on earth. There is no actual fighting at present, although both sides have military forces deployed.

The stakes of this drama are dramatically higher because both countries have nuclear weapons. They are no longer simply enemies whose inability to resolve their differences might lead to war. They are countries whose animosity could trigger a nuclear exchange. The increase in risk has not improved relations. Occasional skirmishes and regular verbal attacks by political leaders continue to this day. During one pointed disagreement in 1999, for example, both sides are reported to have placed their nuclear forces on alert. More recently, India suspects that Pakistan's government was involved in the 2008 terrorist attacks in Mumbai that killed 179 people.

In some volatile regions, there are only a few ways that existing tensions are likely to transform into violence. In other contexts, including the India-Pakistan situation, there can be a whole range of potential triggering events. It would be fruitless to try to identify every possible source of friction and assess how it might lead to violence. Instead, let's look at just one of the many areas of conflict. My goal here is to show how climate change aggravates the relationship between these countries. Although there are already conflicts over resources, climate change will make these much more serious and much more dangerous. As in the Middle East, the problem revolves around access to water.

Imagine two brothers, Ian and Peter, sharing a bottle of soda. If you have children, you can easily imagine how this simple situation can provoke conflict. Suppose Ian drinks from the bottle first. If it is a small bottle, Ian is tempted to drink it all, and he certainly wants to drink more than half. Even if Ian is in a good mood and plans to give half to Peter, he might threaten to drink more than his share just to make the point that he could and to make it seem that Peter should be grateful for whatever he gets. Or perhaps he will offer to give half to Peter only if Peter offers him something in return. Peter, meanwhile, knows all of this and is suspicious from the start. Almost regardless of how much soda is left, Peter is likely to claim that he received less than his share and to protest that he should have more influence over how the drink is divided. If the brothers are already mad at each other for some other reason, of course, the sharing of soda is more likely to cause an escalation in the conflict.

Now, suppose that the bottle is just large enough for both Ian and Peter to feel that each one had a reasonable amount to drink. Because there is enough soda (at least, if neither of them is greedy), the two may be able to manage the tension without the situation devolving into fighting. There will probably still be some arguing and reciprocal accusations, but in the end, with a little luck, one can at least hope that each will get to drink some soda and peace may be maintained. The likely result is different, however, if before either of them gets to drink from the bottle, Ian and Peter's parents take half of the soda for themselves and then return what is left to Ian. With this reduction in available soda, the chances of a fight are dramatically higher. If Ian takes what he judges to be his normal drink, there will be nothing left for Peter. If Peter insists on his normal drink, he will object to any drinking by Ian. If they share, both will still be thirsty at the end. We cannot be sure that Ian and Peter will come to blows in this scenario, but it would hardly be surprising. They may fight even if their parents do not take some of the soda. If the parents do, however, we know that the chances of a fight are much higher.

Access to water issues between India and Pakistan create a situation that is not so different from this little story. I do not mean to minimize the seriousness of the disagreements between these two countries by comparing their conflict to a mundane instance of sibling rivalry. I make the comparison only to show how a shrinking supply of a critical resource can cause problems, especially when one country has first crack at it. Rather than sharing a bottle of soda, the countries share the Indus River, which runs through both of them.

The Indus has always been tremendously important, so much so that it gave its name to India. Although both India and Pakistan rely on the Indus river basin, Pakistan's dependence is nearly complete. Virtually all of its water comes from this one source,[42] and that is really all you need to know to appreciate the problem. Anytime a critical river flows across a border, there is a potential for trouble. When the countries on either side of the border dislike each other, the river can become a weapon used by the upstream neighbor against the downstream one. If the downstream country is completely dependent on the river, the potential for conflict is even higher.

The impact of climate change on India, Pakistan, and the Indus River is easy to understand. A warming planet will affect the flow of the river, causing more floods at some times of the year and more droughts at others. The value of the river will be greatly diminished for both countries and will force both countries to adapt. Because the water reaches Pakistan only after it has passed through India, the former is understandably concerned that its water supply is at risk. Anything India does to secure its own water supply will affect Pakistan, often in negative ways. And because climate change will reduce the overall value of the river, both countries will already be facing shortages and disruption. Because Pakistan will suffer as climate change affects the river and will suffer even more when India tries to protect its own interests, it will look for ways to maintain sufficient access to water.

There are, of course, plenty of rivers in the world that cross borders. Why is this particular river so important? Part of the reason has already been mentioned: the river is absolutely critical to Pakistan's survival. Without it, the country would simply not have enough water. This problem, especially from Pakistan's perspective, is made more serious by the fact that India has toyed with the water supply in the past.

During the 1948 conflict, India blocked the flow of water in two large canals that provided water to crops in Pakistan. This maneuver was politically rather than environmentally motivated; India was not so much in need of the water as interested in asserting its sovereignty over the river. A major crisis ensued, and the eventual resolution only came about because the World Bank, on which both countries depended for access to international finance, brokered an agreement. Any doubt that India could compromise Pakistan's access to water vanished in the wake of this dispute. In 1960, the countries agreed on the Indus Water Treaty, which helped to clarify water

rights over some of the Indus River's tributaries. Most observers credit the
treaty with reducing tensions and limiting the number of wars between India
and Pakistan since that time to two. Although the Indus Waters Treaty has
been useful, it has not fully resolved the issue. Pakistan still remembers when
India denied its access to water and knows that this could happen again at
any time.

The Indus River starts in the Himalayas, and about 80 percent of its water
consists of runoff from glaciers, with the balance coming from tributaries in
India and Kashmir. After passing through India, it continues into Pakistan.
The river's water is heavily used for both hydroelectric power and irrigation;
the Punjab, which straddles India and Pakistan, is one of the most intensively
irrigated regions in the world. The heavy use of the river provides resources
that are essential to the survival of many millions on both sides of the
India-Pakistan border.

Even without climate change, the Indus would be in serious trouble. The
population of India is expected to increase by more than a third over the next
forty years, from its current 1.1 billion to 1.5 billion. Pakistan is growing even
faster. Its current population is 160 million, and it will have 270 million by
2050, an increase of two-thirds. That adds up to more than a half-billion additional people, each of whom will need water.

As population has increased, the river has been affected. Seemingly at every
turn, a portion of the river is diverted into a canal for irrigation or used to generate electricity. Rather than flowing into the Arabian Sea, as it used to, the
Indus is fully consumed by human uses. The sea has responded by pushing
inland forty miles (so far), destroying more than a million acres of agricultural
land. It has also destroyed more than 85 percent of the mangrove-forest ecosystem. At least five animal species in the region have been lost, and fish have
seen a decrease in their reproductive success.[43] The population growth in the
area, by itself, presents a threat to the river and, therefore, to the people who
depend on it.

It is at this point in the story that climate change enters the picture. In some
ways, the story is not so different from that in the Middle East. In both the
Middle East and the Indus river basin, human water needs already outstrip
available supply. Both regions face rapid population growth in the coming
years, which will put further stress on water resources. Preexisting animosities, combined with these conditions, set the stage for a climate-change spark
to ignite a conflict between nuclear powers.

Before discussing the nuclear risk, however, let's think about how climate
change could tip India and Pakistan from animosity to full-blown warfare. We
have to begin at the top of the world, in the Himalayas. More than nine thousand glaciers populate this enormous mountain range and collectively create

a massive freshwater-storage facility. The water from the mountains flows to hundreds of millions of people in China, India, Bhutan, Nepal, Afghanistan, Pakistan, and Bangladesh. The Ganges River, for example, is fed from these mountains and provides water to more than 400 million people.

In chapter 4, I described how glaciers around the world are in retreat and how their gradual disappearance will be disastrous for both water management and food production. Himalayan glaciers are certainly no exception to this pattern of melting. In chapter 4, I focused on how melting glaciers will affect access to water and food. I did not mention, except in passing, another important and dangerous effect: the disappearance of glaciers and mountain snow will provoke a life-and-death competition for resources among countries.

The Indus basin relies primarily on glaciers in the western Himalayas. As these glaciers retreat over the next several decades, their melting combined with more intense rainstorms (another predicted effect of climate change), will aggravate the region's already serious flooding problem. Once the glaciers are gone, the opposite will happen: there will be a precipitous decline in total river flow, leaving the river with perhaps only 60 to 70 percent as much water as exists today.[44]

Quite aside from the total volume of water delivered each year, climate change will create large swings in water flow from season to season. During rainy seasons, water will cascade down the mountains more easily and more quickly, triggering more frequent and more severe flooding. During the dry season, there will be fewer and smaller glaciers (and eventually, no glaciers), which means less runoff and more water shortages.

In July 2010, Pakistan experienced tragic flooding that should be seen as a preview of what is to come. The arrival of the annual monsoons swelled the Indus River, flooding nearly a fifth of Pakistan's total landmass, an area larger than all of England. More than 20 million people were forced from their homes. This is more people than were affected by the 2004 Indian Ocean tsunami, the 2005 Kashmir earthquake, and the 2010 Haiti earthquake combined. Aside from the immediate human toll, the country's already fragile infrastructure was decimated. More than five thousand miles of roads, seven thousand schools, and four hundred health facilities were destroyed.

As the floodwaters receded, they left behind not only the broken country but also a health nightmare. Millions did not have access to safe water, creating the risk of cholera and other waterborne diseases. In early 2011, hundreds of thousands were still living in camps, with only tents as shelter. Food was in short supply, in part because so much of the country's livestock and crops were destroyed. The task of rebuilding continues to be a long-term challenge. To offer just one example, the flood crippled the country's irrigation systems, making recovery in the agricultural sector uncertain and creating an enduring threat to food security.

As climate change increases the flow of water during the rainy season, Pakistan can expect more floods of this type. The problems will be more acute, however, because summer droughts will impede recovery and create their own emergencies.

The World Bank is active in the region, and its senior water adviser in South Asia, David Grey, made the following grim assessment:

> [W]e all have very nasty fears that the flows of the Indus could be severely, severely affected by glacier melt as a consequence of climate change.... Now what does that mean to a population that lives in a desert [where], without the river, there would be no life? I don't know the answer to that question. But we need to be concerned about that. Deeply, deeply concerned.[45]

In fact, I think that Grey does know the answer to the question. I think we all know the answer. The problem is that we shy away from it because it is uncomfortable and brutal. When the flow from the Indus is "severely, severely, affected by glacier melt," as he said, there simply will not be enough water. This means that some people and some crops will die. How many people will die depends on many variables, including how India and Pakistan respond to the crisis, whether people are able to emigrate, and what, if anything, the rest of the world does to help. Those who manage to secure access to water will still face food shortages and, perhaps, famine. We also know something else that will happen: the countries affected by the changes in the river will find themselves competing with one another for this most critical of human needs.

So far, the Indus Water Treaty has held. Its ability to withstand the stresses of climate change, however, is very much in doubt. Even today, there are disagreements between the two countries about the extent to which India is permitted, for example, to build dams on some of the river's tributaries. Here is one way in which the problem presents itself: India wants to build dams to generate hydroelectric power. There are disagreements about what the treaty stipulates in some of these situations. From India's perspective, the dams are harmless because, after the power is generated, the water still flows downstream to Pakistan. From Pakistan's perspective, however, such dams pose an enormous threat, because, even if the water is not removed from the river, the presence of the dam gives India the ability to cut off its neighbor's water supply at will. This puts Pakistan in the position of a supplicant. It is so dependent on the river that if India has the power to turn off the tap, it will have Pakistan at its mercy. India says that it would not exercise such a power, but it is easy to see why such a statement is discomforting to Pakistan (especially since India has done exactly this once before).

Even though India plays down the importance of its dams and its growing control over the water supply, it is clear that Indian officials have not overlooked the potential leverage it affords them. Ashok Jaitly, the former chief secretary of the India-administered portion of Kashmir stated that "[i]f somebody on this side of the border turns off the water and creates a scarcity or suddenly opens it and floods downstream, it would be so obvious. Nobody's going to be that idiotic, unless it's an act of war—which is of course a totally different ball game."[46]

Imagine reading that statement as a Pakistani. It is the farthest thing from reassuring. First, it acknowledges that India could trigger water scarcity or floods in Pakistan, more or less at will. Second, the speaker—a former government official in India—does not seem especially concerned about the fact that doing so would be devastating to Pakistan or that it would violate the Indus Treaty. Instead, he seems to think that it won't happen because it is too "obvious." If the main Indian concern is getting caught, what is to prevent it from disrupting the water flow more subtly? It is difficult to know just how much water should be flowing in the river or how much would flow in the absence of an existing dam. What is to stop India from reducing the supply by 10 percent? As long as India has its hand on the faucet, Pakistan cannot be sure that it is not being cheated. Jaitly also seems perfectly willing to consider such an action in the event of war. These two countries have fought four wars in their sixty-year history. With each new dam project, India increases its ability to use water as a weapon when the next war comes. Knowing that India can do this in the event of war, Pakistan has a strong incentive to avoid a violent conflict. This means that India can take a harder line, because a military response would be devastating to Pakistan. Notice also why Jaitly is willing to consider using water as a weapon during a war: if the countries are at war, India has no reason to worry about an "obvious" manipulation of the water flow. By the same logic, India may be prepared to trigger floods or droughts in Pakistan if there is a conflict short of war but severe enough that India does not care about being obvious. This gives Pakistan one more thing to worry about during its frequent disputes with India.

All of this is inexorably tied up with the disputed territory of Kashmir. Pakistan views Kashmir as its "jugular vein."[47] If India controls the region, it retains the power to shut off Pakistan's water. The concern in Pakistan is heightened by a mistrust of India's motives. *The Nation*, Pakistan's leading English-language newspaper, published the following opinion: "India is violating [the] Indus Water Treaty, and the objective seems to be India's attempt to dry up Pakistan. . . . India's think-tanks have been working on river diversion plans with a view to creating acute water shortage in Pakistan."[48] All of this involves the highest of stakes, and Pakistan knows it. Tariq Hassan, a Pakistani lawyer, former World Bank official, and former Pakistani government official, observes bluntly that water is "one of the most strategic issues facing the subcontinent. If there is a war here in the future, it will be over water."[49]

You can see from the story so far that Pakistan is in a terribly vulnerable position relative to India. Its very existence as a country could be undermined more or less at will by its greatest enemy. Any country in such a situation would look for ways to protect itself. As it turns out, Pakistan does not have many options.

Pakistan cannot hope to sway India with economic pressure. Both countries are poor, but Pakistan is considerably poorer than India. There is trade between the two countries but not enough for Pakistan to use trade sanctions successfully as a weapon. Most important, any attempt by Pakistan to use economic pressure would be frustrated by the fact that India's economy is so much larger than Pakistan's; India's GDP is a little more than $4 trillion, while Pakistan's is $450 billion.[50]

If economic power does not provide leverage, what about military power? Here again, Pakistan is simply not large enough to push India around, at least not with its conventional military forces. India's military is much larger than Pakistan's, generally better equipped, and better trained. It has more manpower, aircraft, warships, and expenditures than Pakistan.

This leaves only one area where Pakistan is able to match India: nuclear weapons. Pakistan has more than enough nuclear capacity to present a threat to India, and it continues to add to it. The reason is simple: nuclear weapons serve as an equalizer between it and the larger, richer, India. Within Pakistan, prominent voices warn that India must change its behavior, or Pakistan must confront it, if necessary, with its nuclear weapons. This position is extreme, but the speakers take the view that India is intentionally depriving Pakistan of water and that things will get much worse if India is not forced to change its conduct. For example, a former Pakistani Supreme Court justice, Javed Iqbal, has stated that the use of nuclear weapons should be threatened in order to stop India from working on dams that Pakistan views as illegal under the Indus Water Treaty. If India refuses to stop, he says, Pakistan "would be bound to wage an atomic war."[51] Najid Nizami, a powerful media figure and editor-in-chief of the *Nation* newspaper in Pakistan, has stated that "Kashmir being the jugular vein of Pakistan, we are bound to liberate it from the cruel clutches of Indian atrocities and if we could not do it, the next generation of Pakistan would die because of thirst as India is hatching conspiracies to grab our water reservoirs and to make Pakistan a land like Ethiopia and Somalia."[52] He has also stated that Pakistan should bomb the disputed Indian dams.[53] Rafique Ahmad, vice chairman of Nazaria-i-Pakistan Trust, a Pakistani think tank, has said that "Pakistan should tackle this problem with courage like Iranians" and that "we should not keep atomic power aside."[54] The water crisis is summed up succinctly in the *Nation*: "if India does not abstain from its course of action, there would be a nuclear war over the water dispute."[55]

These are not official positions of the government of Pakistan, of course, but governments do not need to say things so bluntly. In discussions with India, Pakistan has refused to accept a "no first-use" doctrine for nuclear weapons. In case of a conflict with India, Pakistan is intentionally keeping the nuclear option on the table. On the Indian side, government officials attempt to play down the tensions and hope to keep the Indus Water Treaty in place. This is what one would expect, because India has little to gain from a reopening of the water issue. Nevertheless, the dangers of the situation are not lost on the Hindu nation. The Strategic Foresight Group, a think tank in Mumbai, prepared a report on the India-Pakistan relationship. The report points out that Pakistan's interest in Kashmir stems primarily from its interest in controlling water resources. The report also has the perhaps exaggerated but nonetheless chilling conclusion that "a water war between [India-controlled] Kashmir and Pakistan is inevitable in the future."[56]

There is no way to predict exactly how this sort of serious crisis between countries will be handled. I am certainly not saying that war (much less nuclear war) is inevitable. I am saying, however, that Pakistanis, like all humans, need water to live and that they rely on the Indus River for that water. Climate change will dramatically affect the Indus in ways that are harmful for both India and Pakistan. Whatever India does to manage the resulting water crises will have direct effects on Pakistan. When the flow of water is reduced by climate change (and perhaps before then), both sides of the border will be under pressure to find enough water. On the Indian side of the border, capturing enough water at least to maintain its supply will be a matter of life and death for many people. On the Pakistani side, any Indian effort to deal with the problem will be seen (accurately) as a threat to the country's very existence. War may not be inevitable in this situation, but neither is peace.

V. Terrorism

This chapter has already discussed the crisis in Darfur, an African conflict triggered by resource scarcity. Darfur featured atrocities so severe that they received worldwide attention, despite the fact that the violence did not pose a direct threat to the interests of the United States, Europe, or other important international powers.

Chapter 4 on food security included an account of how climate change will affect Africa in the form of increased frequency and intensity of droughts. In sub-Saharan Africa in particular, some of the world's poorest countries and regions will be further devastated.

In this section, I return to Africa one more time. This chapter is about how climate change will increase the risk of violent conflict and war, and it would be easy to write about how a warming world could trigger bloodshed in Africa. There are many places in Africa where tensions are already high and where conflict already threatens to erupt. Furthermore, climate change will hit Africa as hard as anywhere in the world. In this section, however, I want to consider how violence in Africa, triggered by climate change, represents a threat to American national security. The United States is certainly no stranger to the idea that events halfway around the world influence our interests. We engage in both military and diplomatic efforts in just about every corner of the world, and Africa is no exception.

The United States has plenty of interests in Africa, but the two at the top of the list are almost certainly ensuring access to oil and discouraging and resisting the development of terrorist groups or the radicalization of ideologies and individuals. The drivers of terrorism are complex and multifaceted. No single factor explains why some individuals and groups turn to violence as a tool to express their political grievances. This complexity makes fighting terrorism a difficult and often frustrating task and ensures that there are no guaranteed ways to prevent violent extremism. There are, however, ways to dull the impact of terrorism and reduce the risk that people will be attracted to terrorist groups and ideas. Likewise, there are events and circumstances that we know encourage the growth of terrorism. They do not, on their own, cause, create, or guarantee terrorism. They do, however, provide a more fertile environment for terrorism and terrorist ideas. Like the impact of climate change on war, its impact on terrorism is to increase the risk of disastrous outcomes.

In Africa, threats to American access to oil and the potential growth of terrorism feed on weak and ineffective governments. More than any other part of the world, Africa is home to countries that are, or risk becoming, failed states, states without effective governance. The lack of a working government inevitably goes along with disastrous economic and social conditions and civil unrest. The recipe for terrorism and disruption of oil supplies is fairly straightforward. Start with a desperately poor population, and mix in a dysfunctional (and often corrupt) government. Allow this combination to generate civil unrest and further the collapse of economic growth and government institutions. Bake the mixture on a warming planet to exacerbate the pressure on the system and to precipitate further collapse of social structures. As nations are pushed to the brink of survival, some citizens will turn to extremist elements that promise radical change (Al-Qaeda comes to mind). This rise of radicalism and opposition to existing governments can be counted on to prompt bloody conflicts that impede Western access to oil and give terrorist groups strongholds on the continent.

A. Focus on Nigeria

Historically, Africa has not been an especially significant part of the world in terms of its impact on American interests. This reality has changed, however, as the continent's importance to global oil markets has grown and as the modern threat from international terrorism has reached Africa. Today, any region where ineffective government and law enforcement exist alongside economic, religious, and social conditions that encourage extremism threatens American security. Africa has a number of such places, including, for example, Somalia, Sudan, Chad, the Democratic Republic of Congo, and, the focus of my discussion here, Nigeria (see figure 5.4).

Figure 5.4 West Africa, including Nigeria. Source: https://www.cia.gov/library/ publications/the-world-factbook/maps/nI_largelocator_template.html#.

Nigeria is home to nearly 160 million people, making it the most populous country in Africa. It is a weak and fractured state, with major internal tensions. The demographics of Nigeria's population, 41 percent of which is younger than 15,[57] makes the country vulnerable to extremism. Furthermore, within Nigeria, there are major tensions between the Christian-dominated south and the predominantly Muslim north. The south resents the fact that most of the country's former dictators came from, and/or were backed by, the north; that northerners received the best government jobs; and that in other ways, the north tends to receive more from the government.[58]

Nigeria's cultural fault line—its answer to the Mason-Dixon Line in the United States—is some three hundred miles north of Lagos. Muslim and Christian tribes share the region, sometimes with an uneasy peace and sometimes with violence. Religious and ethnic differences create a good deal of mistrust and suspicion. Against this backdrop, a scarcity of jobs, land, and resources produces the perfect conditions for violence.[59] Until 1999, the country was ruled by military regimes that kept a lid on the violence, but the arrival of democratic, civilian rule has allowed all involved to give greater voice to their complaints and to take action—at times, violent action. Thousands have been killed in riots sprinkled throughout the first decade of the millennium—2001, 2004, and 2008.[60] Violence returned in January 2010, when riots erupted in the town of Jos, located at the center of ethnic tensions. Christians attacked and killed more than two hundred Muslims.[61] In retaliation, Muslims killed several hundred villagers, mostly women and children.[62]

Although these problems are serious enough by themselves, the mere existence of warring groups does not by itself present a threat to U.S. interests. This sort of conflict will only harm the United States and other countries if it interferes with the supply of oil from Nigeria or if it fosters the sort of extremism that threatens global security. As it turns out, Nigeria has something of a tradition of radical insurgencies that do both of these things.[63]

The last decade or so has seen the rise of fundamentalism in the Muslim north. Islamic law (sharia) has been introduced in twelve northern states. In the northern state of Kano, an Islamist group called the Hisbah enforces sharia law and is accused of training militants on behalf of foreign countries. Perhaps not surprisingly, international terrorist groups appear to have been acquiring a presence in Nigeria. It is believed, for example, that Al-Qaeda already has cells in place.[64] There is also a group calling itself the Taliban that has engaged in repeated acts of violence. In 2006, the group attacked Borno, a northeastern city in Nigeria. In 2007, they killed thirteen police officers in the city of Kano.

Nigeria's Taliban is a fundamentalist Islamic sect that, despite its name, does not appear to be connected to Afghanistan's Taliban.[65] Its members are, however, aggressively hostile to the West.[66] A government crackdown in 2004 quieted the group, but it reemerged in 2009, and in that year, more than seven hundred people were killed in conflicts with Nigerian security forces.[67] In 2010, the group declared its support for Al-Qaeda and issued threats directed at the United States.[68] Since mid-2010, the Nigerian Taliban has been active, attacking a prison and freeing more than seven hundred prisoners, carrying out at least two assassinations of critics, and possibly bombing Jos.[69] There is some concern that the group may be receiving support from Al-Qaeda, making the connection to global terrorism crystal-clear. The U.S. State Department considers the Nigerian Taliban to be a terrorist organization. More broadly, the United States is sufficiently concerned about terrorism emanating from Nigeria to have sponsored counterterrorism training and assisted in the creation of Nigeria's specialized counterterrorism unit.[70]

B. Why America Cares

The importance of Nigeria to American energy security is not widely appreciated but cannot be denied. Most Americans do not realize that the country is the fourth-largest exporter of petroleum to the United States.[71] To put this figure in perspective, we import about the same amount of oil from Saudi Arabia as we do from Nigeria. By 2015, just a few years away, it is projected that 40 percent of U.S. oil imports will come from the west coast of Africa.[72]

It is a reality of the modern world that countries depend on one another. The United States has to get its oil from somewhere, and there is no particular reason to think that somewhere should not be west Africa. Unless, that is, reliance on oil from west Africa creates large-scale problems for the United States. This is precisely what may happen. The United States is concerned about some oil-producing states—Venezuela, for example—because the governments of those states are hostile to American interests. This is not the problem with Nigeria (at least, not at the moment). Instead, the problem is that the government is already weak, is likely to grow weaker still, and may not be able to ensure a steady supply of oil. If Nigeria slides further into chaos and dysfunction, U.S. dependence on their oil means that Americans will be along for the ride.

The split between the Muslim and Christian populations is only one of the points of conflict in Nigeria. Although relations between these groups generate violence, there is actually a good deal more violence—and violence of a sort that should concern the Western world—in the Niger Delta region in the south of the country. The Niger Delta is critical to U.S. interests because it contains the country's oil and, for this reason, produces more than 80 percent of the nation's wealth, most of its foreign-exchange earnings, and the majority of its government's revenue. It also produces a large share of the country's bloodshed.

The region's turmoil stems from the fact that the local population does not enjoy the enormous oil wealth that comes out of the ground. In fact, the region's people and its environment seem to get nothing but the negative side effects of oil extraction. Those living in the delta complain that "oil-spill pollution has made their water undrinkable [and] gas flaring has made the air unfit for breathing, while revenue from the oil has paid for mansions to be built in the capital, Abuja."[73]

Imagine the reaction in Texas if that state were told that it could no longer benefit from its oil and gas industry and that the benefits would instead be collected in Washington, D.C., and then distributed to the Northeast. Now imagine how much stronger that reaction would be if we added to the mix religious, cultural, and ethnic differences as strong as those felt in Nigeria. Lacking the political power to gain access to the oil wealth, the region has spawned militia groups prepared to pursue their goals through the use of force. These insurgent groups have taken advantage of the delta's residents' anger toward the government to become major players in the fight over oil and governance in the region. Both the militants and the general population of the Niger Delta are embittered by the region's environmental deterioration and the lack of development and community benefits that should follow such considerable oil resources. They, with some justification, protest that oil revenues do not go to the tens of millions of people who live in the delta.[74]

The militias are the Swiss Army knives of insurgent groups—they do everything. They disrupt oil production and sales, incite local populations, fuel ethnic tensions, attack government facilities and personnel, and threaten the nation's stability. For example, the best known of the militias, a group called the Movement for the Emancipation of the Niger Delta (MEND) has sought what it considers a more equitable distribution of oil revenues and, in particular, wants the indigenous Ijaw tribe—Nigeria's fourth-largest ethnic group—to receive more.[75] MEND has used violence to make its point. On the other hand, Nigeria's security forces have hardly been models of restraint. Nigeria created the Joint Military Task Force (JTF) in response to civil unrest in the delta. The JTF has been accused of human-rights abuses, and there have been many protests and much violence in response to the creation and the actions of this group. MEND was part of the local response, warning foreign oil workers to leave the region, threatening to block the delta's waterways, destroying one of Chevron's largest pipelines, and threatening to use a British hostage held since September 2008 as a human shield.[76]

In another incident, in October 2010, MEND packed two cars with explosives and blew them up in the capital, in the midst of citizens celebrating the fiftieth anniversary of Nigeria's independence. Twelve people died, and dozens were injured in the explosion. MEND claimed responsibility.[77]

With the collaboration of corrupt officials, the militias also steal oil to fund their operations. What they take may exceed $1 billion per year. The money is then used to purchase weapons and fund the militias, which have reduced Nigeria's oil output by 25 to 30 percent. This decrease in production has effects on Nigeria and on international oil prices.[78] As long as the conflict continues, oil production will be curtailed, oil supplies will be unreliable, and oil prices will be higher than necessary. Should the situation take a turn for the worse (from the government's perspective), there is no way to know what might happen to the flow of oil from Nigeria.

American concerns in the region go from significant to deadly serious when terrorism is added to the mix. The unfortunate fact is that Nigeria and other weak or failed states can be breeding grounds for terrorists. The United States is currently engaged in military operations in Afghanistan in an attempt to fight Al-Qaeda and terrorism. We have just recently left Iraq and, along the way, participated in operations in Libya. We hardly need additional fronts in the war on terrorism, yet Nigeria and other weak African countries may become just that.

The easiest way to make the case that Africa is important to U.S. national security is to point out that the American security apparatus itself has reached this conclusion. In 2006, the National Security Strategy of the United States—a document prepared by President George W. Bush and presented to Congress to outline the country's major security concerns—stated, "Africa holds growing geo-strategic importance and is a high priority for this Administration."[79] In 2010, President Barack Obama's National Security Strategy stated that the United States will "reinforce sustainable stability in key states like Nigeria and Kenya that are essential subregional linchpins."[80]

A cynic might be tempted to dismiss these statements by two different presidents as mere political rhetoric. However, during the same period, the United States was taking concrete action to increase its focus on Africa. In 2007, the U.S. military was reorganized, and a new African Command (AFRICOM) was established.[81] This military command is focused on Africa and gives the continent more attention than was achieved by the prior system of parceling out portions of Africa to other commands, including the European Command, the Central Command, and the Pacific Command. AFRICOM seeks to provide a unified security program for the United States in Africa. In short, the military has responded to the growing importance of Africa by devoting more attention and resources to that continent.

Not only does AFRICOM demonstrate how concern about Africa's impact on American security has grown, it also shows that terrorism lies at the heart of that worry. General Carter Ham, the AFRICOM commander, describes the most important tasks of command as detecting and deterring Al-Qaeda and other violent extremist organizations in Africa, strengthening the defense capabilities and rule of law in key African states, ensuring U.S. access to Africa in support of global requirements, being prepared to help protect Africans from mass atrocities, and providing military support to humanitarian assistance efforts when so directed.[82]

Note that combating terrorism earns the first spot on this list and that access to African resources (think oil) is the third item listed. There seems little doubt that the United States views Africa as an important part of its national-security strategy and that its concerns in Africa are centered on two things: natural resources (including oil) and terrorism.

Nigeria is one of the key sources of concern for American security in Africa. This fact is summed up eloquently by Princeton Lyman, a former American ambassador to South Africa and Nigeria: "If there is a prize target for terrorism in Africa, Nigeria should be it."[83]

Finally, Nigeria has provided us with a very clear and frightening sign that these security threats are deadly serious. In December 2009, Umar Farouk Abdulmutallab, a Nigerian citizen, tried to detonate plastic explosives hidden in his underwear while onboard Northwest Airlines Flight 253 from Amsterdam to Detroit. Abdulmutallab grew up in a Muslim family in Nigeria and became radicalized somewhere along the way to early adulthood. He spent the fall of 2009 in Yemen, where he is believed to have met and trained with Al-Qaeda groups. As his flight approached Detroit, passengers on the plane heard popping noises, smelled a foul odor, and saw flames on his pants and on the wall of the plane. Fortunately, the explosives he was carrying were not detonated, and the crew put out the fire while passengers subdued Abdulmutallab.

This incident prompted the addition of Nigeria to the Transportation Security Administration watch list, joining thirteen other countries deemed to have links to terrorism. The list is another way to see that Africa is now critical to antiterrorism efforts. Five of the fourteen countries on the list are in Africa (Nigeria, Sudan, Algeria, Libya, and Somalia).

C. Might Climate Change Provide the Spark?

Like the troubles in the Middle East and the tensions between India and Pakistan, climate change will act as a threat multiplier in Africa. Existing threats, including those present in Nigeria, will grow larger and more dangerous as the climate changes. Here, again, is a situation that can be analogized to Chicago before the Great Fire. Nigeria (among other places in Africa) is ready to burn, and climate change may provide the spark needed for ignition.

In chapter 4, I made the point that Africa will suffer tremendous impacts from climate change. Most obviously, there will be increases in temperature and changes in precipitation patterns. This will reduce soil moisture and accelerate the loss of arable land. These changes will strike at Africa's most important industry, agriculture, which accounts for 40 percent of the continent's GDP. The effects will be especially strong in the Sahel, west Africa, and southern Africa. Yields of some rainfall-dependent crops are likely to experience catastrophic collapses of as much as 50 percent within the decade.[84] By 2020, the agricultural yield in parts of Nigeria that practice rain-fed agriculture may by half of what it was in 2000.[85]

In fact, I should not be speaking of climate change in Africa in the future tense. The present reality of warming is evidenced by the Darfur conflict discussed earlier in this chapter. It is also evidenced by weather patterns on the continent over the last several decades. Since the 1960s, observed temperatures, along with the number of warm spells, have been on the rise throughout Africa.

And while rainfall certainly varies greatly on the continent, observed seasonal variability has increased since 1970 in the form of higher rainfall anomalies and more intense and widespread droughts. For west Africa, this has resulted in measurably less annual rainfall since the late 1960s. Reduced rainfall has had many bad effects, but few are as observable as changes to ecosystems and desertification. The Sahelian, Sudanese, and Guinean ecological zones, for example, have shifted 25 to 35 kilometers (15.5 to 21.7 miles) southward, creating shifting sand dunes and the loss of grasslands, acacia, and other plant and animal species.[86] Forty-six percent of Africa's land area is vulnerable to desertification and climate change. Nigeria has not escaped this reality. The Sahara has expanded into Nigeria, replacing once-fertile land in the north used for agriculture with sand dunes.[87] Every year, a part of Nigeria about the size of Rhode Island turns to desert. Across the continent, the Sahara is spreading southward at a rate of more than three miles a year.[88]

Water sources—critical in a continent marked by arid conditions—are also in retreat. Lake Chad, for example, situated on the edge of the Sahara at the intersection of Chad, Niger, Nigeria, and Cameroon, was the fourth-largest lake in Africa in the 1960s and covered twenty-six thousand square kilometers, roughly the size of Lake Erie. Foreshadowing coming events in many parts of the world, the lake has been devastated by a combination of overuse and arid conditions. Keep in mind that 20 million people from these four countries depend on the lake, so losing this water resource would be a disaster. It would, for instance, exacerbate the ethnic and economic tensions in Nigeria that I have already discussed (and would put the other dependent countries under similar strain).

Today, Lake Chad is on life support. Drought during the 1970s caused the northern half of the lake simply to disappear. The southern half held on but was turned into a swamp with dense vegetation and open pools. Continuing pressure from both climate and population reduced the lake to 5 percent of its original size by the start of the new millennium. It is about that size today, covering less than fifteen hundred square kilometers.[89]

A lack of access to water for the area's population is the most obvious effect of a disappearing lake. Perhaps less self-evident but nonetheless important is that the edges of the lake move as it shrinks. With Lake Chad, Nigeria has seen the portion of the lake located within its boundaries grow smaller and smaller and, eventually, disappear. It now faces the prospect of losing its claim to partial ownership of the lake and, with it, any claim to the water in the lake.[90]

Other consequences also emerge as the lake shrinks. There are too many to enumerate here, but let me point out two more. First, fish stocks are decimated. The catch of fish from the lake is now fifty thousand tons per year. At one time, this would have represented the catch during less than three days. Second, with echoes of the water conflict that triggered the conflict in Darfur, pastoralist nomads and farmers have clashed as the nomads have been denied the access to water that they once enjoyed.

Falling water levels in lakes is bad. The opposite problem exists for oceans. For all of the reasons given in chapter 3, higher sea levels are a threat. The city of Lagos, Nigeria's largest city, is at risk from sea-level rise as soon as 2015. In the Niger Delta (where the oil is), 20 million Nigerians live at or just above sea level.[91] We got a glimpse of what rising seas will do to a large urban population when we examined Bangladesh in chapter 3. Something similar is in store for tens of millions of people in Lagos and the Niger Delta.[92] Moreover, the same risk extends to the 40 percent of west Africans who live on the coast.

All of these problems in Africa feed back into American interests. Reduced water supplies, lower agricultural yields, rising oceans, and a hotter climate will conspire to magnify existing ethnic and religious tensions, intensify competition for resources, threaten oil production and distribution, and incubate terrorist havens.[93]

VI. Conclusion

This chapter has focused on how climate change threatens to aggravate existing tensions and tip them into violence and war that might otherwise be avoided. The world is full of situations that could become violent, and a great deal of time, effort, money, and attention is given to try to prevent them from doing so. The Chicago fire remains a good analogy. All of these difficult and dangerous situations will be made more so by a changing climate. The warming world will turn places that could have avoided war and bloodshed into battlefields.

Whether it is the Middle East busting into flames, India and Pakistan launching nuclear weapons at each other, or a rise of terrorism and disruption of African oil supplies, the results could be devastating for the global community. And I have only mentioned a few of the many possible flashpoints. Darfur may turn out to have been only the first in a series of climate-change wars leading to the deaths of who knows how many millions.

Climate Change Is Bad for Your Health

"Climate change is the biggest global health threat of the 21st Century."
—Lancet, May 2009[1]

Abraham Cowley, the English poet, once observed that life is an incurable disease. Despite our best efforts to prolong and improve the quality of our lives, we all eventually succumb to death. Nevertheless, it is in our nature to delay our demise for as long as possible. In almost all situations, humans are aligned on this one key point: we all want to live as long as we can.

In the never-ending struggle that the human race wages against death, we first look to avoid circumstances and situations that lead to dying. We develop medicines, eat better, wear seatbelts, exercise, and make other life choices that we hope will extend our time on earth. This strategy manifests itself in countless everyday ways. We hesitate before shaking hands with someone who is obviously sick with flu, we think twice before taking the first leap during a skydiving lesson, and we consider alternative routes before we walk down a dark alley.

In addition to the efforts we make as individuals, we also create collective societal programs aimed at preserving life and health. For example, we try to protect ourselves from deadly large-scale events, including extreme weather events, terrorist attacks, and outbreaks of disease epidemics. As is true of individuals trying to reduce the risk of cancer, we are able to improve our odds against these threats, but we cannot eliminate the danger.

Many of our successful strategies to improve and preserve health and life are so deeply embedded in the way we live that it is easy to take them for granted. Most obviously, perhaps, we have developed modern hospitals (at least, in countries wealthy enough to do so), sophisticated emergency-response systems, rescue services, and highly trained doctors and nurses. We have modern sewage systems to protect us from a host of health problems associated with proximity to human waste. We provide services within communities to prevent the piling up of trash that can breed disease. We have water-supply systems that provide safe, clean water to drink. We have food-production and food-distribution systems capable of feeding far more people than was the case in the past, which bring us a great variety of fresh foods from all over the world, all while ensuring that what we eat is safe and free of harmful toxins or bacteria. These systems are imperfect in many ways—they sometimes fail to live up to their promises, they are not present everywhere in the world, and they fail to address some health issues—but collectively, they have an enormously positive impact on the quality and length of our lives.

The end result is impressive. Average worldwide life expectancy in 1900 was thirty years. Today it is sixty-seven years.[2] This average, of course, obscures the dramatic differences among the countries of the world. In some corners of the globe, the average life span has grown steadily for many decades.[3] In other parts of the world, the gains are much more modest, although in almost every country, people live longer and better than their ancestors did. We know we will never conquer death, but we continue to search for ways to delay its arrival.

The flip side of this successful effort to extend life expectancy is that we have a long way to fall if the systems that promote and protect our health fail. We have become accustomed to our longer and healthier lives, but there is no guarantee that they are here to stay. They are the product of the systems mentioned above and many other things. Without these systems, there is nothing to prevent a shortening of life expectancy. We saw something like this happen in sub-Saharan Africa when AIDS emerged and ravaged that continent. In some countries, life expectancy fell by twenty years.[4]

What does all of this have to do with climate change? Climate change poses a unique and unprecedented threat to health and health systems around the world. Climate change threatens the systems we have built and that have extended and improved our lives. This may not be immediately obvious, because for most of us, it is not changing climate itself that presents the greatest threat. It is, instead, the indirect impacts of climate change. Food and water will be less available and more dangerous, disease will be less well contained and more common, and illnesses will be less well treated and more prevalent. Economic hardships will compromise the delivery of health care, weaken systems that protect the safety of food and water, and prevent proper upkeep of infrastructure such as sewage and irrigation systems. Each of these influences, and many more, will have a negative impact on human health.

Health is a complex thing, and it relies on just about everything around us. In a way, this is as good an explanation as any of why climate change affects health: climate change will affect all manner of things we interact with and count on. We have already seem some of these effects: rising seas, creation of deserts and arid lands, changes in local rainfall and river flow, and violent conflict.

Each of the stresses that climate change imposes on individuals and society threatens the systems we have built and upon which we rely to protect our health. A shortage of fresh and safe drinking water, for example, may have a devastating impact on the health of populations in Africa, Asia, and Latin America. Ecosystem changes can cripple food production, leading to shortages and rising prices everywhere. Many areas will simply become uninhabitable, either through desertification or rising sea level, and whole populations of "climate refugees" will be created.

Although I did not focus on health in earlier chapters, drought, famine, flooding, and war obviously affect health in a whole variety of ways. One of the damaging consequences is that institutions developed to protect health may cease to work properly. When food production is dramatically reduced, we can no longer be so picky about safety. When water is scarce, many more people will get sick from using or drinking water that carries diseases. When people are pushed off their land, they will have less access to medical professionals able to care for them. When drought, famine, disease, or war is present, the physical toll on people weakens them and makes them more vulnerable to disease.

Because our health is affected by everything around us, there is an almost endless list of ways in which the impacts brought about by climate change will affect it, and almost all of those effects are negative.

My goal in this chapter is to investigate just a couple of the ways in which climate change threatens human health. There is no way I could catalog the full scope of possible harms. What I talk about here, though, should be enough to give you a sense of how dangerous increasing global temperatures are for our health and even our lives.

I focus on two aspects of the relationship between climate change and health. First, climate change is likely to create conditions that are ideally suited to a global infectious-disease pandemic—a modern-day plague. If this seems far-fetched, consider that such outbreaks are not as rare as you may think. The world faced three pandemics in the twentieth century: 1918, 1957, and 1968. There were four pandemics in the nineteenth century and three in the eighteenth. Some of these, including those in 1957 and 1968, ultimately generated deaths tolls in the low millions—tragically large numbers, to be sure, but perhaps not enough to threaten international systems or structures. The 1918 influenza, however, killed many more—perhaps as many as 100 million—and recent close calls remind us that the risk of a catastrophic global outbreak remains present.

When a person dies in the world today, the odds are about one in four that infectious disease is responsible. You are familiar with many of these diseases: HIV/AIDS (2.7 million deaths per year), tuberculosis (1.6 million deaths per year), and malaria (1.2 million deaths per year). From time to time, a new disease emerges or an existing disease changes in a way that allows it to infect many people and cause severe health consequences, perhaps even death. Experts who study global health pandemics will tell you that the risk of this kind of global pandemic is ever-present, with or without climate change. Climate change will not create this risk, but it will magnify it. As the world warms and our planet is affected in the ways discussed in earlier chapters, ideal conditions for a large-scale infectious-disease outbreak will be created. A person can get lung cancer without being a smoker, but smoking for years makes cancer much more likely. In a similar way, a global pandemic would be possible even without climate change, but a warming world will make it much more likely.

Second, I discuss the ways in which climate change will aggravate illness. Each of these health impacts might be viewed as minor when taken on its own, but collectively, they give a sense of how global warming will chip away at the state of our health. It will create new diseases for new populations; cause old diseases to spread to new places; make everyday acts that we take for granted, including drinking and breathing, more dangerous; and in many other ways wear away the health gains that humanity has made over time.

I. A Modern-Day Plague

A. 1918: The Spanish Flu

World War I was catastrophic. One of the greatest tragedies in history, it caused the slaughter of millions and is, for good reason, taught in schools as a brutal, bloody, and barbaric conflict. What is not often taught is that the war, as devastating as it was, was not even the greatest killer of its decade.

From 1918 to 1919 (with some spillover into 1920), the carnage of World War I was eclipsed by something more lethal: the flu—more specifically, a particular strain of influenza that came to be known as the Spanish flu. This disease spread rapidly around the world toward the tail end of World War I, reaching virtually every corner of the earth and leaving death in its wake.

When it subsided, the death toll was staggering, exceeding that of any other outbreak of disease before or since. The precise number of dead will never be known, because untold millions died in parts of the world where reliable records were not kept. Nevertheless, even the lowest estimates are breathtaking. A reasonable estimate puts the total between 40 million and 100 million worldwide.[5] To put these figures into some kind of perspective, World War I (excluding deaths from influenza, obviously) killed about 8.5 million soldiers and perhaps 7 million civilians. In other words, this outbreak of disease killed at least double, and perhaps as many as six times, the number killed by the Great War.

Even these numbers do not do justice to the horror wrought by influenza in 1918. Even today, 40 million to 100 million people is a chilling number, but the world's population was much smaller in 1918 than it is now. Perhaps the best way to measure the scale of the catastrophe is by the percentage of people in the world who were killed. In 1917, the world's population was about 1.7 billion. This means that somewhere between 2 percent and 6 percent of all of the men, women, and children on the planet were killed by the virus. In other words, in a group of fifty people—think of a school classroom, a small business, or a social group—one or perhaps two (or more) would be expected to die. A similar death rate today would cause 200 million to 400 million deaths, roughly equivalent to killing every single person in the United States.

With or without climate change, the threat of infectious disease is with us. Both existing and new diseases will continue to kill millions every year, and there is always a risk that a new disease will emerge and be as deadly as the Spanish flu. Unfortunately, there is no way to put a precise estimate on the likelihood of another outbreak—there are simply too many factors involved. Two things are clear, however. First, experts in the field all agree that the risks are real. Some go so far as to state that it is not a question of whether there will be another outbreak of this sort but, rather, a question of when it will happen. Second, there have been several close calls since 1918, and we have dodged the bullet of another catastrophic outbreak of disease only through a combination of planning, better science, and, most of all, luck.

The message about infectious disease is simple, clear, and alarming. Despite the advances of science and modern medicine, humans remain vulnerable both individually and collectively. We have adopted strategies to try to manage the risk of future outbreaks, and these strategies have saved many lives. In the end, however, we have not defeated disease, and there is no reason to think that we will do so anytime soon.

While we cannot predict exactly when or where an outbreak of disease may take place, we have a pretty good idea about what makes such events more or less likely. We also know that small changes can cause a disease that would never have come about not only to emerge but also to spread across a large population.

Although climate change itself does not and will not cause disease, it promises to influence negatively just about every one of the factors that make a deadly outbreak more likely. In other words, it will increase the risk of another 1918. In this sense, climate change plays a role similar to the one it plays with respect to war: it takes an already tense and dangerous situation and makes it more dangerous. The key difference is that in the context of violent conflict, climate change can provide the spark that ignites a catastrophe. In the context of disease, it makes the existing conditions more inviting to disease, but an outbreak requires another ingredient: a pathogen (a microorganism such as a virus or a bacterium) capable of spreading and causing severe illness.

The great risk, then, is that climate change will be an important contributing factor to the emergence and spread of diseases that will have catastrophic impacts on humans. It may cause an outbreak that could have been avoided or contained in the absence of climate change.

Although the exact origin of the deadly strain of influenza that ignited the 1918 pandemic is uncertain, evidence points to Haskell County, Kansas.[6] That community had a small outbreak in 1918 that may have been the first sign of a new influenza, the first sign that a flu virus had mutated to become a little more deadly or that a swine virus had acquired the ability to infect humans. Regardless, at some point, a highly transmissible virus became a killer.

If the Spanish flu was going to be a serious problem, it needed a way to reach many more people, far beyond Haskell County. Conveniently enough (for the flu, not for humans), World War I had built the equivalent of a "flu superhighway" which allowed the virus to travel very far and very fast. A few hundred miles away lay Camp Funston, a crowded military installation housing tens of thousands of soldiers, all on the brink of being deployed across the country and around the world. This was the 1918 version of JFK Airport, a large population of people about to spread out in many directions.

There was a steady trickle of people moving between the county and the camp. It is likely that the influenza virus came to the camp with one or more of these people. Before long, the men at Camp Funston started to fall ill. This first outbreak was relatively mild, but the virus was already spreading.

Other military camps provided a critical link in the chain of events that led to the influenza outbreak. In 1917, the United States was frantically preparing for war. In 1914, the U.S. Army was made up of fewer than 100,000 men. By 1918, more than 4 million had joined the Army. These millions of boys and men had to be turned into soldiers, so camps sprang up and opened for business all across the country. The rush to war required many sacrifices. It proved much easier to gather young men in large numbers than to provide proper housing, sanitation, and medical services. It was impossible to equip existing camps properly, let alone build new ones fast enough. Military necessity overrode both comfort and good health practices. Even Army regulations specifying the space required for each man were ignored. Barracks housed more than they were built for, and when no more could be crammed into them, the rest lived in tents, even through the winter. At some camps, men who were already pressed one against the other huddled together for warmth when cold weather arrived.

The military did not have a monopoly on cramped quarters. In cities, too, the war machine had to be geared up. Equipment and supplies had to be built on an unprecedented scale, which meant that an unprecedented workforce was needed. People had to come to the city to make the machines of war, and come they did. They arrived in droves to feed the war's needs. They were not deterred by the fact that cities did not have enough housing or other services. They shared rooms and beds, sometimes sleeping in shifts in a single bed.

As anyone with a small child knows, when pressed together in this manner, people share more than just space. They breathe the same air, use the same bathrooms, and share plates, cups, knives, and forks. Those with children understand this, because whatever illness the child has soon passes to his or her parents. The intimacy and proximity of wartime promoted the sharing of viruses much as the intimacy of parenthood does.

Not only did the close quarters make it easier for the virus to go from one person to another, but once people fell ill, the preparations in the camps proved inadequate. Camp Devens, for example, outside of Boston, was opened in 1917 as part of the mobilization of America. It was built to house as many as 36,000 men. By September 1918, it had 45,000. The hospital seemed ready—it could care for 1,200 patients at a time.[7] The first signs of a flu outbreak came in early September. By September 22, almost 20 percent of the camp reported sick, and three-quarters of those were hospitalized. As the number of sick men grew, they overwhelmed the hospital, and medical care collapsed. Men simply lay sick without seeing a doctor or a nurse. Some slept on beds, many others on the floor. At one point, the hospital had more than 6,000 patients. There was no ability to care for all of these men, no way even to change the linens on the beds. Men too weak to rise simply relieved themselves as they lay, and there was nobody available to clean up the mess.

From the camps, men were sent out in all directions. They, and the disease they carried, were sent to other camps and to cities. Soldiers who were fully trained were sent to Europe to fight. As people moved and came into contact with others, the disease found new victims, and these new victims helped it spread further. When soldiers boarded ships, they were once again in cramped living quarters in which the infected literally rubbed up against the healthy. For the duration of the voyages, ships served as incubators for the disease. Upon their arrival in Europe, a legion of influenza emissaries emerged to mix with other soldiers and civilians. American soldiers soon infected civilians and soldiers from other countries. Cities near military bases were the first to be infected. The people in those cities were also on the move, of course. They, too, were drafted by the flu to carry it to new victims.

Once a highly contagious virus has spread widely enough, it is virtually impossible to stop. This was true in 1918, and it is true today. In 2009, the World

Health Organization abandoned efforts to track individual cases of the H1N1 virus, also known as the swine flu, because it had become too widespread to make that sort of accounting useful. In 1918 and even more so today, there are simply too many interactions among too many people to try to contain a virus once it has started to spread in earnest. Even in 1918, influenza traveled quickly. By late May, for example, it arrived in Bombay aboard a transport ship. Once in India, it spread in the same way it had spread in the United States, by following the movements of people. It traveled along railway lines first, and then it reached into smaller communities.

In the spring of 1918, it seemed that the world had caught a break. To be truly dangerous, an influenza virus must do three things. First, it must be able to infect humans. Many of the viruses that are harmful to humans, for example, are passed to us from animals. Second, it must have a way to be transmitted from human to human. If every human infection must start with an animal host, it is unlikely that the disease can spread widely enough to cause a global crisis. Third, once the virus finds a human host, it must kill.

The influenza of 1918 had accomplished the first two of these tasks but had not (yet) become a deadly virus. We have seen replays of this scenario—where two of the three conditions are met—more recently. The avian flu of 1997 moved from animals to humans and was deadly, but it did not move easily from person to person. To be accurate, I should say that it has not yet learned to move from person to person. Although the outbreak in Hong Kong was contained (as I discuss below), many experts continue to believe that the virus could reemerge and create a major pandemic. The swine flu of 2009 moved to humans and was transmitted easily from person to person. Fortunately, it was not as deadly as it might have been or as many experts feared.

As a virus passes through human hosts, it adapts. This adaptation tends to make it reproduce and spread more efficiently. This does not necessarily cause it to be a better killer, but that is a possibility. In 1918, the earlier outbreak of influenza did, indeed, change into a better and more efficient killer.

B. Climate Change as Catalyst

World War I did not cause the outbreak of the Spanish flu in 1918. It did, however, provide ideal conditions for the disease to emerge and to spread widely. These conditions were not unique to World War I, however. Wherever they have occurred, disease has followed. War, in particular, has always been a friend of disease. Until well into the twentieth century, it was routine for disease, rather than combat, to be the most effective killer in wartime. This was true in the American Civil War, the Boer War, and the Spanish-American War, to name just a few.

War is good for disease for several reasons, most of which are apparent from the Spanish flu example. First, it brings together people from different places with different immunities. This allows the virus to find "virgin" populations without immune defenses needed to thwart an infection. In both army barracks and the rapidly swelling cities of the World War I era, the war brought city folk into contact with country folk. The virus was, in effect, supplied with a steady stream of new, vulnerable victims.

Second, war creates a massing of many people in small spaces, often with poor hygiene and medical care. These conditions make it easier for a pathogen to spread from one person to another and gain a foothold in human populations. When we're told to cover our mouths when we cough or wash our hands before eating, the goal is to lower the chance of disease finding its way from a sick individual to a healthy one. These sensible practices are much less important, however, than ensuring that people have enough space in which to live, that they are treated when they are sick, and that they have access to clean water.

Third, war involves movement—lots of movement. In 1918, soldiers moved from one place to another in response to military necessity, and groups did not always move together. Units formed and reformed, and individuals moved accordingly. Soldiers returned home after their service, once again potentially bringing the disease with them. Similarly, if people moved to cities to help supply the war effort, they traveled. They also traveled back home to visit families. Every move was an opportunity for the disease to move, to find new victims, and to flourish.

Fourth, the infrastructure put in place to mitigate the damage of these sudden health crises is often frustrated, undermined, or simply destroyed by war. During World War I, for example, the propaganda machine put in place in the United States discouraged the public dissemination of knowledge that could hurt morale, preventing health officials from informing the public about the disease or how to stem its spread. Hospitals, likewise, were overflowing, and the availability of doctors and nurses was low. Globally, the health and government infrastructure of many of the infected countries was too fragile to respond effectively.

These four factors allow disease to flourish in times of war and during other crises. They were critical to the catastrophe caused by the Spanish flu in 1918 and 1919. The experience of 1918 is relevant because climate change will create largely the same disease-friendly conditions.

Having learned about 1918, think about what you would do if you wanted to help a disease spread quickly. You would get people from different places and with different immunities to mix. Ideally, they would do so in cramped spaces with poor living conditions. As much as possible, you would want to get people to share space, property, and germs, and you would want to make it as hard as possible to separate the sick from the healthy. When the number of sick overwhelms health services and when basic hygiene cannot be maintained, physical proximity ensures that the healthy will be exposed to the sick, their living spaces, their beds, their food, their drink, and their bodily fluids, making transmission that much more likely.

These are the things that military camps did so well in 1918. Climate change will do the same thing, with refugee camps and cities overwhelmed with migrants fleeing climate change and its impacts. Even places that do not feel the most direct impacts of climate change will have many more refugees within their borders, and these refugees will mix with the local population (which has different immunities) and will live in poor conditions.

You would also want to move people around a great deal so that the pathogen is continually exposed to new, healthy victims. The increased movement of migrants will achieve this at least as well as did the military movements of World War I. People will move from rural areas to cities and camps, from camps to cities, and from cities to other cities, all in search of a chance to settle. Refugees who share space in a refugee camp will be moved out in all different directions as opportunities to find more shelter arise. If a disease breaks out, it will quickly be carried around the world. Globalization also generates a good deal of travel, of course, and this, too, makes a global outbreak of disease more likely. The increase in travel is a feature of the modern world with or without climate change. Climate change will make matters worse in at least two ways. First, some of the most at-risk populations will move farther than they otherwise would. The world's poorest citizens—among those most at risk from an outbreak of disease—are not usually globetrotters. Imagine, for example, an outbreak of disease in an isolated Bangladeshi village. With a small and relatively homogeneous population to infect, the disease might emerge and disappear without finding its way into the rest of the world's population. If, on the other hand, the same illness emerges in a crowded refugee camp where the same Bangladeshi citizens find themselves as climate refugees, it will come into contact with a much larger and more diverse population. It will also have more opportunity to move as refugees are shifted from one camp to another or to more permanent settlement. As these refugees pass through crowded bus stations, train stations, ports, and airports, the potential for a worldwide spread is greatly increased.

Finally, you would want to weaken existing health-care and disease-prevention systems. The impact of climate change here is indirect but no less important. As a changing climate causes economic losses, it will force all countries to make difficult economic choices. Diminished resources translate to less investment in both domestic and international health systems: fewer hospitals to care for the sick, less effective dissemination of health-related information, and weaker international institutions. To this, we can add political problems. Heavily affected countries will have many problems, one of which will be the need to persuade others to accept refugees. This will not only create tensions between governments but will also give countries a strong incentive to keep any new illness a secret. Even a rumor of a potential illness will cause other countries to close their doors to refugees, so a country that desperately needs to open those doors will be reluctant to share information.

It bears repeating that the threat of disease exists regardless of what happens to the climate. As the earth warms, however, every step in the process that can lead to a global disease disaster will be made more dangerous because of climate change. Other factors are also at play, but this does not change the fact that an increase in average global temperature of a couple of degrees makes it more likely that the world will face an outbreak as bad as or worse than the flu of 1918.

C. Making New Diseases

The previous section shows how climate change will make it easier for a disease to spread once it comes into existence. If this were the only effect of climate change, that would be bad enough. But climate change will also make the emergence of disease more likely.

We are, of course, surrounded by viruses, bacteria, and other microorganisms. Most of these are either helpful to us or harmless. A few, however, are dangerous. The reason some microorganisms are dangerous while others are not is complex but can be boiled down to a single word: change.

For most microorganisms and their hosts, including humans, a long-standing relationship has allowed both sides to evolve in ways that allow them to live peacefully together. For example, a virus capable of infecting a chicken or a pig may not be able to infect humans, and so its presence has no impact on our health. Once in a while, however, our tiny friends, which are constantly changing, change in a way that creates problems in our relationship. There are two main ways in which a pathogen can become harmful. First, microorganisms we have lived with for some time (perhaps a very long time) might mutate into something that is harmful to us, that makes us sick or even kills us. Second, a microorganism sometimes "jumps" from some other species to humans. A virus in chickens or pigs or monkeys, for example, may find its way to humans. If we are not equipped to deal with that virus, it may make us sick.

As this suggests, the key here, as with many of the dangers of climate change, is the "change" element. Every time there is a change in average local temperatures, an increase in the amount of standing water, an alteration in the migratory patterns of birds, a change in the reproductive rate of mosquitoes, or even an intermingling of human populations that were previously isolated, it threatens the equilibrium between hosts and microorganisms that has evolved over generations. These changes create opportunities for pathogens to mutate, to jump to new hosts, and to travel outside their traditional geographical locales. When this happens, we are exposed to new viruses or bacteria that humans—either globally or within a local population—may not be equipped to deal with. In short, climate change increases the risk of an outbreak of a deadly pandemic.

This change—through mutation or interspecies migration—can turn a harmless pathogen into a killer. In other words, when it comes to pathogens, new is bad. When the balance between host and pathogen is upset, there is a new opportunity for a deadly disease to emerge. Without the benefit of years of preparation, adaption, and evolution, we're less able to stop these microorganisms from making us sick or, in some cases, from killing us.

There is no doubt that when a disease kills its human host, this is bad news. It does not, however, mean that there will be a major outbreak of the disease. Infectious diseases don't thrive by killing; they thrive by finding ways to be passed from person to person so that they can reproduce themselves. Usually, keeping an infected host alive gives the pathogen more opportunity to reproduce, adapt, and infect new individuals. Like most other organisms, a pathogen "succeeds" if it spread and propagates itself. When it kills the host too early, this opportunity is lost.

A great example of this is Ebola, a type of viral hemorrhagic fever. This virus is thought to be endemic in bats and other rodent species and can infect them without causing too much harm. From time to time, however, it acquires the ability, through mutation and opportunity, to jump into primate species, including humans. When this happens, the results are horrific. Ebola in humans is incredibly deadly. For some strains of Ebola, 90 percent of victims are dead within a couple of days of being infected.

This death rate explains why Ebola is so well known and why it scares us. Yet the actual history of Ebola is much more comforting—or, at least, not terribly alarming. Since the discovery of Ebola in 1976, there have been fewer than thirteen hundred deaths worldwide. To put that number into perspective, during this same period, lightning strikes caused about twice as many deaths in the United States alone.

We are clearly not all dead or dying from Ebola, and that's because it is just too good at killing people. The virus's aggressive nature is also its Achilles' heel. It kills so quickly that it has few opportunities to infect a new, healthy host. It also has very little time to mutate into a form that is less deadly. As strange as it sounds, we are lucky that Ebola is so good at killing. It if killed more slowly or killed a smaller percentage of those it infects while leaving the survivors capable of transmitting the disease, it would be much more threatening.

Ebola, however, is an extreme example. When pathogens become harmful to humans they usually are less deadly. A disease might, for example, kill "only" 5, 10, or even 20 percent of its infected hosts. Or it may create a time lapse between becoming contagious and striking the lethal blow. In either case, the pathogen is then able to replicate and spread before it kills its host. Combine this with the ability to move easily from person to person, say, through the common act of coughing or sexual transmission, and you have the makings of a pandemic.

History provides a long list of diseases that have managed to become very good at both killing people and spreading to new hosts. The grisly catalog reminds us of how dangerous disease can be. The Plague of Justinian in the sixth and seventh centuries killed more than 50 percent of Europe's population. The Black Death in the fourteenth century killed between a quarter and a half of the population of Europe and millions more in Asia and Africa. Smallpox ravaged Mexico in the sixteenth century, reducing its population from 20 million to 3 million within four decades, and killed more than 300 million people worldwide in the twentieth century.[8] In the nineteenth century, tuberculosis killed an estimated one-quarter of the adult population of Europe. Typhus was a threat for more than two thousand years, probably causing the Plague of Athens in 430 BC and killing 3 million people in Russia during World War I. In the late twentieth century, HIV/AIDS emerged and has killed more than 25 million people so far. Diseases will continue to mutate, evolve, emerge, and kill, and there is precious little we can do about it.

The hard truth is that pathogens are more nimble than we are—both in an evolutionary sense and a migratory sense. Environmental changes brought on by climate change create new environments that allow pathogens to evolve into new strains or migrate to new locations. Concentrating people in small places gives pathogens a greater opportunity to spread and reproduce, with a greater opportunity to mutate. This increases the chance of a major outbreak of disease, which is a reason to be very concerned. If climate change is enough to tip us into a global disease disaster, we may pay a price measured in tens of millions or even hundreds of millions of lives.

D. Modern Near Misses

The flu of 1918 seems like a long time ago. Since that time, there have been enormous strides in science and medicine, not to mention the development of stronger public-health systems at both the national and the international levels.

I have already talked about how these changes have extended the quality and length of life and given us a much greater ability to respond to crises.

Assuming that climate change creates conditions that are favorable to disease, it is fair to ask whether the world would respond more effectively today than it did in 1918. Are we really still at such a great risk from disease? Despite the great strides made in science and medicine since the early part of the twentieth century, recent health scares are enough (or, at least, should be) to prevent hubris when it comes to infectious disease. Just within the last two decades, close calls have reminded us that the risk of an outbreak is real. Although these events were not caused by climate change, they serve as a reminder that we remain at risk, and any significant increase in that risk should be taken seriously.

1. Avian Flu: 1997

Despite the advances in our understanding of disease, there is much we still do not know. We do not know, for example, how to identify where disease will come from next. To be sure, we know something about how and where an infectious disease might emerge, but sometimes that knowledge is insufficient. Indeed, as we learned in 1997, sometimes when we think we know something, we are simply wrong.

On May 9 of that year, a three-year-old boy named Lam Hoi-ka complained about a fever, a sore throat, and a tummy ache. His parents took him to their local hospital in Hong Kong, where his doctor assumed that it was a run-of-the-mill case. How many times, after all, are these symptoms seen in children? When the illness did not clear up, however, his parents took the boy to a different hospital. The doctors there were not sure what was wrong with him and decided to transfer him to the larger Queen Elizabeth Hospital. Still, the doctors could not figure out what was wrong. His condition deteriorated, and on May 21, 1997, he died.

This private tragedy for the boy's family soon became something more. Shortly before the boy died, fluid from his throat was collected for analysis. A few days later (but after his death), the infectious agent was identified as influenza. By itself, this was unremarkable; people die from influenza every year. Worldwide, there are between 3 million and 5 million cases of severe illness attributed to influenza each year, and between 250,000 and 500,000 people die.[9]

What made this case special was what happened after it was determined that the boy had died from influenza. Having identified an influenza virus, the next step was to "type" it, meaning to determine the type of influenza. Three types of virus were known to cause influenza in humans. These are known as the H1, H2, and H3 viruses. It was believed that this exhausted the list of harmful influenza viruses.

When Lam Hoi-ka's influenza was tested, however, it proved negative for each of the human strains of influenza. In other words, he had died of influenza but not of any of the strains that cause illness in humans. This presented a puzzle. To scientists, this was like testing someone's blood type only to discover that it is was not any of the known blood types: A, B, O, or AB.

Stumped, Hong Kong's top virologist sent the samples to several labs around the world: the Centers for Disease Control and Prevention in Atlanta, the National Institute for Medical Research in London, and the Dutch National Institute of Public Health in Bilthoven, Netherlands. Dutch virologists Jan de Jong and Albert Osterhaus eventually solved the mystery. They discovered that Lam Hoi-ka had been killed by the H5N1 virus.[10]

H5N1 was known to cause disease in birds but was thought to pose no threat to humans. In other words, this little boy had gotten sick and died from something that the entire scientific world thought was harmless to humans. The boy's influenza was what is sometimes referred to as a black swan, something that was thought impossible but came to be.[11]

Virologists have nightmares about black-swan viruses. Remember the three things a virus must do to cause a pandemic: it must infect humans, be transmitted from person to person, and kill. Lam Hoi-ka's influenza had shown that it could infect a human and kill—two of the three ingredients. If it was also able to move from person to person, there was no limit to the potential damage it could cause. The boy's death could be the first sign of a major disease crisis, perhaps even another 1918.

Because the H5N1 virus had not previously infected humans, exactly zero people on the planet would have protective immunities. Making matters worse, the modern world provided endless opportunities for the virus to spread. Suppose Lam Hoi-ka was, indeed, the first victim. Suppose he had infected just one other person, but that person had boarded a plane in Hong Kong and flown to London. The passengers from that flight would have then boarded connecting flights to destinations across Europe and the rest of the world. By the time the threat was identified, it might have already been too late. Keiji Fukuda, who at the time was the chief of epidemiology at the Centers for Disease Control and Prevention, was among the first experts consulted in the very early days of the investigation. His reaction upon learning that it was an H5 virus that had killed the boy was to think to himself, "This is how it begins."[12]

In 1997, Rob Webster was the world's foremost expert on avian flu. He was part of the international team that descended on Hong Kong to try to find out where the virus came from and what to do about it. He, and many other experts, believed that the virus would find a mutation that would allow more efficient transmission from person to person. If it did—if, for example, it became airborne so that you could catch it simply by breathing—the death toll could quickly grow into the millions.

The avian-flu crisis was eased by several bits of good fortune. One was that the scientific team was able to assess the situation quickly. Another was that the Hong Kong health authorities took drastic but effective steps. Dr. Margaret Chan, director of Hong Kong's department of health, called for the extermination of every one of the 1.2 million chickens within Hong Kong and Kowloon Island.[13] During the final days of 1997, a small army of government workers fanned out across the territory to collect all of the birds from one hundred sixty chicken farms and more than one thousand chicken wholesalers and retail chicken stalls. The birds were either killed by market owners or carted away by local authorities to be killed with poisonous gas. In just a few days, more than a million chickens were killed, as were hundreds of thousands of other birds.

Chan, who was later elected director general of the World Health Organization in 2007, is widely credited with making a courageous decision in stemming this threat. Tourism in Hong Kong dropped, jobs were lost, and the mass slaughter of fowl caused losses of tens of millions of dollars. The success of the effort relied on rapid political action, proper infrastructure, and the courage of this one official.

This decision appears to have been the right one, or, at least, it was enough to prevent further illnesses. Study of the H5N1 virus conducted after the crisis showed that it was quickly adapting to its new human hosts and mutating in ways likely to increase its ability to replicate in human tissue. It is probable that the virus was only months away from being able to move easily among humans. A global pandemic was just around the corner.[14] Months later, talking with a journalist, Webster said that if the chickens in Hong Kong had not been killed, "I predict that you and I would not be sitting here talking now. Because one of us would be dead."[15]

For a brief but terrifying period, the avian-flu crisis threatened to turn into another 1918. It was a combination of quick work by experts, tough political decision making in Hong Kong, and good fortune that the virus did not mutate into a more dangerous form before action was taken. Consider how things might have been different—or how they might be different in the future as a result of climate change. If the disease first emerged in a cramped refugee camp or in a country staggering under the weight of a climate crisis, Lam Hoi-ka's illness might have never come to the attention of authorities able to discover that he represented an early warning sign. It might have been months before we learned of the new virus. In that time, many more people would have been infected, both because more time would have passed and because the initial victims would have been in very close contact with others. In that time, the virus would have also had a chance to mutate, perhaps in ways that would allow its transmission from person to person. By the time international experts heard about it, it might have already spread too far to be contained.

Even if the disease had been discovered quickly, would a country already facing food and water crises brought on by climate change have the will and the ability to slaughter millions of chickens on which its population depended for food? If it tried, would its already-hungry population tolerate it without resistance?

The answers to these questions would depend on many factors that we cannot predict in advance. There are two things we can say with confidence. First, we just barely managed to avert a major disaster in 1997. Second, if a similar situation emerges in the future, climate change reduces our chances of success. And if containment had not succeeded in 1997, the millions of dead might have been human beings rather than chickens.

2. SARS

The avian flu illustrates the fact that there is nothing we can do to prevent the emergence of new and deadly infectious diseases. When the avian flu emerged, we were lucky that it was identified quickly and containment was still possible. If the flu had spread more widely, it might have been too late to prevent a massive international crisis on the scale of 1918.

In 2002, a new flulike illness emerged in China. Its symptoms—fever, dry cough, headache, and body aches—resembled those of pneumonia, a fact that delayed its identification as a distinct disease. Some symptoms were different from pneumonia's, so the disease was initially described as "atypical pneumonia." Before long, however, it came to be known as severe acute respiratory syndrome, or SARS.

The SARS epidemic began in China's Guangdong Province in 2002. The first case is thought to have been in November 2002. China's response to the disease is generally considered to have been poor, which might have contributed to the international spread of the disease.[16] National health officials learned of the early cases within weeks, and by early January 2003, experts had diagnosed the disease as a viral infection.[17] A report was submitted at the end of January but was classified as "top secret," preventing it from reaching a wide audience. Any occurrence of the disease was also deemed to be a state secret, meaning that anyone who reported on the disease could face prosecution. China did inform the WHO about the disease by mid-February but continued to downplay the magnitude of the outbreak. This included, for example, hiding patients from WHO inspectors.[18] A national bulletin on how to prevent the spread of SARS was not released until early April. By mid-April, China changed course and fully acknowl-edged the problem. The resulting months of delay, however, were critical and likely contributed to the spread of the disease and made containment much more difficult.

While China was dragging its feet, the disease spread and attracted seri-ous international attention. In late February 2003, Dr. Liu Jianlun traveled from the city of Guangzhou in Guangdong Province to Hong Kong, where he stayed at the Hotel Metropole. Liu was eventually admitted to the Kwong Wah Hospital with a diagnosis of severe pneumonia. Within a month of admission, he was dead.

Before going to the hospital, however, Liu infected several others at the Metropole. It is believed that he infected three people from Singapore, two from Canada, one from Vietnam, and one from Hong Kong, all of whom had rooms on the same floor as his. This is how the disease spread from one person to seven. These seven carried the disease with them back to their respective homes, where it spread further.

In Vietnam, the disease came to the attention to Dr. Carlo Urbani, a WHO physician. Urbani alerted the WHO to the outbreak and is credited with bring-ing proper international attention to the disease. He himself contracted SARS and died in March 2003.

In Hong Kong, meanwhile, SARS was becoming a serious problem. The Hong Kong resident who had contracted SARS while staying at the Metropole was treated at the Prince of Wales Hospital in Hong Kong and discharged on February 28. He returned on March 4 and was admitted.

Over the next few weeks, the hospital was afflicted by what is sometimes called a "doctor's plague," as hospital staff contracted SARS and grew ill. More than one hundred medical personnel would eventually get sick from SARS.

From the initial emergence of the disease in November 2002 until the real-ization that an international response was necessary was only four months. Within weeks of its emergence from China, however, SARS had spread to more than thirty-seven countries. The WHO and national health authorities around the world faced the challenge of trying to contain a virus that was already in many places and spreading more widely every day.

The WHO issued a global alert on March 12, 2003. On March 15, it issued an emergency travel advisory, stating that people with SARS-like symptoms should not travel and recommending that airlines alert health authorities at the destination if a passenger or crew member showed symptoms. The same travel advisory labeled SARS as a "worldwide health threat" and identified possible cases in Canada, Indonesia, the Philippines, Singapore, Thailand, and Vietnam. Containment efforts included aggressive quarantine of individuals with SARS symptoms, surveillance at airports, and substantial international cooperation.

Supplies and specialists were dispersed throughout the world to assist in control efforts. A concerted effort was made to ensure that countries reported cases to the WHO immediately. When an outbreak was identified, the WHO followed up to ensure that containment measures were in place and the risk of further spread was evaluated. The organization provided guidance and advice for dealing with the new disease to countries around the world, including an electronic meeting of physicians in many countries that was convened to share information on the disease and its treatment.

In the meantime, the WHO's laboratory network around the world began researching the disease to determine its cause and try to develop a vaccine. The virus that caused SARS was soon identified, improving the ability to treat those who were infected.

By early June, in large part because of the organization's efforts, the WHO announced that the outbreak of SARS had peaked globally, and it began gradually to lift the travel warnings against countries that had been affected.

In total, SARS caused some eight thousand infections and about eight hundred known deaths. The international response to SARS was admirable. Thousands were quarantined, travel advisories were issued, and surveillance teams were deployed. Governments came together and took charge in order to stem a deadly, rapidly spreading disease. This kind of cooperation was not possible when the Spanish flu emerged (both because of World War I and because of technological limitations). As climate change strains domestic institutions and international relations, the ability of countries to work together will be compromised. Cooperation, to be sure, will remain better than it was in 1918, but it may not be as effective as it was in response to SARS.

The SARS case shows that we can sometimes stop a dangerous disease in its tracks. The difference between success and failure might be tens of thousands or even millions of lives. It also gives us a sense of the tools we rely on to prevent the spread of disease. Needless to say, if we lose these tools, we will be much less able to contain new diseases.

The story of SARS has another lesson. It shows that an outbreak of disease, even if it is contained and ultimately does not cause large numbers of deaths, can be very expensive. News of the SARS outbreak triggered a dramatic slowing of tourism, described as the "most dramatic shutdown of tourism [the World Travel and Tourism Council] has ever seen." The cost was more than $7.5 billion, 28 million jobs lost, and a 25-percent reduction in the growth of the travel sector.[19] The economic harm from an outbreak of disease can also reach far beyond tourism. It can discourage foreign investment, cause other countries to limit international trade, and hurt local economies by preventing people from engaging in productive activity.

The World Bank has estimated that the cost of a "moderate pandemic" could be 3 percent of world GDP or, in a serious outbreak, 5 percent.[20] Global GDP is about $60 trillion, meaning that a pandemic could cost the world in the range of $1.8 trillion to $3.0 trillion, or somewhere between the GDPs of Brazil and Japan.

3. H1N1: 2009

The avian flu of 1997 was deadly, but it fortunately did not acquire the ability to spread easily from human to human. Had it developed that ability (or if the virus, which still exists in birds, develops the ability to do so in the future) without losing its lethality, the results could easily have been disastrous.

One of the reasons the virus did not become more contagious was that there was a rapid response that limited the time it had to mutate into an easily transmitted form. The avian-flu crisis, then, should be scored as a victory for modern medicine and international cooperation on infectious-disease issues. That is the good news.

Just a few years ago, however, a different disease reminded us that our defenses are still porous and that when international systems are degraded, the risks increase. H1N1, also known as the swine flu, emerged in March 2009 in La Gloria, a pig-farming village in Veracruz, Mexico. It claimed its first victim, Maria Adela Gutierrez, on April 13. As was the case with the avian flu, government authorities appear to have reacted well. It was immediately obvious that this virus was cause for serious concern. By the time it was investigated, it was capable of doing two of the three things that a virus must do in order to cause a major disease crisis. It was able to infect humans, and it could be transmitted easily from one person to another. In fact, it had also shown that it could kill, although whether it would kill a large share of those infected remained to be seen.

At this point, the best hope was to contain the disease. If it could be prevented from spreading too widely, its impact could be limited, and it would eventually run out of victims (or perhaps a treatment or vaccine could be found). The Mexican government was a critical player. It announced a health alert on April 6, cooperated with the World Health Organization, and instituted strict control measures, including the closing of schools. To Mexico's credit, all of these actions happened very quickly once the disease was recognized. In fact, the national and international responses were both impressive.

In the fight against disease, however, only outcomes matter. The best efforts of Mexico, the international system, and many other countries were not enough. The disease quickly spread beyond Mexico's borders and around the world. The first American cases appeared in March 2009, the same month the first case arose in Mexico. By the end of April, Canada, New Zealand, the United Kingdom, Israel, Spain, Germany, Austria, Switzerland, and the Netherlands all reported confirmed cases within their borders. Containment efforts continued, including the closing of some three hundred schools in the United States, but became increasingly futile. By June, three months after its emergence, there were almost thirty thousand cases worldwide, in seventy-two countries. Containment had failed.

Once containment was abandoned, the key global strategy was to cross our fingers. The disease was out and spreading fast. It was clear that many millions would be infected worldwide. Although the race to develop and mass-produce a vaccine was under way, the best hope to avoid a global catastrophe was that fate would be kind and the disease would not become an effective killer.

Fortunately for all of us, this is just what happened. By December 2009, it was estimated that the disease had killed almost twelve thousand people in the United States, but this number is tiny compared with what could have been. Consider that about 57 million people in the country caught the disease, roughly one out of every six. With so many infected, it is clear that a more deadly virus would have been a catastrophe. We were saved by simple good luck.

The explosion of H1N1 illustrates how difficult it is to contain a virus in the modern world. People and products move so often, so quickly, and so far that it is almost impossible to stay ahead of a virus once it starts spreading. This flu spread around the world faster than any flu at any time in the past.

In the end, the swine flu spared us all from the worst-case scenario. Because it did not take on an especially deadly form, the damage was limited. Even so, it took a toll on our health-care systems and warned us against hubris. Consider how the United States fared—a country that you might assume would be well positioned to respond to an outbreak of disease. Even with good information and a rapid response from both national and international organizations and governments, the virus could not be contained. The lesson is that sometimes we will simply not be able to prevent the spread of a disease, even if we learn of it and identify it quickly, publicize it widely, and take quick action.

H1N1 demonstrates that while we are better prepared for a pandemic today than we were in 1918, we are still no match for a fast-spreading virus. Some of the conditions that allowed the 1918 flu to spread so quickly not only remain in place today but have become even friendlier to the spread of disease. For example, people are always traveling from one part of the planet to another, and products move all around our globe. A traveler can go from JFK Airport in New York to Charles de Gaulle Airport in Paris to Beijing International Airport. If that traveler has a contagious disease, he or she can infect several hundred people on the airplanes themselves and many more in the airports. Most of these newly infected people are, of course, travelers, who will take the disease to wherever they are going. A single person on a single trip can spread the disease to virtually every corner of the world. Living conditions provide another example. In some parts of the world, conditions have improved dramatically in the last century, but in other parts, that has not happened. Meanwhile, the world's cities have become more crowded. Seven cities in the world have populations greater than 19 million people. The higher the concentration of people in cities, the easier it is for a virus to spread. More than at any other time in history, we have made it easy for infectious disease that comes about in one part of the world to come into contact with people from other parts. A study by the RAND Corporation states that "the risk of a new or reemerging infectious disease being introduced into the United States is perhaps higher now than ever."[21]

E. How to Cause a Pandemic

The history of both actual pandemics and near misses teaches us that infectious diseases are ever-present threats. In this century alone, we have narrowly avoided catastrophe on at least two occasions: SARS in 2003 and H1N1 in 2009. If we go back five more years, we can add the 1997 avian flu to the list. Each of these had the potential to become a worldwide crisis, and it was only a combination of good luck, rapid and effective response, and courageous political decisions that defused these dangers. There is no reason to think that future threats will have such positive outcomes.

All of this demonstrates the fact that our society remains vulnerable to disease and that the best we can do is try to reduce the risk of a major outbreak and, should one occur, hope to minimize its impact. But this chapter is not about the threat of infectious disease in general. My goal is not to illustrate the dangers of disease. Rather, the chapter is about how climate change will affect the way we live. Climate change is relevant to disease because the former increases the risks humanity faces from the latter.

You can think of the relationship between climate change and disease in the same way you think of the relationship between forest fires and droughts. Forest fires have the potential to cause considerable damage, and anywhere you find a forest, you find the risk of a fire. In particular, a forest fire can happen even in the absence of a drought. Droughts, for their part, can happen without triggering a forest fire. So fires and droughts can exist separately from each other. A drought is neither necessary nor sufficient to cause a fire. Nevertheless, you do not have to be a forest ranger to know that the presence of a drought greatly increases the risk of a forest fire. Not only that, but when a fire starts, a drought makes it more difficult to bring it under control.

Climate change affects the risk of infectious disease in the same way that drought affects forest fires. Infectious disease kills millions every year, and there is always a risk of a disastrous outbreak that could kill many more millions. This is true even in the absence of climate change. Climate change, for its part, cannot by itself cause a pandemic. So, like drought and forest fires, climate change and disease can each exist without the other. Climate change is neither necessary nor sufficient to cause a catastrophic outbreak of disease. Just as drought increases the likelihood of a forest fire, however, climate change increases the risk of a disastrous global disease epidemic.

Earlier in this chapter, I discussed the balance between microorganisms and hosts. Over the years, we have developed intricate and sophisticated immune systems to avoid serious attack. We also reward pathogens that avoid being too lethal with an evolutionary advantage: they have the opportunity to spread more efficiently. This balance allows us to coexist with pathogens that sometimes make us ill. When a new pathogen is introduced, however, this balance is upset in a way that can lead to many deaths.

Time and time again, climate change will tilt things in favor of infectious disease and against human efforts to respond. It will add another entire layer of risk, beyond whatever dangers already exist as a result of globalization and other factors. A warming planet will drive people into living conditions that are ideal for both the outbreak and the spread of disease. It will help pathogens spread to new regions and encounter new populations that lack immunities to fight them off. It will cause national governments to be less forthcoming with critical health information while eroding the capacity of those governments, international institutions, and private groups to identify, track, and respond to the outbreak of disease. It will force people into crowded and unsanitary living conditions where a pathogen can move easily from person to person. It will trigger hunger, thirst, and poor nutrition in millions upon millions, making them vulnerable to infection and reducing their ability to resist. Each of these changes will be triggered by climate change, and each of them will increase the risk of a global health crisis. Should such a crisis emerge, each of them will also make it more devastating than it would otherwise be.

1. Bringing People Together Can Be a Bad Thing

Let's start with some of the circumstances that are believed to have contributed to the 1918 influenza outbreak. Although other factors were relevant, there is no doubt that the crowding together of people as a result of the war, poor sanitary conditions, and frequent movement all played a role in the outbreak. John Barry, author of *The Great Influenza*, describes how preparing for war created ideal conditions for an outbreak of influenza in a chapter aptly titled "The Tinderbox":

> These circumstances not only brought huge numbers of men into this most intimate proximity but exposed farm boys to city boys from hundreds of miles away, each of them with entirely different disease immunities and vulnerabilities.[22]

Note that Barry is pointing to two distinct influences that make it easier for disease to spread. First, bringing large numbers of people into close contact makes it easy for disease to spread from one to another. Second, bringing together people from different places gives pathogens a chance to encounter hosts who have never developed relevant immunities, once again making it easier for the disease to spread and making it more likely that the new hosts will grow ill.

Bringing so many people from different places together was an enormously important factor in the outbreak and spread of the 1918 influenza. Paul Ewald, a biologist at the University of Louisville, argues that the conditions created by World War I were so critical to the influenza outbreak that an outbreak is unlikely in the absence of such conditions. A new outbreak of disease is unlikely to be as powerful or as deadly as what was witnessed in 1918, he argues, because there were unique circumstances in 1918 that created an ideal environment for the virus to spread. Millions of men (and a much smaller number of women) were crammed into close quarters in military facilities across the United States and abroad, in trenches in Europe, in trains, and on troop ships. In these cramped quarters, a virus could jump easily from one person to another. Without the extreme conditions, the flu would have had more difficulty in moving from person to person. A sick person, after all, may not travel much, and certainly after death, people normally do not infect others. But when people are living one against the other and sleeping inches apart, there is no way to escape a sick neighbor.[23]

My own view is that Ewald understates the risk of a devastating outbreak under current conditions, but the more important point, on which he is surely correct, is that the crowding together of people is an important factor in the spread of disease.

Ewald's argument is intended to be an optimistic one. This optimism, however, cannot survive consideration of climate change. Climate change will deliver exactly the kind of crowding that Ewald says is needed to trigger another 1918-style crisis.

In earlier chapters, I discussed some of the ways people will be displaced from their land. Rising seas will claim territory and force people away from their homes, water crises will force farmers to abandon their land, food shortages will drive people to cities, and warfare and violence will cause populations to flee in search of safety. There is no way to know how many people will be displaced, but it could easily be in the tens of millions or even hundreds of millions.

Many of these people will go to cities in the hope of finding a way to survive. These cities will lack the space or infrastructure to handle the swelling population. As the population increases, people will crowd closer together, and sanitation, health-care, sewage, and other systems will all be overburdened. Others, especially those who find no shelter in their own countries and so are driven to seek survival in other nations, will no doubt be housed in camps that offer only the barest of subsistence, are severely overcrowded and dirty, and provide insufficient infrastructure.

Notice how the forced movement of people because of rising seas resembles the movement prompted by World War I. All of the ingredients present during World War I will be reproduced, including crowded conditions, poor sanitation, movement of people from group to group, and the mixing of the sick with the healthy. Millions of people will move to the cities in search of work and survival. Once there, many will live on the margins of society, as there will simply not be enough work. They will live in crowded slums, sharing what little space they have. Basic sanitation services—already missing from the poorest communities in much of the world—will be absent. The sick will remain next to the healthy, allowing disease to pass from one to another. The sick will also have to survive. Only debilitating illness will be enough to prevent them from doing whatever they must to provide for themselves or their families. Laborers will go to work even if they are sick. Beggars will still beg when they are sick. This will bring the sick into contact with a wider population within the city, allowing disease to cross class and ethnic lines easily.

In refugee camps, the story will largely be the same. People will have little space and poor sanitation. It is a safe bet that medical services will be undersupplied, so the sick will, once again, remain with the healthy. New arrivals to the camps may bring disease with them—in which case, it will spread easily—or may quickly be exposed to disease that is already there. When people leave the camps to find more permanent living quarters, they will take disease with them into cities and other places.

In both cities and camps, people will mix in new ways. Individuals from populations that otherwise do not interact very much will be thrown together out of necessity. Farmers from the country who are pushed off their lands will mix with city dwellers. Citizens of one country will flee across borders into other countries. These movements will bring people with different immunities together, giving a pathogen new populations and fresh victims without immunity.

The most obvious differences between the experience during World War I and what we can expect in the coming decades suggest that climate change will do even more to promote disease than the Great War did. The population movements will be larger, for example (recall that sea rise in Bangladesh alone may displace 20 million people), the effects will be longer-lasting (World War I lasted just four years, after all), and the political commitment and economic ability to provide livable conditions will be weaker.

To be sure, massive population movements and crowding do not guarantee a global pandemic. World War II, for example, did not produce a crisis resembling the Spanish flu. When considering the future, however, we have to think in terms of risk. Leaving your car unlocked does not guarantee that it will be stolen, but you should still lock it, because an unlocked car is more likely to be stolen. In the same way, a world dealing with climate change is more likely to face an outbreak of disease that kills many millions. That no such outbreak happened during World War II is evidence of good fortune more than anything else.

2. Government and International Institutions

The experiences of the avian flu in 1997 and the SARS outbreak in 2003 demonstrate the importance of quick and decisive action by both international health experts and domestic governments in response to the emergence of a dangerous infectious disease.

The same lesson is clear from some of the greatest health victories of the twentieth century. In 1988, for example, a coalition of national governments and several international organizations (including the WHO and UNICEF) launched the Global Polio Eradication Initiative, which would become the largest international public-health project in history. By 2008, more than 2 billion children had been immunized against polio. As a result of this effort, the number of cases diagnosed each year has fallen from several hundred thousand to about fifteen hundred. It is anticipated that polio may be completely eradicated in the near future. Without a major and coordinated effort by both governments and international organizations, it would have been impossible to bring this killer under control. If polio is eradicated, it will be only the second time in history, along with smallpox, that humans have completely defeated a disease.

Global efforts to combat disease rely on international cooperation. Without effective international coordination, the response to the avian flu in 1997 would have been much slower and less well informed. If countries fail to work together, the resulting delays could give a disease enough time to mutate into a form that can be transmitted easily from person to person. A well-coordinated international response system relies, in turn, on information from local health-care providers. In Hong Kong in 1997, it took only days from when Lam Hoi-ka entered the hospital until a virus sample was sent to labs around the world. This swift action allowed the rapid identification of his illness as influenza. The mystery of what caused the boy's death was solved because help was sought from outside the territory. This action required that local health professionals identify the issue at hand and then pass relevant information to specialists and experts. It also required that these specialists recognize the gravity of the problem and seek foreign assistance. The containment of a virus is obviously a race against time. Every day lost increased the danger that the virus would mutate and find a way to pass between humans. If that had happened, there may not have been any hope for control.

The point here is that the international system intended to deal with infectious disease is heavily reliant on domestic health systems working fairly well. It was fortunate that the outbreak of avian flu happened in Hong Kong, where health services were available and doctors were well trained. In some places, there are so few qualified doctors that the earliest signs of a new disease are unlikely to be recognized. In some areas where doctors are available, they are overtaxed and perhaps undertrained, so they may have neither the opportunity nor the ability to investigate the cause of a death thoroughly. Where doctors and other health-care providers are able to identify new diseases, that information still must be communicated to national and international authorities. If national health-care systems are not functioning well, that communication system may break down. Even when domestic systems work well, there is a risk that national authorities will decide not to announce the presence of a disease internationally.

Informing the international community that a potentially harmful contagious disease has emerged within your borders is an expensive proposition.[24] Entire industries can be injured when the world learns of a local disease. The most obvious is tourism, but the news can also deter foreign business travel and foreign investment. On top of this, other countries may react (or perhaps overreact) with travel warnings, trade embargoes, and so on. After the world learned about the swine-flu outbreak, for example, close to twenty nations (including China and Russia) banned the importation of pigs, pork, and other meat from the United States, Canada, and Mexico. It is hard to understand this being a reasonable safety measure, because the virus involved is not foodborne. There was no danger from these products, and yet they were banned.

As I already mentioned, the SARS crisis caused the most dramatic shutdown of tourism in recent world history.[25] Given the high economic stakes, it is easy to understand why a government might be slow to draw attention to an illness that may not even turn out to be a serious threat. Recall how China reacted to the initial outbreak of SARS. In part because of concerns about the economic impact of publicizing the illness, China was slow to inform the international community, admit the full scope of the disease, or take forceful action to contain SARS.

Assuming that the consensus predictions about climate change reported by the IPCC are even in the ballpark, many countries will be much worse off economically as a result of climate change, and they, their citizens, and their businesses will thus have even greater and more desperate reasons to fear the consequences of reporting possible outbreaks.

The fear that governments will fail to report disease is more than speculation. It is a problem that already exists. Pakistan, for example, has failed to report the many cholera outbreaks it has experienced in the last thirty-five years.[26] Many countries underreport the prevalence of HIV/AIDS within their borders. Outbreaks of plague in Africa have also gone unreported.[27]

All of the existing reasons that countries fail to report disease will grow in importance as the economic hardships of climate change make governments even more gun-shy about publicizing outbreaks that will cause further economic pain. Strain on domestic reporting systems will also make it more likely that domestic authorities fail to learn about disease outbreaks quickly or fail to report them as they focus on other priorities.

The international system for monitoring and responding to the threat of infectious disease relies on a chain of information and communication that includes several links. The disease has to be noticed as something unusual by a doctor, the issue must be communicated to national health officials, those officials must investigate the illness, and, in the case of an infectious disease that has the potential to spread widely, national authorities must share the information with appropriate international bodies such as the WHO.

Climate change will weaken every link in this chain. The numerous challenges presented by climate change, from rising seas to food shortages to conflict with neighbors, will tax government budgets and resources. Simply put, governments will have to do more with less. Inevitably, public services, including health services, will suffer.

Social, economic, and political factors already inhibit acknowledgment of the emergence of a pathogen, even if public-health infrastructure is sufficient to detect that the outbreak exists in the country.[28] As the world warms, these problems will only get larger. Even when a disease is identified, countries already facing economic difficulties brought on by climate change will be reluctant to inform the world of a disease. Consider that all of the relevant resources, including the detection infrastructure, will be severely stretched by the other impacts of climate change: lack of food and water, flooding, severe weather events, heat waves, and so on. It seems highly probable, if not definite, that countries will struggle even more with disease-control measures—such as finding funds to compensate for destroyed livestock—as a result of climate change. It also seems very likely that underreporting or delays in reporting will increase. This happens now because individuals, along with regional or national governments, fear the consequences of reporting. Businesses fear a loss of livelihood. This fear led large agricultural companies in Asia to pay poultry owners to remain silent about infected animals.[29] Governments, too, fear loss of revenues from trade, tourism, and other sources:

> No country wants to bear the stigma or the economic costs associated with disease. In a world where international trade and investment are the main engines of prosperity, a disease, or any other condition that discourages foreign traders and investors from visiting and doing business, is a kiss of death. Disease is invariably associated with huge business losses.[30]

Even on the international level, the response will be less effective. Climate change will tax international institutions and structures just as it will tax domestic ones. International resources will be harder to come by, because the countries that contribute to international institutions will face their own climate-change challenges. The resources that are available will have to be spread over many areas, and some will be much more expensive than today. An obvious example is the cost of dealing with the large number of displaced people. All of this means that there will be fewer resources available for international health efforts, so the international response to an outbreak of disease will be slower, weaker, and less likely to succeed.

The threat extends far beyond the set of countries most affected by climate change. Bangladesh will experience much worse flooding and displacement of people than will the United States, for example, but the United States cannot protect itself from the increased risk of infectious disease caused by climate change. The United States depends on every other part of the world to guard against infectious disease. The reality of this dependence on other nations means that efforts by the United States to limit or prevent importation of infectious elements will be undermined by climate change. In countries where the impact is expected to be far worse than that projected for the United States, it is reasonable to assume that public-health infrastructure will be more strapped, not less; that public officials will be more overwhelmed, not less; and that governments and firms will be more concerned, not less, about the economic consequences of reporting outbreaks. Thus, the United States can likely expect more delays and less openness from affected nations when it comes to reporting potential infections. This is in direct opposition to what the World Health Organization says is necessary to prevent widespread outbreaks: "[a]n integrated global alert and response system for epidemics and other public health emergencies based on strong national public health systems and capacity and an effective international system for coordinated response."[31]

II. A Better Killer

A large-scale pandemic in the style of the 1918 influenza is the most frightening way in which climate change and disease might interact. On a national scale, a widespread epidemic can stretch health resources, disrupt national productivity, and cause political instability. On a global scale, emerging diseases can cost billions in trade losses, threaten tourism industries, and instigate international tensions. The more you think about this sort of global outbreak of disease, the more you find yourself hoping that we simply get lucky. You cannot help but seek comfort in the fact that a major worldwide event is not certain, because uncertainty is just about the only hopeful part of the story. Climate change will increase the risk of such a disaster, but even if we do nothing to mitigate the effects of climate change, we may be lucky enough to avoid this particular catastrophe.

Even if we are lucky enough to avoid an outbreak of disease that kills tens of millions or even hundreds of millions, however, climate change will be harmful to human health in several other ways. Put most simply, many more people will die as a result of existing (or possibly as yet unknown) diseases and health problems because of climate change. These deaths will be less dramatic than those caused by a massive global outbreak of disease or, for that matter, than those caused by floods, large-scale famines, or wars, but the affected people will be no less sick and no less dead. And because the impact will be felt so widely, the number of affected people may be enormous. Suddenly, we are back to thinking about millions and millions of people.

We now have to surrender the comforting possibility that bad health events won't happen. As the world warms, we can be certain that there will be more sickness and more lives lost to illness. And the more the world warms, the greater the impact. The only way to prevent these consequences is to prevent climate change.

Actually, to say that climate change will increase the spread of diseases is correct but incomplete. The reality is that this has already happened. Empirical studies that look at both weather data and the incidence of disease have confirmed this fact.[32] The impact has been greatest in developing countries where malaria, dengue fever, and encephalitis, among other diseases, have spread more easily as a result of climate change.[33] Like any increase in incidence of disease, this spread of disease imposes costs in a number of ways. It reduces economic productivity, because people spend more time sick and less time engaged in productive work; it requires costly treatment; it burdens medical systems that are often already weak and facing extremely limited resources; and it extracts a high human toll in terms of suffering and disruption of the lives of families.

Compared with what is to come, climate change to date has been limited. Yet even this small change has increased the frequency of disease. Between the mid-1970s and the year 2000, for example, climate change caused the annual loss of more than 150,000 lives (Kofi Annan, the United Nations secretary general, puts the figure at 300,000) and more than 5.5 million "disability-adjusted life years" (DALYs).[34] DALYs are a commonly used measure of quality of life. One lost year of life as a result of death is equal to one DALY. For years lost to disease, the corresponding number of DALYs is the result of a formula that takes into account time spent with the disease, the age at which the disease is contracted, and the severity of the disease. The result is that less severe diseases are given less weight, and more severe diseases are given more weight. To give you a sense of scale, the burden of malaria was measured at 30 million DALYs in 1998.[35]

To date, then, climate change is having a real impact on human health, but the numbers are still relatively modest (although it is telling that 150,000 deaths and 5.5 million DALYs per year can be considered modest). If the numbers stayed at current levels, the effect of climate change would justify concern and some efforts to respond but could not be described as a major crisis. The world is a big place, and these numbers are not enough to prompt major global policy changes. As climate change gets worse, however, it is virtually certain that the numbers will grow quickly.

A. Disease, Delivered

There are two important ways in which people can be exposed to "new" diseases. First, the disease itself may be new to humans. I have already discussed several examples of this sort: AIDS, avian flu, H1N1, and others. Second, an existing disease may find a new population of potential hosts. I will discuss a couple of examples below, including malaria and dengue fever.

One of the major factors that trigger the emergence of new diseases and the spread of existing ones is change—change in type or extent of contact between the pathogen and humans, change in environmental circumstances, changes in the host population. Even relatively small environmental changes can have surprising effects on health and disease. From 1987 to 1992, for example, the southwestern United States experienced a period of prolonged drought. This had a series of effects, including one that would not normally be considered important by most people: the population of raptors, coyotes, and snakes declined. The change in the population of these animals had an impact on the ecosystem. The one thing that these species have in common is that they like to eat rodents. When the drought ended in 1993 and the El Niño storm season brought heavy rains, rodents suddenly had an abundant food supply and few predators. Their population exploded, growing more than tenfold in a short period of time. That population acted as a host for what at the time was an existing but dormant virus known as the hantavirus. As the rodent population grew, the number of rodents in homes and farm buildings grew with it. This multiplication of rodents increased human exposure to rodent droppings, which is believed to have led to a disease outbreak caused by the hantavirus, called hantavirus pulmonary syndrome (HPS). Although HPS did not spread widely, it was deadly. It caused respiratory problems in its victims, and the fatality rate exceeded 50 percent.[36]

With respect to many of the diseases that already pose a threat to humans, climate change will alter their range and expose them to new populations. Consider malaria, for example. Malaria is a horrible disease that is estimated to kill a million people each year, most of them children.[37] Beyond those who are killed, 300 million people—almost 5 percent of the world's population— suffer a bout of malaria every year. The symptoms of the disease include fever, chills, headache, sweats, fatigue, and nausea. Those who are infected but recover often have to deal with lifelong effects, including permanent disability.

The disease also extracts a large economic cost and can reduce a country's growth by more than 1 percent.[38] Although 1 percent may not seem like much, this loss compounds year after year and can make a huge difference to a country's economic well-being. During a ten-year period, a country that grows at an annual rate of 2 percent rather than 1 percent, for example, will be 10 percent larger. Over thirty years, the faster-growing economy will be a full third larger than the slower-growing one. Add to this the fact that just the treatment of malaria can consume a country's health resources. In some countries, malaria accounts for as much as 40 percent of public-health expenditures, 30 percent to 50 percent of inpatient hospital admissions, and as much as 60 percent of outpatient health-clinic visits.[39]

One of the reasons that so many people suffer from malaria is that about 45 percent of the world's population is at risk of contracting the disease based on where they live.[40] As the climate changes, the number of people at risk will change. The World Health Organization predicts that if global temperatures increase by 2° to 3° C, malaria will present a risk to an additional 3 to 5 percent of the globe's population.[41] Even at the low end of this estimate, this means that an additional 200 million people will be at risk.

Today, the vast majority of malaria cases are found in Africa, in part because poverty hampers eradication efforts and in part because of climate. The key climatic factors affecting malaria are temperature, precipitation, and relative humidity. Malaria is transmitted by a parasite called plasmodium, which is transmitted via the bite of an infected mosquito. Once in the body, the parasite multiplies and infects red blood cells. The parasite reproduces more slowly when temperatures are lower. At low enough temperatures (around 18° C, or 64° F), it does not have time to mature within the life span of the mosquito. At slightly higher temperatures (20° C, or 68° F), the parasite matures quickly enough to infect people when the mosquito bites them.

You can now see how climate change may change the areas in which malaria is a serious problem. As temperatures increase, the parasite will be able to reproduce more quickly in places where, until now, malaria has been absent. There are signs that exactly this is happening in some higher-elevation areas in Kenya, Tanzania, Uganda, and Ethiopia.[42] Forty years ago, these areas were malaria-free. They were simply too cool for malaria to exist. Today, malaria has arrived.

The threat reaches beyond the highlands of east Africa, of course. Around the world, where malaria's range is limited by temperature, an increase of a couple of degrees will extend the range into new territory. Putting more people at risk is a terrible thing, but it is not the worst part of this change. The larger problem is that epidemics of contagious disease are much more likely to take place at the edge of the disease's range, especially as that range expands.

People living in areas that are at risk for malaria develop an uneasy but relatively stable relationship with the disease. Most people are exposed to the disease when they are children. Some do not survive, but those who do survive acquire a partial immunity. As adults, then, they are less prone to the disease. Malaria remains a deadly disease that imposes large health and economic costs on a society, but it may not bring a population to its knees.

When malaria or some other infectious disease reaches new territory, it encounters people who have never been exposed. Immune systems are not ready for the disease, and so those who are infected pass it on to others, who also lack immunity. With little to stop it, the pathogen spreads widely and quickly, perhaps creating a devastating epidemic. A larger share of the population falls ill, health services are overwhelmed, more people die, and the community itself may have trouble carrying on.

In the highland regions of east Africa, which were once malaria-free, there are now about 12.4 million cases per year. This represents about 2.5 percent of the world total. Those who contract the illness die more frequently than the world average; between 12 percent and 25 percent of annual worldwide deaths come from these regions.[43]

Malaria is not the only disease that will be affected by a changing climate. Another important example is dengue fever. Before 1970, only nine countries had experienced cases of dengue hemorrhagic fever. Today, more than sixty countries have had cases, earning dengue the title of "most important mosquito-borne viral disease in the world," according to the WHO.[44] Something in the neighborhood of 50 million people are infected each year. Of these, 500,000 experience the much more serious dengue hemorrhagic fever, and 22,000 die.[45] There are no effective vaccines or drug treatments currently available.

At the moment, two out of every five people on the planet live in an area where dengue exists. And dengue's reach continues to grow. The continuing warming of the earth will lead to further expansion of dengue's range.[46] Assuming a temperature increase of 2.5° C, it is expected that between 5 billion and 6 billion (yes, *billion*) people will be at risk, an increase of 40 to 70 percent from the number we could expect if the climate were not changing.[47] In other words, climate change will be responsible for putting 2.5 billion people at risk of contracting dengue fever.

B. Don't Drink the Water

In addition to expanding the reach of disease, climate change will tend to create conditions favorable to disease. Diseases that already do harm in the world will have more opportunities.

On January 12, 2010, a devastating earthquake struck Haiti. Measuring 7.0 on the Richter scale, the quake killed 300,000 people and left 1.5 million homeless. Haiti's preexisting poverty ensured that the damage from the earthquake itself would be just the beginning. Without the resources to respond effectively, it was inevitable that the creation of a large homeless population and the destruction of the already meager public infrastructure would exact a heavy toll. Around the same time, cholera emerged in Haiti for the first time in more than one hundred years. The obvious temptation is to blame the earthquake for the epidemic, but the evidence does not point that way. There is little doubt that the natural disaster impeded Haiti's ability to cope with cholera, but the outbreak is attributable to something else: higher temperatures and increased salinity in river estuaries. These are, of course, two consequences of climate change.

The actual death toll in Haiti was more than seven thousand. This is a large number, but perhaps not catastrophic for the country. This event, however, is a good illustration of how climate change and other events interact. If, as is generally believed, warmer temperatures are responsible for the cholera epidemic in Haiti, then climate change has added one more problem to Haiti's already challenging existence. While it rebuilds from the earthquake—a task that will take decades—it also has to find a way to improve its water system to protect people from cholera. To provide clean water and treat waste is likely to cost more than a billion dollars that Haiti does not have. Yet until water and sanitation systems are rebuilt, cholera will thrive.[48] Cholera is caused by bacteria and is transmitted through drinking water. Plankton in the water carries the disease. The plankton thrives in warm salt water. Plankton is dormant in cooler water, but as the temperature increases, it blooms, taking the cholera bacteria along for the ride. More infected plankton means a higher risk of cholera for anyone who drinks the water.

Those who are infected suffer from watery diarrhea and can sometimes die within two hours of when they first start showing symptoms.[49] During a typical year, cholera is a serious disease but perhaps not serious enough to cause global alarm. On average, there are 3 million to 5 million cases of cholera per year in the world and a little more than 100,000 deaths.[50] The disease is easily avoided by drinking only clean water. When access to clean water is interrupted, large populations may be exposed to the disease. We are once again faced with the central role of water in human events. When people do not have clean water, they have little choice but to drink whatever is available. Major disasters, then, have two effects: they increase the risk of cholera by disrupting access to clean water, and they undermine our ability to respond to cholera because they create so many other urgent needs.

Climate change has many ways to disrupt access to clean water, several of which have come up in this book. When it displaces people from their homes (whether because of rising seas, drought, war, or disease), those people may not be able to find easy access to clean water. In addition to other challenges, then, these displaced persons will face a greatly increased risk of disease.

The same risk will arise when people do not move but water supplies are interrupted. In areas that rely on water from glaciers, for example, there will be shortages during dry periods, forcing people to rely on water that is less safe. The same will be true when sub-Saharan Africa and other places suffer through droughts. In 2009, for example, northern Kenya faced a cholera epidemic in the wake of a severe drought.[51] People had little choice but to drink the water they could get, even if it was infected with the cholera bacteria.

As these comments suggest, cholera has the potential to emerge suddenly when the conditions for an outbreak are suitable. This is why the limited number of cases during good years should not be taken to mean that the problem is small. As water systems are strained by climate change (and population growth, for that matter), the risk of regular large-scale outbreaks increases.

In 1991, there was an outbreak of cholera in Peru. In that year alone, more than 300,000 people were infected. In 1992, another 160,000 cases were reported. The numbers fell to 22,000 by 1995. Among the causes was an unusually strong El Niño event that lasted several years and allowed the cholera bacteria to spread. This raises the inevitable question of whether climate change bears some responsibility for the El Niño event. The answer, as I have discussed a couple of times already here, is that while climate change makes such events more likely, whether this one in particular was caused by global warming is impossible to know. The underlying conditions in Peru also played a major role. Poor water supply helped spread the disease, as did the overcrowding of cities and shanty towns. Population growth in these centers simply exceeded the capacity to deal with fecal contamination of water supplies.

Cholera, then, is a very opportunistic disease. It can pop up following just about any major disaster or during any water crisis. As climate change disrupts the lives of billions of people; forces displacement through rising seas, floods, famines, and war; and interrupts our existing system for providing fresh water, it will also be putting out the welcome mat for cholera.[52] The story here resembles in some ways that of the risk of a modern-day Spanish flu-type epidemic. Cholera does not threaten a death toll in the hundreds of millions, of course, and so lacks the cataclysmic potential that a global outbreak of deadly disease might have. On the other hand, as the conditions for its emergence become more common, there is no doubt that it will exact a human toll. It is less deadly but more certain.

Today, cholera outbreaks occur most often in areas near the equator, where temperatures are relatively consistent year-round.[53] Outbreaks do occur in other areas, but they tend to have a seasonal pattern. As temperatures rise, more of the globe will have cholera-friendly temperatures all year long. Not only will climate change increase the incidence of cholera by creating conditions that promote epidemics, but higher temperatures themselves will also allow the disease to do more damage in more places than it does at present.[54]

The dangers are not limited to cholera or to poor countries, of course. Even well-functioning, modern water systems can develop a dramatic increase in health risks in the face of unexpected change. For example, unusually heavy rainfall is associated with increases in waterborne disease. Climate change, of course, will increase the frequency of severe precipitation events around the world. This translates into an increased risk of disease. To illustrate, the Great Lakes are the primary water source for more than 40 million people and are expected to see an increase in both average precipitation and the frequency of extreme precipitation events. Scientists have estimated that this change in precipitation patterns could increase the incidence of waterborne disease by 50 to 100 percent.[55]

C. Heat Waves: Nickels and Dimes Add Up

Nobody likes to be nickel-and-dimed, forced to pay small amounts in order to get some service or product. The problem is not that any single payment is significant but, rather, that we seem to have to pay over and over, in a way that adds up. Many of us are familiar with a version of this approach as practiced by banks and credit-card companies. There is a seemingly endless parade of fees and charges (and endless changes to those fees and charges). Having to pay a service fee to a bank or credit-card company once may be irksome, but it is bearable and not that much money. When we have to pay repeatedly, however, the charges add up to a lot of money, both for consumers and for banks. Airlines also know how to play the game and charge fees for checking bags, changing tickets, and using frequent-flyer points.

To the extent that this chapter has sought to demonstrate that climate change is bad for human health, it is incomplete, because it does not examine how climate change will nickel-and-dime us. Just as banks and airlines seem to find more and more ways to hit us with fees, climate change will create more and more ways in which human health is compromised. Each incident by itself may seem minor, at least when measured in terms of the number of people affected. But when the many impacts are added up, they become more important and more threatening to the system. For many people, climate change will literally nickel-and-dime them to death.

In writing on the subject of climate change, it is necessary to focus on the most consequential effects. Leaving out smaller impacts is misleading, however, because there are many ways in which climate change will have less dramatic but still deadly effects.

I will discuss in detail just one of these "minor" effects: the increase in the number of heat waves. Other problems will be aggravated by climate change, of course. I could, for example, have opted to include a discussion of air quality. People with respiratory problems, including asthma which affects about 300 million people in the world, are likely to experience more acute symptoms in a warmer world. Higher temperatures also promote smog formation, which, in turn, leads to a small increase in urban mortality and morbidity rates. This small increase translates into a lot of human lives, because so many people live in cities and breathe urban air. Alternatively, I could have decided to talk about foodborne illness, which is also expected to become more common. This is a serious problem in poor parts of the world where diarrheal disease—often acquired by eating contaminated food—is one of the leading causes of death among children.

I have chosen instead to talk about heat waves because, at first glance, an increase in heat waves seems like a minor thing and because heat waves will affect both rich countries and poor ones, and I want to emphasize that it is not only the poor who will pay the price of climate change.

An increase in temperature of a couple of degrees initially seems almost irrelevant to the frequency or impact of heat waves. There is, after all, not much difference between, for example, 30° C (86° F) and 32° C (89.6° F). But an increase of a couple of degrees on average also means more extremes. It is the extreme temperatures that cause most of the problems, and raising average temperatures by a couple of degrees leads to many more days of extreme heat. If temperatures increase by just a bit more than 2° C, for example, it is expected that the number of "heat-wave days" (defined as periods of three or more consecutive days with temperatures above 32° C, or 89.6° F) will more than triple in Los Angeles, going from an annual average of twelve days to forty-four days.

Heat waves kill people, and more heat waves kill more people. Among their other ways to kill, they cause an increase in heart attacks and strokes and can aggravate chronic respiratory diseases. People living in urban environments are at particular risk, because housing is not well designed to stay cool and because the "urban heat island" effect (basically, cities trap a lot of heat and therefore heat up more than other areas) amplifies temperature increases. To get a sense of scale, an increase in average temperature of two degrees is expected to cause an additional four hundred deaths per year in Los Angeles.[56]

Four hundred deaths—we would obviously like to avoid any unnecessary deaths, but that number is probably not enough to trigger great concern or action and certainly seems small compared with many of the other impacts I have discussed. Then again, this is the number for Los Angeles alone. It does not include other large American cities—Dallas, Houston, Chicago, Miami, New York, Boston, Atlanta, and so on. If we include the estimates from all of those cities and from smaller U.S. population centers, the numbers start to add up. One credible estimate is that by 2050, heat-related deaths in the United States will be three thousand to five thousand people every year, compared with seven hundred today.[57]

The United States is home to only a small share of the world's population—a little more than 4 percent. So if we really want to consider the global impact of heat waves, we need to consider the rest of the world, too. Now the numbers rise quickly. Many of the world's largest cities, some much more populous than Los Angeles—Beijing, São Paulo, Lagos, Delhi, Istanbul, Moscow, and on and on—will face the same problem. As our grim count reveals that death will harvest an additional ten thousand souls, is that enough to get our attention? Fifty thousand? More?

Some recent events make this discussion more than just theoretical. The best example may be the 2003 heat wave in Europe. As is true of virtually any specific weather event, we cannot be sure that climate change caused this heat wave, but it certainly may have. More important, it will certainly cause similar—and worse—heat waves in the future. This European experience is a useful early warning of what we can expect. Across Europe, the death toll from the heat wave reached 35,000 by the time it was done. The economic cost was $13 billion.

This example is useful in part because it has been studied very carefully. Trying to determine the number of people killed by a heat wave is a little tricky, because you have to exclude those people who would have died anyway. A study in France compared the number of deaths in thirteen French cities during the heat wave with the number of deaths during the same period in prior years. The results are a good estimate of the number of people killed by the heat wave itself.

One important result is that there was an increase in the number of deaths in every one of the cities. The most striking results were from Paris, which endured a heat wave from the end of July until August 15. The peak of the heat wave was August 9–13, 2003. During the first few days of the heat wave, there was only a small increase in the number of deaths above what one would expect.[58] After this period, though, the death rate climbed, going from a normal (no heat wave) rate of 50 per day to 100 and, for a few days at the peak of the hot weather, much higher, reaching 320 people on the worst day.[59] For the period from August 1 to August 19, the overall death rate was 240 percent of normal. In other words, for every two people who would have died if the weather was normal, five actually did so. Nor was this simply a displacement of deaths that would have happened soon thereafter. If the heat wave simply accelerated the deaths of people who were already near the end, there would have to be a decline in the death rate (relative to normal) after the heat wave ended. There was no evidence of such a decline.[60]

One of the world's richest and most developed cities was simply unable to respond effectively to this heat wave. The same thing happened throughout Europe. Many thousands died as a result. As the earth warms, this will become more common. The heat waves will be hotter and will last longer, and death rates will be higher. This will affect rich and poor countries alike, nickel-and-diming victims into the grave.

7

Where Do We Go from Here?

"We can't solve problems by using the same kind of thinking we used when we created them."

—Albert Einstein

I am the first to acknowledge that this is not a feel-good book. I did not set out to put a happy face on the subject of climate change. I have tried instead to present the harsh reality of climate change as we actually face it. It is important to understand, as well as we can, the full scope of the problem and the consequences of inaction. A competent businessperson trying to turn around a failing business would want to know as much as possible about the market and the competition, even if this knowledge was mostly bad news. A good coach preparing for a game wants to know the strengths and weaknesses of his own team and those of the opposition as accurately and objectively as possible. He cannot prepare properly unless he knows what he is up against. In short, any forward-looking decision process needs to work with the most accurate available information. Deciding what to do in response to the climate-change threat is no different, so this book has tried to present the human consequences of climate change honestly and accurately.

I have also tried to focus specifically on the threat that climate change poses to humans. Many others have written in more detail about how the climate itself will change, how animals will be affected, how coral reefs are threatened, and so on. All of these issues are important and worthy of consideration, and all of them have consequences for humans. In the end, however, what we need to understand, above all, is how human beings will be affected. The greatest impediment to action is not a lack of scientific information or the efforts of deniers to make the evidence seem uncertain. Nor is it an inability to identify policies that would effectively reduce GHG emissions or in some other way avoid some of the harms discussed in this book. It is not even the challenges, as great as they are, of getting agreement among the world's countries to take some form of coordinated action in which everyone will have to bear some of the costs of responding to this threat. Although each of these contributes, at least to some extent, to our failure to combat climate change, I am persuaded that the most significant hurdle has been the public's lack of enthusiasm for strong action. This stems from a disconnection between the scientific reality of climate change—an increase in average temperatures of two degrees or more, melting ice caps, rising seas, and so on—and the human experience. As is true with most important issues, our political leaders will act only when they see that the public wants them to do so.

With that in mind, this book has tried to explain as clearly and honestly as possible how the effects that scientists have identified will actually affect people. If it is successful, readers will appreciate that the climate-change crisis will affect more than just our physical world. The consequences we really care about are those that affect humans, and, as the book shows, many hundreds of millions of people—indeed, probably billions—will be badly hurt as the earth warms, and just about every human being on the planet will face at least some negative effects.

Focusing on the human consequences of climate change has a downside. There is a risk that readers will not simply be distressed by the bad news but will also feel that the problem is too big to solve and throw up their arms in despair. This is exactly the opposite of what the world needs. Reducing the harms from climate change is a manageable task, but only if voters demand that their leaders make difficult political choices. Specifically, policies that come with a short-term economic cost will have to be accepted, and politicians who put forward such plans will have to be applauded rather than punished at the polls. The only way to avoid devastating long-term harms is to accept short-term costs.

Although it often seems as though our political system is incapable of prioritizing the future over the present in this way, there is reason for optimism. We have put in place all sorts of policies based on the idea that we must make investments today to secure a better future. The closest in spirit to what is needed for climate change are environmental regulations. Everything from emissions standards on cars to waste-disposal regulations to bans on substances that harm the ozone layer shows that we are willing to accept costs today in order to secure future benefits. In the United States, the Clean Air Act and the Clean Water Act have been at the center of an effort during several decades to reduce air and water pollution.[1]

Beyond the environment, we make investments in public education today so that tomorrow's workers are more productive, we maintain a large military to protect against future and uncertain threats, and we invest through private and public efforts in research and development. All of these actions involve costs today and benefits tomorrow. Perhaps the most like climate change is education. We pay taxes to support the cost of children's education. The payoff from this investment comes only many years later, when those children become adults and enter the workforce. Despite the time between when we pay for the education and when society receives the benefits, we understand the importance of providing a quality education to our children. We realize that a better educational system produces more capable adults, who, in turn, power a more productive and vibrant economy. The battle against climate change should be seen in the same way. By making relatively modest investments now, we earn large returns in the form of less warming in the future.

One can even find instances of climate-change policy that show a willingness to accept costs today with the goal of reducing harms tomorrow. The EU, for example, has tried to adopt serious policies on the issue, as has California. Even the Environmental Protection Agency in the United States may succeed in generating significant reductions in emissions. These efforts are far short of what we need, but they at least signal that action is not impossible.

Once we, as a global community, decide that we want to do something about climate change, there remains the question of just what that something should be. What policy options do we have, and which of them seem most promising?

We have to acknowledge that it is too late to eliminate all harms. People all over the world are already suffering from the effects of climate change. Think of the Uru Chipaya in Bolivia, who have relied on mountain glaciers for thousands of years and who are now running out of water. Think of the citizens of the Maldives or the millions of others around the world whose livelihood is threatened by rising seas. Think of the victims of climate-related violence in Darfur or the Middle East. Think of those whose health is compromised by more frequent and more intense heat waves all around the world. Within the United States, think of the increased threat from hurricanes along the East Coast, the severe droughts in the Midwest and Southwest and the increase in wildfires that accompany them, and the water crises in California that will only get more severe as time goes on. Although we cannot prevent these harms altogether, all of these impacts, the many others discussed in this book, and an even larger number that have not been discussed can be reduced by sensible policies enacted today.

It would take another whole book (or perhaps several) to explore fully the many different ways in which we might respond to climate change. With that in mind, the closing chapter of this book is intended to provide a glimpse of some of those options and a sense of some of their advantages and disadvantages. What matters most is that we do *something* to address the problem. We obviously want to act in the most efficient and effective way possible, but the search for the perfect solution should not get in the way of adopting policies that will make things better.

Before considering policies aimed at curbing GHG emissions, I want to offer a few words about some other strategies that are sometimes advocated. To be more accurate, these should be called nonstrategies. They are arguments for inaction combined with the crossing of fingers and hoping that everything will be all right. I call these pixie-dust strategies, because in the end, they are a good idea only if you believe that humanity is blessed with some form of magical protection against calamity.

I. Pixie-Dust Strategies

A. *Hiding under the Covers*

Faced with a scary situation, especially one that is unfamiliar and beyond his control, a small child might seek comfort and a sense of safety by hiding under the covers of his bed. The bed obviously does not provide any actual protection, but to a child, it offers the illusion of having made the threat disappear. The bed is perceived as a sanctuary, a place associated with security. He retreats to hide from the insecurity he feels in the face of a threat. For a child in a safe and caring home, there is no reason to discourage this kind of activity. Most likely, there is no real reason for him to be frightened to begin with, so there is no harm in his finding comfort in his bed.

One approach to climate change is to mimic the child who hides in his bed. It is surprisingly easy simply not to think about the problem and hope it goes away. This is perhaps because it can feel like such an enormous challenge that it is easier to ignore it.

Not only is this approach easy and comforting, but it is being actively advocated by many people. Any argument about climate change along the lines of "We should not take action until we have a more complete understanding of the problem" amounts to a call for hiding under the covers and hoping everything will be all right. Those in the climate-change-denial industry also play on our reluctance to face the problem honestly. Because it is a huge global problem, they know it is tempting to embrace claims that there is no threat at all. They are, in effect, inviting us to hide under the covers and pretend that the threat does not exist.

To appreciate just how misguided it is to ignore the problem, let's imagine, contrary to fact, that there is serious scientific disagreement on the question of whether or how humans are causing the earth to warm. Keep in mind that only the most ardent and least credible of deniers claim that we can say with confidence that there is no warming. The claim, instead, is that it is not certain, that we need more evidence before acting, or something along those lines. Put aside the fact that we have all of the evidence that any objective person could ask for, and assume that they are right about the issue. Isn't it still foolhardy to rely on this uncertainty working out in our favor? A child hiding under the covers (again, assuming a safe and caring home) is making a good bet; it is almost certain that either there is no threat or his parents will protect him. Indeed, even if there is a real threat, he is probably too young to do much to protect himself, anyway. If we hide under the covers in an attempt to avoid the climate-change crisis, we are in a different position. We are making a terrible bet. Even according to deniers, there is a good chance that the threat is real. To ignore it is to leave ourselves defenseless. Rather than emulating the child, we should think about how his parents should behave. If they hear suspicious sounds outside their house, they should lock the doors, check the windows, and turn on the outside lights. If the signs of danger are significant, they should call the police and maybe find a place in the house to hide until help arrives. If the parents simply cowered in their own bed without taking any precautions and without looking out for their children, they would be endangering themselves and their children, and we would surely consider them irresponsible.

Any strategy that relies on the idea that by doing nothing we will somehow come out all right should be recognized as equivalent to hiding under the covers. This is true whether it is based on denial of the science, reliance on action in the future instead of now, or simply an unwillingness to grapple with the issue. It is also true of approaches that rely on as-yet-unknown scientific solutions, which I discuss next.

B. Procrastinating

A variation on hiding under the covers is putting off any difficult responses to climate change until some unspecified future time. If hiding under the covers is what a child would do, procrastinating is how a teenager might respond. To be fair, the case for procrastination is, at least superficially, stronger than the case for ignoring the problem altogether. The argument relies on two economic ideas. The first is that the greatest harms from climate change are in the future. If we care more about the present than the future, as economists and others normally assume, those future problems are not such a big deal today. In the context of climate change, the question is what economic costs are we prepared to pay today in order to get benefits in twenty or fifty or eighty years? A second, related argument in favor of procrastination relies on the assumption that the world will be richer in the future and thus better able to bear the costs of dealing with climate change. Why pay now, when we are relatively poor, rather than paying later, when we will be richer?

There is something to these arguments, but I don't think either of them makes a persuasive case for inaction. This is in part because climate change will change our world in ways that cannot be reversed, even if the world is much richer than today. Land lost to rising seas and saltwater intrusion cannot be reclaimed in any significant amount. Communities and even entire countries ruined by those same rising seas or vanishing glaciers or drought will vanish permanently. No future economic gains can compensate for famine and bloodshed experienced in sub-Saharan Africa. If India and Pakistan were to tip into war, perhaps nuclear war, nobody would argue that future economic prosperity could erase the resulting disaster. One problem with waiting, then, is that much of the harm from climate change is irreversible. It is not possible to undo that harm, even if we are richer tomorrow than we are today.

The assumption that we will be richer tomorrow than we are today is also a problem for the procrastination argument. It is comforting to believe that the world will continue to experience sufficient economic growth to make us, on average, richer. Just because it is comforting, however, does not make it true. Climate change will affect every part of the planet, including its economy. To pick just one critical sector of the economy, the food industry, prices will rise as climate change disrupts production. For billions of people on the planet, that is enough, by itself, to make them significantly poorer. At the same time, all of the stresses discussed in this book, not to mention many that have not been addressed here, will also have economic consequences. Tens of millions (or more) of displaced people will be less economically productive, at least until they find new and permanent homes; regions affected by war or civil strife will produce less; and water crises will hurt the economy. Perhaps most important, economic growth, like every aspect of economic activity, will be slowed by climate change. Growth depends on investment and increases in productivity. Persistent economic crises, food shortages, massive human movements, and the like all undermine the foundation of a strong global economy, making economic growth slower and more painful. One study, for example, estimates that existing estimates of the harm from climate change should be doubled to account for the impact of economic growth rates.[2] The procrastination argument only works if doing nothing now is the best strategy for long-run growth. The evidence that climate change will slow growth suggests just the opposite. Taking action today to reduce the impacts of climate change will promote growth. This means that we can expect a richer future if we respond to climate change now rather than waiting.

The real procrastination argument—the one you always end up with if you offer the above responses—is the discount rate. The discount rate reflects the extent to which we care about the future. The problem is that whether one cares about the future and how much one cares about the future are subjective questions. Every person is entitled to his or her own view on the issue. When pressed, a procrastination advocate can simply assert that we should not care about human life twenty-five or fifty years from now. No evidence about climate change, no matter how severe, can overcome that focus on the present. This extreme myopia seems quite odd, and it is hard to believe that people really have such disregard for the future. One way to determine this is to ask them if they are saving for retirement or for their children's college education. For anyone younger than fifty, the time horizon for retirement is not so different from the time horizon relevant to climate change. Even better, ask them if they would advise a thirty-year-old to save for retirement. Anyone willing to dismiss the costs of climate change because they are in the "distant future" should, for the same reason, be opposed to saving for a retirement that is thirty-five years away. There is plenty of other evidence that we care about the future. I pointed out above that spending on education and the military reflects this forward-looking attitude. Consider one more, less scientific illustration. Look into the eyes of a grandparent meeting his or her grandchild for the first time. When my parents first saw my children, it was clear to me that they were looking at the future and that they cared deeply about it. The idea that we should refuse modest investments today that will yield benefits one or two generations from now is simply impossible to reconcile with the way humans treat their children and grandchildren.

C. Geoengineering

If simply dismissing the problem or finding some other way not to think about it is not enough to bring comfort, some people turn to an approach that relies on science. The basic idea here is that science will somehow play the role of superhero and swoop in to save the day just in time to prevent us from having to take any serious action in response to the threats posed by climate change.

Technological change has dramatically altered the way we live in just the last couple of decades. I can recall, for example, the first time I "surfed the Web" (as it was then referred to), but today I cannot imagine how I would function without easy access to the Internet virtually everywhere I go. It is fair to say that technology has provided answers to many of humanity's most serious problems, not just in recent years but throughout history: medical advances have dramatically increased life expectancy; technological advances have generated consistent improvement in the quality of human life from before the Industrial Revolution to today; the invention of the printing press forever changed the way humans communicate with one another; the domestication of plants and animals allowed people to live in stable communities; and the discovery of fire gave us a source of light and heat that transformed human existence.

So maybe it is not surprising that we look to technology as a solution to the problem of climate change. Indeed, it is certain that technological advances will play a critical role in combating climate change by reducing GHG emissions, removing and sequestering carbon, and helping us to cope with the warmer world in which we will be living. Alternatives such as solar or wind power, for example, will be necessary and will surely become more economical. Heat- and drought-resistant crops may be developed to help reduce agricultural losses. And who knows what other innovations will prove vital in the future?

It is a mistake, however, to think of technology as *the* solution rather than as part of a series of steps we have to take. It would be swell if we could count on science to deliver us from climate change through some gizmo that corrected GHG levels in the atmosphere and, in so doing, prevented climate change. Unfortunately, that is not going to happen. The closest thing we have to a technological "solution" to climate change is a set of ideas about large-scale projects to protect our climate, often referred to as geoengineering projects. These are examples of scientists and others thinking on a large scale. They involve massive interventions that would allow humans to tinker intentionally with the global thermostat. Their scale, ambition, and power make them thrilling to consider. Some of these projects may even one day be practical solutions to climate-related problems. None, however, offers a silver bullet capable of solving the problems we face.

Only the human imagination limits the ways in which we might try to find technological fixes for climate change, so we cannot hope to canvass every possibility here. Let's take a look at just a couple of the most commonly discussed options that are sometimes proposed. As is true of the two strategies I describe below, these large-scale geoengineering projects tend to be staggeringly expensive, require technology that we do not yet possess, have enormous side effects that we can immediately identify, and generate massive unintended consequences. Nothing is perfect, of course, and it may be possible to find a project along these lines that is worth pursuing. Before any such project is set in motion, however, it should satisfy several criteria: it must succeed in preventing (or reducing) warming; have minor, if any, negative side effects; provide a means to keep up with continued and growing GHG emissions; and be cheaper than the alternative ways of reducing emissions. Unless these requirements are met, we are better off with other approaches.

Faced with the task of preventing the earth from growing warmer, the most obvious (though not necessarily the easiest) strategy is to prevent some of the sun's energy from reaching the earth. If we controlled the flow of energy from the sun, we could set the earth's thermostat to any temperature we wanted. Perhaps the most frequently cited proposal along these lines involves injecting droplets of sulfur dioxide into the stratosphere, where they would oxidize rapidly, creating tiny droplets of sulfuric acid that would remain suspended for several years. These droplets would reflect solar radiation back into space and reduce the amount of energy (and therefore heat) added to the earth's system. It is a little like holding up a giant mirror to reflect some of the sun's heat. If done just right, this approach could prevent the earth from warming. In fact, we have at least some evidence of this sort of thing at work, because some volcanic eruptions have generated a measurable cooling effect.

Even if it worked, however, it would come at a cost. There would still be higher levels of carbon dioxide in the air, which means that the oceans would continue to become more acidic, threatening the marine ecosystem. There would also be an increase in acid rain and ozone depletion. Less sunlight would reach the earth's surface, which could harm agricultural production and might reduce our ability to generate solar energy. Furthermore, this solution would alter the temperature differences between the oceans and large landmasses such as Africa and Asia, which would have a major impact on weather patterns and, therefore, agriculture and virtually every other human activity.

Because the sulfates emitted into the atmosphere will last only a few years, they would have to be replaced on a consistent basis. Even at present emission rates, the concentration of GHGs in the atmosphere is rising every year. This means that to keep the system in balance, more and more sulfates would have to be added each year. The ever-increasing need to pump sulfates into the atmosphere will grow still more quickly as global emissions increase, something that is sure to happen if no effort is made to limit them. This would, of course, lead to larger side effects over time, larger costs to maintain the practice, and unintended consequences that will also grow indefinitely.

A main weakness of a sulfate-based approach is that it treats the symptoms of climate change rather than the problem itself. Rather than addressing the underlying problem—that GHG concentrations are rising—the sulfate strategy offsets the secondary warming effect by reflecting radiation back into space. If this policy were used successfully, we would be committing ourselves to continuing it forever (and maybe committing to increasing our use indefinitely). Because the sulfates exit the stratosphere after a few years, any halt in the addition of sulfates to the atmosphere would cause temperatures to rocket upward much faster than they are doing today, causing unimaginable catastrophe.

Nor can we ignore the realities of implementing a massive geoengineering scheme. Like any other human activity, this one will involve errors in design, manufacturing, and operation. Administrative questions about who controls the project and how oversight takes place would be enormous. Tremendous amounts of money would be involved, and there would have to be systems in place to ensure that the project's goals respond to the earth's needs rather than to those of self-dealing participants. Even if it all worked, different countries would have different priorities, and the question of who gets to set the earth's thermostat would be a matter of life and death in many parts of the world.

To treat the disease rather than the symptoms requires reducing the level of GHGs and, in particular, CO_2 in the atmosphere. Lowering emissions would achieve this, of course, but so would a technology capable of capturing and storing CO_2 or in some other way removing it from the atmosphere. We already know one easy way to remove CO_2: planting trees. Trees serve as carbon "sinks," places where carbon is collected and stored. There is no doubt that planting more trees could help, but the reality is that the world's forests are being cut down much faster than trees are being planted. The growing need for agricultural land (and land for other uses) makes the planting of tress on a sufficient scale impractical.

An alternative strategy is to look for ways to increase carbon storage in the oceans. One common proposal is to encourage growth on the ocean's surface of organisms that absorb CO_2. The idea is to fertilize sections of ocean with iron dust. Iron is a critical ingredient in the growth of phytoplankton, microscopic plants that support much of the marine food chain. Phytoplankton takes CO_2 from the atmosphere and converts it into organic carbon. When the phytoplankton dies, it sinks to the ocean floor, where the carbon is "stored." If this were done on a large enough scale, the notion is that we could remove carbon from the atmosphere in large enough quantities to affect the pace of climate change.

There has been some investigation of this possible strategy, and the results suggest that our enthusiasm for the approach should be limited. One serious problem is that the efficiency of the process is fairly low, meaning that only a small percentage of the phytoplankton carbon is ultimately sequestered, and the large majority is returned to the atmosphere as CO_2. This means, among other things, that it would take massive amounts of iron to operate such a plan on a large enough scale to have an impact. It is also important to note that adding iron to the oceans in this way would have other impacts, only some of which we understand. It would, for example, affect the phytoplankton in unpredictable ways and may cause "toxic blooms," with harmful plankton species poisoning the water. In the end, capturing carbon in this way is a possibility worthy of further study, but it remains uncertain whether it will one day prove effective. It is certainly not something we can rely on to save us from having to change the rate at which humans emit CO_2 into the atmosphere.

To these two examples—adding sulfates to the stratosphere and encouraging phytoplankton blooms in the oceans—one could add many other ideas that range from serious to fantastical. Given the nature of the problem, geoengineering solutions are necessarily massive in scale. Any action capable of affecting the climate will involve an intentional and enormous intervention in the natural systems of the planet unlike anything humans have ever attempted. It will inevitably have other large impacts on the planet, which will be all but impossible to predict in advance. And we will not know if it will succeed in lowering the earth's temperature until we try it. We would literally be gambling with the entire planet. Common sense dictates that such a program be carried out with great caution, because the risks and uncertainties are so immense.

Imagine that someone you know is suffering serious health problems as a result of exposure to some toxic substance. She is informed by a doctor about an experimental surgery that might improve her health, but there is no way to know for sure if it will do her more harm then good. Furthermore, even if the surgery is successful, she will suffer from major negative side effects, only some of which are known. An alternative to the surgery, she is told, is to stop exposing herself to the toxic material. Making this behavioral change will cause her health issues to fade, and she will return to health. It does not take a medical degree to know that the better solution is for the patient to avoid the toxic material rather than take on the risks associated with the surgery.

A similar lesson applies to geoengineering and climate change. The planet is warming as a result of excessive emission of GHGs. A geoengineering solution is like experimental surgery: there is a chance it will help, but it may do more harm than good, and it will certainly have major side effects, not all of which can be identified in advance. A better alternative is to find ways to reduce the GHGs we are pumping into the atmosphere; this achieves the same result but without the enormous risks of geoengineering solutions.

I do not wish to be entirely dismissive of geoengineering proposals. There may well come a time when we will need them, or they may come to be understood well enough to be practical. It may also turn out that it makes sense to use such techniques in moderation, as part of a suite of strategies to combat climate change. For the moment, however, it is fairly clear that these strategies do not offer a credible alternative to reducing emissions. They are too expensive and too risky. They even carry the potential to make things much worse than they already are. Rather than responding to a reasonably well-understood human influence on climate with a complex, untested, elaborate, and expensive technological experiment, it is much more sensible to think about how to reduce the GHGs we are adding to the atmosphere.

II. Grown-Up Strategies

When one looks at the climate crisis honestly, there is no way to avoid the conclusion that we have to reduce the speed with which we are pumping GHGs into the atmosphere. The problem certainly will not go away simply by being ignored. Nor can reducing the amount of energy that enters the earth's system (by, for example, injecting sulfates into the atmosphere) or removing and storing carbon (by, for example, seeding the oceans with iron) offer practical alternatives to dealing with the rate of GHG emissions. If we are to prevent catastrophic warming, we simply have to find a way to reduce our emissions of GHGs.

A. How Low Should We Go?

Once we turn to the question of *how* we can reduce emissions, it is almost inevitable that we start to think in terms of some target for GHG concentration. Having a target helps us understand the scale of the problem and can help countries negotiate on the question of how much each of them needs to do. On the other hand, we should not let ourselves become so consumed by debates about the ideal target that we fail to get started on efforts to reduce emissions. The costs of climate change rise very quickly with higher concentrations of GHGs, so any reduction is welcome.[3]

Ultimately, the proper target for GHGs is a matter of science. The correct target is one that prevents warming or, more accurately, prevents too much warming. The planet has already warmed some and will continue to do so for a time even if GHG emissions drop to zero tomorrow. The question of how much warming is too much concerns more than science, of course, because it raises policy questions about what we are prepared to do to reduce warming. The key issue, though, is still science. We need to know the point at which the changing climate will have such enormous impacts that our very way of life is threatened.

There is no certainty here, so we have to move forward with our best guess. Without delving into the details of the scientific issues, we can observe a couple of positions that have emerged. One approach is to assume that warming of more than 2° C would be too much. It would be too much for the reasons given in this book: the harms to humans would be enormous, and the planet would be quite different from what it is today. This target of 2° C, which is measured against temperatures in the 1800s and represents an increase of barely more than 1° C relative to today's temperatures, corresponds to a concentration of carbon dioxide equal to 450 ppm (parts per million). In other words, to keep temperatures from rising more than 2° C from what they were in the 1800s would require that we not allow CO_2 levels to rise above 450 ppm, keeping in mind that today's level is about 387 ppm.

Keeping CO_2 below 450 ppm would require significant action, and if this were the target, we would have every reason to view the situation as urgent.

A competing perspective, however, is that 450 ppm would be far too high. In fact, among those who reject 450 ppm as a target is James Hansen, one of the most important voices in climate-change debates and one of the leading figures who initially put forward 450 ppm as a sensible goal. As climate science developed, however, Hansen became convinced that 450 ppm was much too high. He now argues that we must target a much lower limit: 350 ppm. This change in perspective does not reflect some failure on Hansen's part. In fact, it shows just the opposite. As evidence accumulated about the speed with which the climate is changing and the pace of the climate's impacts, Hansen behaved as a good scientist should: he updated his views to reflect the new information. The evidence Hansen observed, which is available to anyone interested in the subject, was that ice sheets were melting faster than expected, glaciers were disappearing, coral reefs were suffering, and so on. Again and again, it turned out that earlier predictions about the climate's impact proved to be overly optimistic. Throughout the natural world, things are changing faster than expected, and this means that the target of 450 ppm is probably too high.

The implication of the 350-ppm target is that we have to find a way to reduce the actual concentration of carbon in the atmosphere if we hope to avoid the most severe effects of a warming world. This is a tall order, which will require an unprecedented level of global commitment and cooperation. It is even more difficult because we live in a world with a rapidly growing population and a desperate need for economic growth. Unfortunately, the climate is not concerned with how hard humans must work to avoid the problem. If Hansen is right, and there are lots of reasons to think that he is, humanity has already passed the stage where merely stabilizing emissions at current levels will be enough.

Hansen's voice is not the only one in this discussion, and some observers propose higher targets. My own instinct is to accept 350 ppm as a target, because I have confidence in the scientists who support it. Whether someone agrees with a target of 350 ppm or not, however, is not critical to me. I am much more concerned with the fact that there is no significant disagreement among climate scientists that the current path is not sustainable. If we act responsibly and adopt sensible policies to reduce climate change, we will eventually have to decide on a target. In the short term, however, the target is not our biggest problem. Our immediate challenge is to decide that we are prepared to take some action to slow the rate of GHG emissions. Until we get to that point, we do not need a specific target. In other words, while determining an appropriate target makes sense, we do not need to make a collective determination on that front in order to make the critical policy decision to respond to the threat of climate change.

B. What Can or Should Be Done?

Although the debates about climate change often focus on scientific questions, the greatest hurdle may be political. How can we get people to accept that sacrifices must be made today in order to protect future generations? If we manage to persuade individuals, how can we ensure that this translates through the political system to national policies? If countries are persuaded of a need to act, how can we get them to cooperate in a way that distributes the burden of reducing emissions effectively and fairly? Progressing from recognition of the problem to appropriate policies is not easy. It is, however, necessary, and the first step is for people to recognize the problem. That is what I hope this book helps to achieve; I hope it shows that we face a real crisis and that action must be taken, even if that action involves some economic costs today.

Because this book is about the enormity of the problem, I cannot possibly provide a full-blown investigation of possible policy solutions. Nevertheless, it is important at least to touch on the basics of what must be done to reduce GHG emissions and discuss the most promising options for moving forward.

1. It Is All About Price

Although there is some potential for government to regulate economic activity directly, no government regulation is as effective at controlling behavior as prices. When the price of an item goes up, everybody who uses it adapts to the new, higher price. People buy and use less of it, and they find substitutes. This drives up the price of substitutes, and producers of these alternative products respond by increasing production. The story of how best to combat climate change is essentially a pricing strategy. By changing the price of carbon, we can reduce its use and so reduce GHG emissions.

At this basic level, the solution could not be simpler. To reduce emissions of carbon, we have to increase the price of those emissions. Higher prices generate a whole array of reactions in the carbon market, just as they do in any market. In this case, those reactions all contribute to the fight against climate change.

Consumers faced with higher prices would cut back on the amount of carbon they emit through, for example, the use of fossil fuels. We are all familiar with how higher gasoline prices affect our behavior by making us take public transportation, walk more, or even buy more fuel-efficient cars. Those same high prices give businesses an incentive to improve the efficiency of their energy use, finding ways to do the same things while releasing less carbon. Higher prices also make alternative energy sources more attractive to develop and bring to market. The world needs energy, and a stable climate will require large-scale use of solar, wind, and other forms of clean energy.

You might reasonably think that use of alternatives is, at least currently, expensive, and you would be right. It is precisely because they are expensive that traditional energy sources—oil, coal, gas—continue to form the backbone of the world's energy supply. These carbon-emitting energy sources are less expensive and are therefore heavily used. But when we say that they are less expensive, we are talking about the price paid by whoever is buying them or, if we trace the production process back to the source, whoever extracts them from the earth. This price, however, ignores the costs that the use of the energy source imposes on the general public. The full cost of fossil fuel is not paid by the consumer. Specifically, the harm to the climate must also be included as a cost (it is what economists term an externality). These costs, however, are not reflected in the price of the fuel. They are instead paid by everyone in the form of a warmer world and the disastrous consequences that brings.

If we take into account the full cost of energy—including the climate costs—it is not nearly so easy to say that fossil fuels are cheaper than other energy sources. Any economist will agree that prices do a great job of getting people to use resources efficiently. But those same economists will agree that prices play this role properly only when they reflect the true cost of whatever is being bought and sold. The problem with fossil fuels is that the price at which they are bought and sold is far below their true cost, because it does not reflect the catastrophic harm done to the planet.

2. Alternative Energy

Because the full cost of fossil fuels is not reflected in their price, people consume too much. The obvious (and necessary) solution is to find a way to raise the price of carbon so that it accurately reflects the true cost. Before I turn to discuss the two most promising strategies for doing this, it makes sense to look at alternative energy sources. There are several other ways to produce energy that are, or at least may be, less harmful to the climate. These include nuclear energy, wind power, solar power, geothermal energy, biofuel, and hydrogen. Each of these has advantages and disadvantages in terms of availability, the state of technology, and risks. Nuclear power, for example, is capable of producing large amounts of energy but presents well-known safety issues.

Each of the above-listed alternatives holds the promise of reducing the future level of GHG emissions, but none of them is currently operating in a way that can be expected to prevent a 2° C (or more) warming. The appeal of these alternatives is increased by an awareness of the threat posed by climate change. There is no doubt that nuclear power presents risks, as evidenced so catastrophically by the Fukushima nuclear disaster in 2011. It would be foolish to deny these risks, but if turning away from nuclear power means continued growth in GHG emissions, we may be embracing an even greater threat. Funding research into solar or wind energy may seem expensive, and subsidizing the development of these energy sources may seem unnecessary, but these actions are easier to understand once we appreciate that carbon is not being priced at its true cost.

My goal here is not to provide anything resembling a complete analysis of alternative energy sources. All I really want to emphasize is that once we understand the size of the threat posed by climate change, efforts to pursue alternatives to fossil fuels become more attractive and more urgent.

3. A Carbon Tax

There are essentially two ways to raise the price of carbon to account for its true cost. The first, and simpler, option is simply to tax it. We could, at least in principle, collect a tax on every unit of fossil fuel that came out of a mine or well. Taxing the product at its source would be enough to have the cost of the tax passed through to consumers. If the tax accurately reflects the full cost, including the harm to the world's climate, then everybody in the chain from production to consumption will adjust his or her behavior accordingly, which is what is needed. The revenue from the tax can then be spent or simply distributed to the public (e.g., in the form of lower taxes in other areas). Note that if the tax revenue is distributed to the public, then there is no overall increase in taxes (since the public gets back the same amount it pays in). The impact of the tax, however, is to increase the cost of using fossil fuels, which, in turn, encourages people to reduce their use of fossil fuels and adjust their behavior toward less harmful forms of energy. Among the benefits of a tax on carbon is that it raises the cost of all fossil fuels at the same time. This avoids an outcome in which a tax on one source, such as oil, serves to increase demand for another source, such as coal.

4. Cap-and-Trade

The second widely discussed approach to regulate carbon is cap-and-trade. The idea here is simple, although the actual implementation is quite complex. A limit (cap) is placed on the total amount of GHG emissions that will be permitted in the country during a given year. Large emitters of GHGs must acquire permits in order to release GHGs, and the total number of permits is equal to the cap. In brief, the government limits the permitted level of GHGs, which, obviously, affects the rate of climate change. Limiting the supply of permits also drives up the price of carbon, causing people to move away from carbon-emitting energy sources in the same way that a tax would. In terms of its effects, cap-and-trade can do exactly what a tax would do.

To make cap-and-trade work, however, the emissions permits have to be distributed somehow. One solution would be to auction them off. Those who can get the most out of each unit of fossil fuel would be willing to pay the most for the permits. Another option is to hand the permits out. The case for this approach is that we could give them to industries and firms that would be most affected by the implementation of a cap-and-trade system and, in that way, reduce the impact of the policy on these businesses.

Thanks to the trade part of cap-and-trade, the way in which the government distributes the permits is not critical. Once distributed, the permits can be traded freely. This means that the most efficient energy users will be willing to pay the most for the permits, and less efficient energy users will do better by selling the permits rather than using them. The result is that the market will direct permits into the hands of those that emit fewer GHGs for any given level of production.

The case for cap-and-trade, then, is that it is a more efficient way to regulate GHG emissions. The short-term drawback is that it is more complex, as should be clear even from the very brief description above. In the long term, it has another disadvantage, which is that its effect on GHG emissions can fade over time. Dealing with climate change ultimately requires a shift to carbon-free energy sources. This cannot happen all at once. A carbon tax, if set appropriately to account for the full costs of carbon, will remain in place even if and when we reach the point where carbon-free energy or carbon-saving approaches make the use of fossil fuels more expensive than the use of alternatives. The result would then be what we need: fossil fuels will be left in the ground, and carbon that would heat the planet if released into the atmosphere will remain stored.

Cap-and-trade does less well in this situation. It is not realistic (either politically or economically) to limit fossil fuel use immediately to the level we need to reach in the long term. We will initially have to set the cap higher. As demand for fossil fuels falls, so will the demand for permits. This makes the cost of the permits fall, and so fossil fuel prices fall, too, allowing them to remain a competitive form of energy. Cap-and-trade can respond effectively to falling demand of fossil fuels only by lowering the cap, something that makes it politically more precarious. To be fair, a cap-and-trade policy can solve this problem by setting a floor on the price of emissions. If the market price of permits falls below the floor, the number of emissions permits would be automatically reduced, pushing the price up again.

5. *Choosing a Policy*

A reasonable response to the two options above would be to ask why we would use a cap-and-trade system when it seems to do exactly the same thing as a tax and yet is so much more complex and so much more susceptible to abuse or political manipulation. The handing out of permits may not directly matter to the goal of reducing emissions, but it does give politicians enormously valuable goodies to distribute. Predictably, this attracts lobbyists trying to capture as much of those goodies—the permits—as possible, which has the potential to create all sorts of bad outcomes. The distribution of permits risks being a matter of political favoritism and cronyism, for example. The process of lobbying to get this benefit will consume time and money that could be more efficiently used elsewhere (although lobbying efforts will also tend to drive up energy prices, since the lobbyists are then part of the cost of energy production). Perhaps worst of all, faced with demands for the permits, there is a temptation to increase the cap so as to satisfy the demand from industry. Getting a permit can be of great value to a firm, so it will be willing to spend money on lobbyists to persuade politicians to deliver the permit. For a politician, delivering the permit to the firm generates rewards in the form of political support and campaign contributions. (My point here is not that politicians will take illegal bribes but, rather, that in the American system, industry groups and firms make contributions to politicians in order to curry favor with them. When politicians deliver for those firms, more contributions typically follow.) You can see how it is tempting to increase the cap so as to be able to generate support from more firms and industries. Increasing the cap, of course, means increasing emissions and undermining the climate-change benefits.

Returning to the question of why anyone would support cap-and-trade, the answer is that, on one hand, cap-and-trade is thought to be better than dictating to firms the permissible level of emissions, and, on the other hand, it is more politically achievable than a straight carbon tax. The above description of a carbon tax leaves out the question of politics, and that is why it sounds so appealing. But think about how the American political system reacts to proposals for new taxes. Now, consider that the carbon tax in question, if done properly, would raise gasoline prices by a dollar per gallon or more. In fact, it would raise all fossil-fuel prices—most energy prices, in other words—significantly. Even if it were combined with a promise to return the tax revenue to the public in the form of a dividend or a reduction in some other taxes, it would be an exceptionally difficult thing to sell politically. Here we see one of the most pernicious effects of the climate-change-denial industry: by refusing to accept the science on climate change, deniers make it much more difficult even to propose, let alone adopt, a serious policy response to the problem in the form of a carbon tax. Any politician making such a proposal would be taking an enormous risk.

By comparison, cap-and-trade is less politically toxic. Although it may achieve the same result, it is easier to implement, because it is less transparent. It is relatively easy to understand how a tax on fossil fuels translates to increased prices at the pump, and it is easily communicated in the media. The way a cap on overall emissions affects prices is much harder to know in advance and requires a longer explanation. This makes it less controversial. The same is true of what is sometimes called a command-and-control approach, in which a government agency dictates prices or quantities to energy firms. Like the other two approaches, this could achieve the goals of raising energy prices and reducing emissions. It relies, however, on the ability of the government to allocate production quotas efficiently. Americans have some considerable, and well-founded, skepticism about the government's ability to manage the economy in this way. A cap-and-trade approach, by comparison, allows the market to determine who ultimately gets the emissions permits, and there is a good deal more confidence that this will lead to efficient outcomes.

A cap-and-trade approach has an additional political advantage. Although it invites all sorts of harmful lobbying in pursuit of permits, the ability to allocate permits can also be used by the government to placate political opposition. This provides some compensation to groups that will be negatively affected by the policy and therefore makes it more likely to be adopted.

The choice, then, boils down to one's view of the political system. Cap-and-trade is easier to adopt but harder to implement effectively once adopted. If it is adopted, it is more likely to be weaker than desired, and it is certain to create entire industries of lobbyists and to attract financial institutions that will profit from trading the permits. A carbon tax is much simpler in concept and implementation but more difficult to adopt in our political system.

A lot more could be said about possible strategies to combat climate change and the various advantages and disadvantages of each. That is a critically important discussion but cannot be delved into here.

If you are convinced of the need to act, the next step is to press your elected leaders to do so. Whatever they do must be judged based on whether it will contribute to reducing the level of GHG emissions. We must demand this. The political forces arrayed against these efforts are considerable; powerful business interests continue to earn enormous profits from energy, and they are happy to continue to do so without paying for the impact of their business practices on the climate. On the other side are voters, people who care about their own futures and those of their children and grandchildren. My own children are not yet teenagers. By 2050, they will be middle-aged adults, not much older than I am today. If we do not act now, they will face a much more severe, costly, and urgent climate-change problem. Their world will be experiencing massive consequences and getting worse each year. Countless millions will be displaced by rising seas; refugees around the world will be looking for places to live; food and water supplies will have failed in many parts of the world, triggering famine and humanitarian crises on a new and horrific scale; countries will be going to war over water and other resources necessary for survival; some states will dissolve into chaos, making them ideal places for terrorist organizations to operate; and human health around the world will be under attack from heat waves, water- and foodborne illnesses, and possibly major outbreaks of deadly contagious disease.

If we fail to act now, my children's generation may be the first to find their entire way of life under attack as a result of climate change, and later generations will know nothing else. All of the challenges facing my children will be multiplied several-fold for any grandchildren I may have.

The adults in the world today face a choice about what we are going to do. We cannot wish away climate change, and we should not pin our hopes on a miracle to save us. What we must do is recognize the seriousness of this challenge and decide what is necessary to halt the warming of the globe. There should be no mistaking the fact that this will involve some economic sacrifice. Our lives are easier because energy is plentiful and inexpensive, but we can no longer ignore the impact of our energy use on the climate. We must raise the price of carbon sufficiently to keep the planet from overheating. If we don't, we will trigger human tragedy on a scale the world has never seen.

NOTES

Chapter 1

1. Robert Strom, *Hot House: Global Climate Change and the Human Condition* (New York, Copernicus, 2007), 184.
2. Gerard Wynn, "Climate Change Expert Said He Underestimated Threat," Reuters, April 16, 2008.
3. Peter M. Cox et al., "Acceleration of Global Warming due to Carbon-Cycle Feedbacks in a Coupled Climate Model," *Nature* 408 (2000): 184.
4. *An Inconvenient Truth*, directed by Davis Guggenheim, Paramount Classics, 2006.
5. Paul Krugman used the metaphor in his newspaper column, "Boiling the Frog," *New York Times*, July 13, 2009, A19. The ABC News television program *Earth 2100* also used the frog metaphor (directed by Rudy Bednar, American Broadcasting Co., 2009). The story of the frog is the focal point in "Boiled Frogs and Path Dependency in Climate Policy Decisions," a chapter by Mort Webster in *Human-Induced Climate Change: An Interdisciplinary Assessment*, ed. M. Schlesinger et al. (Cambridge, U.K.: Cambridge University Press, 2007), 255–264.
6. The year 2007 is tied for the second-warmest year on record. NASA Goddard Institute for Space Studies, "GISS Surface Temperature Analysis," http://data.giss.nasa.gov/gistemp/2007.
7. *Human Impact Report: The Anatomy of a Silent Crisis* (Geneva: Global Humanitarian Forum, 2009), 1.
8. Ibid.
9. See, e.g., Richard A. Kerr, "Latest Forecast: Stand by for a Warmer, but Not Scorching World," *Science* 312 (2006): 351.
10. Seth Borenstein, "Global Warming Said Killing Some Species," *USA Today*, November 21, 2006, http://www.usatoday.com/tech/science/2006–11–21-warming-species_x.htm.

Chapter 2

1. Peter T. Doran and Maggie Kendall Zimmerman, "Examining the Scientific Consensus on Climate Change," *EOS* 90 (2009): 23.
2. George Monbiot, "Monbiot's Royal Flush: Top 10 Climate Change Deniers," Guardian Online, March 9, 2009, http://www.guardian.co.uk/environment/georgemonbiot/2009/mar/06/climate-change-deniers-top-10.
3. Steven Milloy, "There's a New Global Warming Consensus in Town," Junk Science, Fox News Online, May 23, 2008, http://www.foxnews.com/story/0,2933,357201,00.html.
4. Carolina A. Miranda, "10 Questions for Al Gore," Time.com, November 27, 2006, http://www.time.com/time/magazine/article/0,9171,1562957,00.html.

5. Gro Harlem Brundtland, Speech to UN Commission on Sustainable Development, May 10, 2007.
6. Arthur Max, "U.N.: Ignoring Global Warming Is 'Criminally Irresponsible,'" *USA Today*, November 12, 2007, http://www.usatoday.com/weather/climate/globalwarming/2007–11–12-united-nations_N.htm.
7. William Anderegg et al., "Expert Credibility in Climate Change," *Proceedings of the National Academy of Science U.S.A.* 107 (2010): 12107–12109; Doran and Zimmerman, "Examining the Scientific Consensus," 22–23; Naomi Oreskes, "The Scientific Consensus on Climate Change," *Science* 306 (2004): 1686; Robert Strom, *Hot House: Global Climate Change and the Human Condition* (New York, Copernicus, 2007), 3.
8. "Remarkably, none of the [928] papers disagreed with the consensus position. Admittedly, authors...might believe that current climate change is natural. However, none of these papers argued that point." Oreskes, "The Scientific Consensus," 1686.
9. Naomi Oreskes, "The Scientific Consensus on Climate Change," *Science* 306 (2004): 1686.
10. Anderegg et al., "Expert Credibility," 12107–12109.
11. In addition to the IPCC (discussed later in this chapter), a few of the books explaining how the climate is changing are: Tim Flannery, *The Weather Makers* (New York: Grove, 2005); James Hansen, *Storms of My Grandchildren* (New York: Bloomsbury, 2009); Strom, *Hot House*; and James Hoggan, *Climate Cover-Up* (Vancouver: Greystone, 2009).
12. Patrick Michaels, "The Climategate Whitewash Continues," *Wall Street Journal*, July 12, 2010, http://online.wsj.com/article/SB10001424052748704075604575356611173414140.html.
13. Republican National Committee, 2008 Republican Platform: Environment, http://www.presidency.ucsb.edu/ws/index.php?pid=78545.
14. There were, and are, prominent members of the Republican Party who remain skeptical about climate change, at least in their public remarks. The most prominent Republican skeptic is probably Sarah Palin, the Republican vice-presidential candidate in 2008. In 2008, Palin said of climate change, "I'm not one though who would attribute it to being man-made." Rick Klein, "Palin: Global Warming Not Man-Made," ABC News, August 29, 2008. This is not full-throated skepticism, as it does not directly dispute that we face a climate crisis or even affirmatively assert that it is somehow natural rather than man-made. While Palin's perspective was different in emphasis, her state, Alaska, is quite vulnerable to climate change, and Palin appears to have recognized this fact. In an administrative order issued in September 2007, Palin states, "climatologists tell us that the current rate of warming is unprecedented within the time of human civilization." Sarah Palin, Governor Sarah Palin's Report on the Climate Change Sub-Cabinet, http://www.climatechange.alaska.gov/docs/govrpt_jul08.pdf.
15. James M. Inhofe, "The Science of Climate Change," Senate Floor Statement by U.S. Sen. James M. Inhofe (R-Okla.), Chairman, Committee on Environment and Public Works, Floor Speeches, July 28, 2003.
16. Inhofe has made similar statements many times. James M. Inhofe, "Inhofe Calls 2009 the Year of the Skeptic," U.S. Senate Committee on Environment and Public Works, Minority Page, November 18, 2009; "'Consensus' in Freefall: Inhofe Global Warming Speech," James M. Inhofe: Press Room, Press Releases, January 8, 2009.
17. Matthew Yglesias, "Rep Shimkus Says We Need Uncapped Carbon Emissions Because Carbon Is 'Plant Food,'" Yglesias, March 28, 2009, http://yglesias.thinkprogress.org. The same source points out, "of course, if there was no carbon dioxide in the atmosphere, that would have dire implications for the world's plants. But even if there were no carbon dioxide emissions in 2010, that would still leave plenty of carbon dioxide in the atmosphere. The point about our CO_2 emissions is that the rate at which fossil fuel use puts new carbon into the atmosphere greatly exceeds the rate at which plants remove it. The aim is not to eliminate CO_2 from the atmosphere but to stabilize the amount of CO_2, which means curtailing emissions to a level much closer to the rate at which plants consume it."
18. Paul Krugman, "Betraying the Planet," *New York Times*, June 29, 2009, http://www.nytimes.com/2009/06/29/opinion/29krugman.html.

19.. "U.S. Senate Minority Report: More Than 700 International Scientists Dis-sent over Man-Made Global Warming Claims," U.S. Senate Committee on Environment and Public Works: The Inhofe EPW Press Blog, December 11, 2008,http://www.epw.senate.gov/public/index.cfm?FuseAction=Minority.Blogs&ContentRecord_id=10fe77b0–802a-23ad-4df1-fc38ed4f85e3.

20. Mark Hertsgaard, "On the Front Lines of Climate Change," *Time*, March 29, 2007, http://www.time.com/time/magazine/article/0,9171,1604879,00.html.

21. "2010 Tied for Warmest Year on Record," NOAA, January 12, 2011, http://www.noaanews.noaa.gov/stories2011/20110112_globalstats.html.

22. Steve Cole and Leslie McCarthy, "NASA Research Finds Last Decade Was Warmest on Record, 2009 One of Warmest Years," NASA Press Release Archives, January 21, 2010, http://www.nasa.gov/home/hqnews/2010/jan/HQ_10–017_Warmest_temps.html.

23. Ibid.

24. IPCC, "Activities," http://www.ipcc.ch/activities/activities.htm#1.

25. IPCC, "Principles Governing IPCC Work," April 28, 2006, 1, http://www.ipcc.ch/pdf/ipcc-principles/ipcc-principles.pdf.

26. Ibid.

27. IPCC, "Activities Archive," http://www.ipcc.ch/activities/activities.shtml#.UCWik-ESL5FU.

28. IPCC, "Procedures for the Preparation, Review, Acceptance, Adoption, Approval and Publication of IPCC Reports," last updated September 4, 2008.

29. IPCC, "Summary for Policymakers," in *Climate Change 2007: The Physical Science Basis. Contribution of Working Group I to the Fourth Assessment Report of the Intergovernmental Panel on Climate Change*, ed. S. Solomon et al. (Cambridge, U.K.: Cambridge University Press, 2007), 10.

30. Strom, *Hot House*, 84.

31. Ibid., 86.

32. NOAA Satellite and Information Service, http://www.ncdc.noaa.gov/paleo/global-warming/instrumental.html.

33. IPCC, "Summary for Policymakers," 13.

34. Strom, *Hot House,* 123.

35. The conference was organized by the International Alliance of Research Universities. It included more than fourteen hundred presentations. Following the conference, a "Synthesis Report" was prepared. I rely on this report for the conclusions of the conference.

36. Katherine Richardson et al., Synthesis Report from Climate Change: Global Risks, Challenges, and Decisions, Copenhagen, 2009, 8.

37. Rebecca Lindsey, "Climate and Earth's Energy Budget," NASA Earth Observatory, January 14, 2009, http://earthobservatory.nasa.gov/Features/EnergyBalance.

38. James F. Kasting, "The Carbon Cycle, Climate, and the Long-Term Effects of Fossil Fuel Burning," *Consequences: The Nature and Implications of Environmental Change* 4 (1998), http://www.gcrio.org/CONSEQUENCES/vol4no1/carbcycle.html; Lindsey, "Climate and Earth's Energy Budget"; John F. B. Mitchell, "The 'Greenhouse' Effect and Climate Change," *Review of Geophysics* 27 (1989): 115–139.

39. Strom, *Hot House*, 109.

40. Ibid.

41. G. A. Meehl et al., "Global Climate Projections," in *Climate Change 2007: The Physical Science Basis. Contribution of Working Group I to the Fourth Assessment Report of the Intergovernmental Panel on Climate Change*, ed. S. Solomon et al. (Cambridge, U.K.: Cambridge University Press, 2007), 790; P. Forster et al., "Changes in Atmospheric Constituents and in Radiative Forcing," in *Climate Change 2007: The Physical Science Basis. Contribution of Working Group I to the Fourth Assessment Report of the Intergovernmental Panel on Climate Change*, ed. S. Solomon et al. (Cambridge, U.K.: Cambridge University Press, 2007), 135.

42. Xander Olsthoorn, "Carbon Dioxide Emissions from International Aviation: 1950–2050," *Journal of Air Transport Management* 7 (2001), 87.

43. P. Falkowski et al., "The Global Carbon Cycle: A Test of Our Knowledge of Earth as a System," *Science* 290 (2000), 292.
44. Ibid., 293.
45. J. D. Sterman and L. Booth Sweeney, "Understanding Public Complacency about Climate Change: Adults' Mental Models of Climate Change Violate Conservation of Matter," *Climatic Change* 80 (2007): 213–238; L. Booth Sweeney and J. D. Sterman, "Bathtub Dynamics: Initial Results of a Systems Thinking Inventory," *System Dynamics Review* 16 (2000): 249–294.
46. "350 Science: What Is 350?" 350.org, http://www.350.org/en/about/science.
47. Johan Rockstrom et al., "A Safe Operating Space for Humanity," *Nature* 461 (September 24, 2009): 472–475.
48. A. Tripati, C. Roberts, and R. Eagle, "Coupling of CO_2 and Ice Sheet Stability over Major Climate Transitions of the Last 20 Million Years," *Science* 326 (2009): 1394–1397.
49. Geoff Brumfiel, "Academy Affirms Hockey-Stick Graph," *Nature* 441 (2006): 1032–1033; Committee on Surface Temperature Reconstructions for the Last 2,000 Years, *Surface Temperature Reconstructions of the Last 2000 Years* (Washington, D.C.: National Academies Press, 2006).
50. Brumfiel, "Academy Affirms," 3.
51. P. D. Jones, T. J. Osborn, and K. R. Briffa, "The Evolution of Climate over the Last Millennium," *Science* 292 (2001): 662; Rosanne D'Arrigo, Rob Wilson, and Gordon Jacoby, "On the Long-term Context for Late Twentieth Century Warming," *Journal of Geophysical Research—Atmospheres* 111 (2006): 1–12; K. R. Briffa et al., "Low-frequency Temperature Variations from a Northern Tree Ring Density Network," *Journal of Geophysical Research* 106 (2001): 2929–2941; J. Oerlemans, "Extracting a Climate Signal from 169 Glacier Records," *Science* 308 (2005): 675–677; E. Jansen et al., "Palaeoclimate," in *Climate Change 2007: The Physical Science Basis, Contribution of Working Group I to the Fourth Assessment Report of the Intergovernmental Panel on Climate Change*, ed. S. Solomon et al. (Cambridge, U.K.: Cambridge University Press, 2007), 467; Anders Moberg et al., "Highly Variable Northern Hemisphere Temperatures Reconstructed from Low- and High-resolution Proxy Data," *Nature* 433 (2005): 613–617.
52. Committee on Surface Temperature Reconstructions for the Last 2,000 Years, *Surface Temperature Reconstructions.*
53. U.S. Senate Environment and Public Works Committee (Minority), "Over 400 Prominent Scientists Disputed Man-Made Global Warming Claims in 2007," U.S. Senate Committee on Environment and Public Works, December 20, 2007, http://epw.senate.gov/public/index.cfm?FuseAction=Minority.Blogs&ContentRecord_id=f80a6386–802a-23ad-40c8–3c63dc2d02cb.
54. Dan Shapley, "Inhofe's 400 Global Warming Deniers Debunked," Daily Green, November 1, 2008, http://www.thedailygreen.com/environmental-news/latest/inhofe-global-warming-deniers-scientists-46011008.
55. Joe Wiesenthal, "The Ten Most Important Climate Change Skeptics," Business Insider, July 30, 2009, http://www.businessinsider.com/the-ten-most-important-climate-change-skeptics-2009-7?op=1.
56. Ibid.
57. Bjorn Lomborg, *Cool It: The Skeptical Environmentalist's Guide to Global Warming* (New York: Vintage, 2007), ix.
58. Bjorn Lomborg, *Smart Solutions to Climate Change* (Cambridge, U.K.: Cambridge University Press, 2010).
59. Juliette Jowit, "Bjorn Lomborg: The Dissenting Climate Change Voice Who Changed His Tune," *Guardian* (London), August 30, 2010, http://www.guardian.co.uk/environment/2010/aug/30/bjorn-lomborg-climate-change-profile.
60. Tom de Castella, "Top Scientists Share Their Outlook," *Financial Times,* November 20, 2009, http://www.ft.com/cms/s/0/f1d9f856-d4ad-11de-a935–00144feabdc0.html#axzz23C0aRgcf.
61. R. M. Carter, "The Myth of Dangerous Human-Caused Climate Change," *Science and Public Policy Institute* (July 2007): 8–9, http://scienceandpublicpolicy.org/images/stories/papers/reprint/CarterMyth/carter_myth.pdf.

62. Research, Computational Science and Engineering, http://cse.berkeley.edu/research.

63. U.S. Consumer Product Safety Commission, Press Release 06–122, March 29, 2006, http://www.cpsc.gov/cpscpub/prerel/prhtml06/06122.html.

64. National Highway Traffic Safety Administration and Bureau of Transportation Statistics, U.S. Department of Transportation, National Survey of Pedestrian & Bicyclist Attitudes and Behaviors, Highlights Report, 2002, 2.

Chapter 3

1. "Maldives Cabinet Makes a Splash" BBC News, October 17, 2011.

2. W. T. Pfeffer et al., "Kinematic Constraints on Glacier Contributions to 21st-Century Sea-Level Rise," *Science* 5 (2008): 1340–1343.

3. Ahmed Shaig, "Climate Change Vulnerability and Adaptation Assessment of the Maldives Land and Beaches," James Cook University, Center for Disaster Studies, 2006, 3.

4. Maldives Ministry of Environment, Energy, and Water, "Maldives National Adaptation Plan of Action Draft for Comments," 2006.

5. Hans-Martin Fussel, "An Updated Assessment of the Risks from Climate Change Based on Research Published since the IPCC Fourth Assessment Report," *Climatic Change* 97 (2009): 469, 471.

6. Shaig, "Climate Change Vulnerability," 8.

7. Maldives Ministry of Planning and Development, "Maldives Country Review Report on the Implementation of the Brussels Programme of Action for LDCs," 2006.

8. "Maldives Cabinet Makes a Splash."

9. Steven D. Levitt and Chad Syverson, "Market Distortions When Agents Are Better Informed: The Value of Information in Real Estate Transactions, National Bureau of Economic Research, Working Paper Series No. 11053, 2005.

10. Andrew C. Revkin, "Maldives Consider Buying Dry Land If Seas Rise," *New York Times*, November 11, 2008, http://www.nytimes.com/2008/11/11/science/earth/11maldives. html.

11. Randeep Ramesh, "Paradise Almost Lost: Maldives Seek to Buy a New Homeland," *Guardian*, November 10, 2008, http://www.guardian.co.uk/environment/2008/nov/10/ maldives-climate-change.

12. Ibid.

13. Kiribati is looking to purchase land, too. Nobuo Mimura, "Vulnerability of Island Countries in the South Pacific to Sea Level Rise and Climate Change," *Climate Research* 12 (1999): 137–143.

14. Fred Pearce, *With Speed and Violence: Why Scientists Fear Tipping Points in Climate Change* (Boston: Beacon, 2007).

15. "Tuvalu Refugees 'Last Resort,'" Adelaide Now, October 26, 2008, http:// www.adelaidenow.com.au/news/south-australia/tuvalu-refugees-last-resort/ story-e6frea83–1111117856091.

16. Jane Resture, "Tuvalu and Global Warming," October 17, 2010, www.janeresture.com. Reprinted in O. H. Pilkey and Rob Young, *The Rising Sea* (Washington, D.C.: Island Press, 2009).

17. "Climate Change," Alliance of Small Island States, http://aosis.info/2010/ climate-change-and-sids.

18. "AOSIS Climate Change Summit," Alliance of Small Island States, http://aosis.info/2010/ climate-change-and-sids.

19. "National Security and the Threat of Climate Change," CNA, 2007, 24; John Podesta and Peter Ogden, "The Security Implications of Climate Change," *Washington Quarterly* (Winter 2007–2008): 117.

20. "GNI per Capita," World Bank, 2008, http://data.worldbank.org.

21. Joshua B. Busby, "Climate Change and National Security: An Agenda for Action," Council on Foreign Relations, CSR No. 32, November 2007, 8.

22. Golam Mahabub Sarwar and Mamunal H. Kahn, "Sea Level Rise: A Threat to the Coast of Bangladesh," *Arnold Bergstraesser Institut* (2007): 375–397.

23. Helene Franchineau, "Bangladesh Fears Climate Change Will Swallow a Third of Its Land," *Washington Times*, September 18, 2009, http://www.washingtontimes.com/news/2009/sep/18/bangladeshi-fears-land-will-vanish/?page=all.

24. N. Myers, "Environmental Refugees: A Growing Phenomenon of the 21st Century," *Philosophical Transactions of the Royal Society B* 357 (2002): 609–613.

25. Sarwar and Kahn, "Sea Level Rise," 375–397.

26. Collete Augustin, "Case Studies on Climate Change and World Heritage," UNESCO World Heritage Centre, 2007; Hermann M. Fritz and Chris Blount, "Protection from Cyclones," in *Coastal Protection in the Aftermath of the Indian Ocean Tsunami: What Role for Forests and Trees?* ed. Susan Braatz et al. (Bangkok: Food and Agriculture Organization of the United Nations: 2007): 37–50.

27. David Sterman, "Climate Change in Egypt: Rising Sea Level, Dwindling Water Supplies," Climate Institute, July 2009, http://www.climate.org/topics/international-action/egypt.html.

28. "Migration, Climate Change, and Environmental Degradation: A Complex Nexus," International Organization for Migration, http://www.iom.int/jahia/Jahia/pid/2068.

29. John Vidal, "Migration Is the Only Escape from Rising Tides of Climate Change in Bangladesh," *Guardian*, December 4, 2009.

30. "Climate Change: Bangladesh Facing the Challenge," World Bank, http://web.world-bank.org/WBSITE/EXTERNAL/COUNTRIES/SOUTHASIAEXT/0,,content MDK:21893554~menuPK:2246552~pagePK:2865106~piPK:2865128~theSiteP K:223547,00.html.

31. Ibid.

32. "Bangladesh," United Nations World Food Programme, 2010, http://www.wfp.org/countries/bangladesh.

33. Ibid.

34. "National Security and the Threat," 24; Podesta and Ogden, "The Security Implications," 117.

35. Lawyers Committee for Human Rights, *Seeking Shelter: Cambodians in Thailand* (New York: Human Rights First, 1987).

36. Vikram Kolmannsko, "Climate Change: People Displaced," Norwegian Refugee Council, 2009.

37. Koko Warner et al., "Human Security, Climate Change and Environmentally Induced Migration," United Nations University–Institute for Environment and Human Security, June 2008.

38. Shann Frank and Duke Trevor, "Twenty-three Thousand Unnecessary Deaths Every Day: What Are You Doing about It?" *Pediatric Critical Care Medicine* 10 (2009): 608–609.

39. European Environment Agency, "Vulnerability and Adaptation to Climate Change in Europe," *EEA Technical Report* 7 (2005): 22.

40. "US National Assessment of the Potential Consequences of Climate Variability and Change, Educational Resources Regional Paper: The Southeast," United States Global Change Research Program, 2004.

41. "Delta Subsidence in California: The Sinking Heart of the State," United States Geological Survey, April 2000.

42. Ibid.

43. Ibid.

44. "Dealing with the Delta: Envisioning Futures, Finding Solutions," Public Policy Institute of California, February 2007, 2.

45. "Our Changing Climate: Assessing the Risks to California," California Climate Change Center, July 2006; Tamara Keith, "California Delta at Risk," National Public Radio, January 8, 2008.

46. Joe Palca, "Crucial California Delta Faces a Salty Future," National Public Radio, January 14, 2008.

47. Mike Taugher, "Levees Put Delta in Danger," *Contra Costa Times*, March 29, 2007, http://www.mercurynews.com/news/cI_5434764?source=pkg.

48. Palca, "Crucial California Delta."

49. Taugher, "Levees Put Delta in Danger."

50. Douglas Fox, "California's Sinking Delta," *Christian Science Monitor*, December 2, 2009, http://www.csmonitor.com/Environment/2009/1202/californias-sinking-delta.

51. In November 2009, Governor Arnold Schwarzenegger reached an agreement with law-makers on a plan intended to address the threat to the water supply. Part of the plan is an $11.1-billion bond, which will be on the ballot for voters to decide in November 2010 and which contemplates a restoration project for the delta. "2009 Comprehensive Water Package Special Session Policy Bills and Bond Summary," Office of the Governor, California Department of Water Resources, November 2009; Samantha Young, "California Water Deal No Quick Fix for Struggling Farms," Associated Press, November 13, 2009.

52. Subir Bhaumik, "Fears Rise for Sinking Sundarbans," BBC News, September 15, 2003.

53. Anil Ananthaswamy, "Sea Level Rise: It's Worse Than We Thought," *New Scientist*, July 1, 2009, http://efdl.cims.nyu.edu/publications/public_media/newscientist_sealevel_09.pdf.

54. "Observed Impacts of Climate Changes," in *Encyclopedia of Earth*, ed. Stephen C. Nodvin (Washington, D.C.: Congressional Research Service, 2009).

55. Geoffrey Lean, "For the First Time in Human History, the North Pole Can Be Circumnavigated," *Independent*, August 31, 2008, http://www.independent.co.uk/environment/climate-change/for-the-first-time-in-human-history-the-north-pole-can-be-circumnavigated-913924.html.

56. Ananthaswamy, "Sea Level Rise."

57. Sharon Begley, "Heat Your Vegetables," *Newsweek*, May 5, 2008, http://www.thedailybeast.com/newsweek/2008/04/26/heat-your-vegetables.html.

58. "Retreat of the Gangotri Glacier," NASA Earth Observatory, January 7, 2011, http://earthobservatory.nasa.gov/IOTD/view.php?id=4594.

59. "Glaciers and Icecaps: Storehouses of Freshwater," United States Geological Survey, March 31, 2011.

60. Ananthaswamy, "Sea Level Rise."

61. Aradhna K. Tripati, Christopher Roberts, and Robert Eagle, "Coupling of CO_2 and Ice Sheet Stability over Major Climate Transitions of the Last 20 Million Years," *Science* 326 (2009): 1394–1397.

62. Ananthaswamy, "Sea Level Rise."

63. Pfeffer et al., "Kinematic Constraints."

64. Richard A. Kerr, "Both of the World's Ice Sheets May Be Shrinking Faster and Faster," *Science* 326 (2009): 217.

65. Ananthaswamy, "Sea Level Rise."

66. Katherine Richardson et al., "Synthesis Report from Climate Change: Global Risks, Challenges, and Decisions," University of Copenhagen, 2009, 9, http://www.preventionweb.net/files/12038_CopenHagenclimatecongress1.pdf.

67. Ibid.

68. James Hansen, *Storms of My Grandchildren: The Truth about the Coming Climate Catastrophe and Our Last Chance to Save Humanity* (New York: Bloomsbury, 2009), 256.

69. Hansen, *Storms of My Grandchildren*, 38.

70. P. J. Webster et al., "Changes in Tropical Cyclone Number, Duration and Intensity in a Warming Environment," *Science* 309 (2005): 1844–1846; K. Emanuel, "Increasing Destructiveness of Tropical Cyclones over the Past 30 Years," *Nature* 436 (2005): 686–688.

71. Webster et al., "Changes in Tropical Cyclone Number, Duration and Intensity."

72. G. Holland, "Climate Change and Extreme Weather," *IOP Conference Series: Earth and Environmental Sciences* 6 (2009).

73. "Myanmar Cyclone Survivors Still Need Shelter: UN," Reuters, November 25, 2009.

74. "A Year after Storm, Subtle Changes in Myanmar," *New York Times*, April 29, 2009, http://www.nytimes.com/2009/04/30/world/asia/30myanmar.html?pagewanted=all.

75. "Burma: Widespread Cyclone Damage in Major Rice Production Regions," United States Department of Agriculture Foreign Agricultural Service, May 15, 2008.

76. Cheng Fang et al., "Special Report: FAO/WFP Crop and Food Security Assessment Mission to Myanmar," FAO Global Information and Early Warning System Special Reports and Alerts, January 22, 2009.
77. "Hydrological Disasters," United Nations Statistical Division, 2010, http://unstats.un.org/unsd/environment/Hydro_disasters.htm.
78. Christine Gibson, *Extreme Natural Disasters* (New York: HarperCollins, 2007), 96.
79. Ibid..
80. "Report of the National Flood Relief Commission 1931–1932," NFRC, Shanghai, 4–5.
81. Ibid., 5.
82. Ibid., 303.
83. Ibid., foreword.
84. Ibid., 147.
85. Ibid., 147, 295.
86. Mike Brunker, "CDC Tests Confirm FEMA Units Are Toxic," MSNBC.com, February 14, 2008, http://www.msnbc.msn.com/id/23168160/ns/us_news-life/t/cdc-tests-confirm-fema-trailers-are-toxic/#.UCffvUJ9ndk.
87. Hallett Abend, "Millions Fighting for Life in China: Conditions in Refugee Camps of Flooded District Almost Beggar Description," *New York Times*, October 11, 1931, E8.
88. "Hankow Is Feeding Flood Refugees: The City, Army and Charitable Groups Are Aiding 400,000 Destitute in Camps," *New York Times*, August 27, 1931, http://select.nytimes.com/gst/abstract.html?res=9E03E6D6133BE433A25754C2A96E9C946094D6CF&scp=5&sq=hankow+feeding&st=p.
89. Ibid.
90. Ibid.
91. "Report of the National Flood Relief Commission," 68.
92. "Halving Hunger: It Can Be Done," *UN Millennium Project, Task Force on Hunger* (London and Sterling, Va.: Earthscan, 2005), 28–29.
93. "Water-Related Emergencies and Outbreaks," Centers for Disease Control and Prevention, August 25, 2010, http://www.cdc.gov/healthywater/emergency.
94. Ibid.
95. "Communicable Diseases following Natural Disasters: Risk Assessment and Priority Interventions," World Health Organization, 2006, http://helid.digicollection.org/pdf/s13416e/s13416e.pdf.
96. Ibid.
97. Gibson, *Extreme Natural Disasters*, 97.
98. "Report of the National Flood Relief Commission," 69.
99. Ibid.
100. Ibid., 70.
101. "Environmental Health in Emergencies and Disasters: A Practical Guide," ed. B. Wisner and J. Adams, World Health Organization, 2002, 168.
102. Abend, "Millions Fighting for Life."
103. Ibid.

Chapter 4

1. D. Evans et al., "A Comprehensive Archaeological Map of the World's Largest Pre-industrial Settlement Complex at Angkor, Cambodia," *Proceedings of the National Academy of Sciences* 104, no. 36 (2007): 14277–14282.
2. Richard Stone, "The End of Angkor," *Science* 311 (2006): 1364; Richard Stone, "Divining Angkor," *National Geographic* (July 2009), http://ngm.nationalgeographic.com/2009/07/angkor/stone-text.
3. Roland Fletcher et al., "The Water Management Network of Angkor, Cambodia," *Antiquity* 82 (2008): 658, 662.
4. Stone, "The End of Angkor," 1364, 1367.
5. Stone, "The End of Angkor," 1364, 1365.

6. Leigh Dayton, "Water Warning in Angkor Ruins," *Australian* (March 2007), http://www.theaustralian.com.au/news/health-science/water-warning-in-angkor-ruins/story-e6frg8gf-1111113157821; Stone, "Divining Angkor."

7. Stone, "The End of Angkor," 1367.

8. Ibid.

9. Stone, "Divining Angkor."

10. Juliette Jowit, "Many Glaciers Will Disappear by Middle of Century and Add to Rising Sea Levels, Expert Warns," *Guardian*, January 19, 2009, http://www.guardian.co.uk/environment/2009/jan/19/glacier-rising-sea-levels.

11. NOAA, "Average U.S. Temperature Increases by 0.5 Degrees F," June 29, 2001, http://www.noaanews.noaa.gov/stories2011/20110629_newnormals.html.

12. S. H. Schneider et al., "Assessing Key Vulnerabilities and the Risk from Climate Change," *Climate Change 2007: Impacts, Adaptation and Vulnerability. Contribution of Working Group II to the Fourth Assessment Report of the Intergovernmental Panel on Climate Change*, ed. M. L. Parry, O. F. Canziani, J. P. Palutikof, P. J. van der Linden, and C. E. Hanson (Cambridge, U.K.: Cambridge University Press, 2007), 781.

13. Rory Carroll and Andres Schipani, "Bolivia: Water People of Andes Face Extinction," *Guardian*, April 24, 2009, http://www.guardian.co.uk/world/2009/apr/24/andes-tribe-threat-bolivia-climate-change.

14. Ibid.

15. Ibid.

16. Ibid.

17. World Bank, "Retracting Glacier Impacts Economic Outlook in the Tropical Andes," April 23, 2008, http://web.worldbank.org/WBSITE/EXTERNAL/COUNTRIES/LACEXT/0,,contentMDK:21739254~pagePK:146736~piPK:146830~theSitePK:258554,00.html.

18. James Painter, "Huge Bolivian Glacier Disappears," BBC News, May 12, 2009, http://news.bbc.co.uk/2/hi/8046540.stm.

19. Mathias Vuille et al., "Climate Change and Tropical Andean Glaciers: Past, Present, and Future," *Earth-Science Reviews* 89 (2008): 82.

20. Carroll and Schipani, "Bolivia."

21. Andrea Kobeszko, "A Glacier Gone," *E* 21 (March/April 2010): 2, 10.

22. Painter, "Huge Bolivian Glacier Disappears."

23. W. Vergara et al., "Economic Impacts of Rapid Glacier Retreat in the Andes," *EOS* 88 (2007): 261.

24. David Shukman, "Glacier Threat to Bolivian Capital," BBC News, December 4, 2009, http://news.bbc.co.uk/2/hi/8394324.stm.

25. Andres Schipani, "Bolivian Villagers Want Compensation as Glaciers Melt," BBC News, April 19, 2010, http://news.bbc.co.uk/2/hi/americas/8629379.stm.

26. Shukman, "Glacier Threat."

27. Stacey Combs, Michael L. Prentice, Lara Hansen, and Lynn Rosentrater, "Going, Going, Gone! Climate Change and Global Glacier Decline," World Wildlife Fund, http://assets.panda.org.

28. Vergara et al. "Economic Impacts," 261; Shukman, "Glacier Threat."

29. Elisabeth Rosenthal, "Bolivia, Water and Ice Tell a Story of Climate Change," *New York Times*, December 14, 2009, http://www.nytimes.com/2009/12/14/science/earth/14bolivia.html?pagewanted=all; William Stevens, "The Warming World: Coping with Climate Change," *New York Times*, September 30, 1997, http://www.nytimes.com/1997/09/30/science/warming-world-coping-with-climate-change-if-climate-changes-who-vulnerable.html?pagewanted=all&src=pm.

30. Vergara et al., "Economic Impacts," 261.

31. Anji Seth et al., "Making Sense of Twenty-First-Century Climate Change in the Altiplano: Observed Trends and CMIP3 Projections," *Annals of the Association of American Geographers* 100 (2010): 835.

32. Oxfam International, "Bolivia: Climate Change, Poverty and Adaptation," October 2009, 23, http://oxf.am/ZRc.

33. "Bolivia," World Factbook, https://www.cia.gov/library/publications/the-world-factbook/geos/bl.html.
34. Bolivia can expect five main impacts as a result of climate change: less food security, glacial retreat affecting water availability, more frequent and more intense "natural" disasters, an increase in mosquito-borne diseases, and more forest fires. Oxfam International, "Bolivia," 12.
35. World Bank, "World Development Indicators," http://data.worldbank.org/data-catalog/world-development-indicators.
36. California Rural Policy Task Force, "California Agriculture: Feeding the Future," Governor's Office of Planning and Research, 2003, 3.
37. John Steinbeck, *The Grapes of Wrath* (New York: Penguin, 1939, repr. 2002), 441.
38. David Carle, *Introduction to Water in California* (Berkeley: University of California Press, 2004), 146.
39. Ibid., 147.
40. Ibid., 90.
41. Data360, "Average Water Use per Person per Day," http://www.data360.org/dsg.aspx?Data_Set_Group_Id=757.
42. Ibid.
43. California Department of Water Resources, "Climate Change," http://www.water.ca.gov/climatechange.
44. Ibid.
45. Resources Agency, "Managing an Uncertain Future: Climate Change Adaptation Strategies for California's Water," California Department of Natural Resources, 2008, 4.
46. T. P. Barnett, J. C. Adam, and D. P. Lettenmaier, "Potential Impacts of a Warming Climate on Water Availability in Snow-Dominated Regions," *Nature* 438 (November 17, 2005): 303–309.
47. Ibid.
48. Katharine Hayhoe et al., "Emissions Pathways, Climate Change, and Impacts on California," *PNAS* 1010 (August 2004): 12422–12427, table 1, 12423.
49. Ibid.
50. Francis Chung et al., "Using Future Climate Projections to Support Water Resources Decision Making in California," California Climate Change Center, April 2009, http://www.energy.ca.gov/2009publications/CEC-500-2009-052/CEC-500-2009-052-D.PDF.
51. B. P. Kaltenborn, C. Nellemann, and C. Vistnes, "High Mountain Glaciers and Climate Change: Challenges to Human Livelihoods and Adaptation," UNEP (2010), http://www.grida.no/publications/high-mountain-glaciers.
52. J. Oerlemans et al., "Modelling the Response of Glaciers to Climate Warming," *Climate Dynamics* 14 (1998): 267–274.
53. Jurgen Bohner and Frank Lehmkuhl, "Environmental Change Modelling for Central and High Asia: Pleistocene, Present and Future Scenarios," *Boreas* 34 (2005): 220–231.
54. C. Rosenzweig, G. Casassa, D. J. Karoly, A. Imeson, C. Liu, A. Menzel, S. Rawlins, T. L. Root, B. Seguin, and P. Tryjanowski, "2007: Assessment of Observed Changes and Responses in Natural and Managed Systems." *Climate Change 2007: Impacts, Adaptation and Vulnerability. Contribution of Working Group II to the Fourth Assessment Report of the Intergovernmental Panel on Climate Change*, ed. M. L. Parry, O. F. Canziani, J. P. Palutikof, P. J. van der Linden, and C. E. Hanson (Cambridge, U.K.: Cambridge University Press, 2007), part 10.6.2.
55. This statement was made by the chair and vice chairs of the IPCC and the cochairs of the IPCC working groups. "IPCC Statement on the Melting of Himalayan Glaciers," Geneva, January 20, 2010.
56. Dirk Scherler, Bodo Bookhagen, and Manfred Strecker, "Spatially Variable Response of Himalayan Glaciers to Climate Change Affected by Debris Cover," *Nature Geoscience* 4 (2011): 156–159.
57. Emilio Godoy, "As Andean Glaciers Recede, Region Steps Forward to Adapts," Inter Press Service, December 13, 2010, http://www.ipsnews.net/2010/12/climate-change-as-andean-glaciers-recede-region-steps-forward-to-adapt.

58. Raymond S. Bradley, Mathias Vuille, Henry F. Diaz, Walter Vergara, "Threats to Water Supplies in the Tropical Andes," *Science* 312 (June 23, 2006): 1755.

59. Rosenzweig et al., "2007: Assessment," 87.

60. Ibid.

61. Kaltenborn et al., "High Mountain Glaciers."

62. "Climate Change Science Compendium 2009," *United Nations Environment Programme,* ed. C. McMullen and J. Jabbour, 2009, 15.

63. Associated Press, "Alps Glaciers Gone by 2050, Experts Fear," MSNBC.com, http://www.msnbc.msn.com/id/16754462/ns/world_news-world_Environment/t/experts-alps-glaciers-will-vanish/#.UCfn0kJ9ndk.

64. B. Zierl and H. Bugmann, "Global Change Impacts on Hydrological Processes in Alpine Catchments," *Water Resources Research* 41 (2005): 1.

65. J. Alcamo, J. M. Moreno, B. Nováky, M. Bindi, R. Corobov, R. J. N. Devoy, C. Giannakopoulos, E. Martin, J. E. Olesen, and A. Shvidenko, "2007: Europe," *Climate Change 2007: Impacts, Adaptation and Vulnerability. Contribution of Working Group 2 to the Fourth Assessment Report of the Intergovernmental Panel on Climate Change,* ed. M. L. Parry, O. F. Canziani, J. P. Palutikof, P. J. van der Linden, and C. E. Hanson (Cambridge, U.K.: Cambridge University Press, 2007), 549–550.

66. Stephen Devereux, "Famine in the 20th Century," IDS Working Paper 105: 1, http://www.ntd.co.uk/idsbookshop/details.asp?id=541.

67. Matthew O. Berger, "Hunger Drops Mere Half a Percent over Last Decade," IPS, September 16, 2010, http://www.ipsnews.net/2010/09/hunger-drops-mere-half-a-percent-over-last-decade.

68. Amartya Sen, *Poverty and Famines: An Essay on Entitlement and Deprivation* (Oxford: Oxford University Press, 1981), 39.

69. National Center for Atmospheric Research, "Learn More about Climate," 2010, http://ncar.ucar.edu/learn-more-about/climate.

70. Nicholas Stern et al., *The Stern Review: The Economics of Climate Change* (Cambridge, U.K.: Cambridge University Press, 2006), 139.

71. James Stuhltrager, "Global Climate Change and National Security," *Natural Resources and Environment* 22, no. 3 (2008): 39.

72. Shenggen Fan and Anuja Saurkar, "Strategic Agricultural Growth Options for Poverty Reduction in Africa and Implications on the Democratic Republic of Congo," International Food Policy Research Institute, 2008; Gerdien Meijerink and Pim Roza, "The Role of Agriculture in Economic Development," in *Markets, Chains and Sustainable Development Strategy and Policy Paper #5* (Wageningen: Stichting DLO, 2007), http://65.54.113.26/Publication/10636116/markets-chains-and-sustainable-development-strategy-&-policy-paper-4-the-role-of-agriculture-in.

73. M. I. Boko et al., "Africa," in *Climate Change 2007: Impacts, Adaptation and Vulnerability. Contribution of Working Group 2 to the Fourth Assessment Report of the Intergovernmental Panel on Climate Change,* ed. M. L. Parry et al. (Cambridge, U.K.: Cambridge University Press, 2007), 435.74. Ibid.

75. Ibid., 437.

76. Raj Patel, *Stuffed and Starved* (New York: Melville House, 2007), 148.

77. Food and Agriculture Organization of the United Nations, "Hunger: Frequently Asked Questions," 2011, http://www.fao.org/hunger/hunger-home/en.

78. Nafissa Abdel Rahim et al., *Greenwar: Environment and Conflict* (Budapest: Panos, 1991), 13.

79. Sen, *Poverty and Famines,* 115.

80. Ibid.

81. Ibid., 116.

82. Carolyn M. Somerville, *Drought and Aid in the Sahel: A Decade of Development Cooperation* (Boulder, Colo.: Westview, 1986), 28.

83. Ibid., 29.

84. U.S. Department of Health, Education, and Welfare, "Vital Statistics of the United States," *II—Mortality* (1973), 1–2, table 1–1.

85. CIA World Factbook, "Death Rate," https://www.cia.gov/library/publications/the-world-factbook/fields/2066.html.
86. Somerville, *Drought and Aid*, 30.
87. Boko et al., "Africa."
88. Asmerom Kidane, "Mortality Estimates of the 1984–85 Ethiopian Famine," *Scandinavian Journal of Social Medicine* 18 (1990): 281–286.
89. Kurt Jansson, Michael Harris, and Angela Penrose, *The Ethiopian Famine* (London: Zed, 1987), xii.
90. Patel, *Stuffed and Starved*, 148.
91. Kidane, "Mortality Estimates."
92. Martin Fletcher, "Zimbabwe's MDC Plans to Extradite Mengistu Haile Mariam to Ethiopia," *Sunday Times*, February 5, 2009; Fred Bridgeland, "Calls for Mengistu Extradition," Institute for War and Peace Reporting, April 11, 2008, http://iwpr.net/report-news/calls-mengistu-extradition.
93. Thomas P. Ofcansky and LaVerle Berry, eds., *Ethiopia: A Country Study* (Washington, D.C.: Library of Congress, 1991).
94. Jan McGirk, "Millions Face Famine as Drought Hits Central America," *Independent*, September 4, 2001, http://www.highbeam.com/doc/1P2–5180058.html.
95. William R. Cline, "Global Warming and Agriculture," *Finance and Development* (March 2008): 24.
96. Ibid.
97. Ibid.
98. Daniel R. Taub, Brian Millier, and Holly Allen, "Effects of Elevated CO_2 on the Protein Concentration of Food Crops: A Meta-Analysis," *Global Change Biology* 14, no. 3 (March 2008): 565–575.
99. Cline, "Global Warming and Agriculture."
100. Ibid.

Chapter 5

1. "Water Dispute Can Trigger Nuclear War with India: Nizami," *Nation* (Pakistan), June 6, 2009, http://www.nation.com.pk/pakistan-news-newspaper-daily-english-online/Lahore/07-Jun-2009/Water-dispute-can-trigger-nuclear-war-with-India-Nizami.
2. Richard F. Bales and Thomas F. Schwartz. *The Great Chicago Fire and the Myth of Mrs. O'Leary's Cow* (Jefferson, N.C.: McFarland, 2005), 52.
3. Robert Cromie, *The Great Chicago Fire* (New York: McGraw-Hill, 1958, repr. 1994).
4. Oliver Read, "Crisis in Sudan—Janjaweed Militia." Online News Hour, PBS, April 7, 2006, http://www.pbs.org/newshour/indepth_coverage/africa/darfur/militia.html.
5. Alexander De Waal, *Famine That Kills: Darfur, Sudan* (Oxford: Oxford University Press, 1989), 28; Stephan Faris, *Forecast: The Surprising—and Immediate—Consequences of Climate Change* (New York: Holt, 2009).
6. Samantha Power, "Dying in Darfur," *New Yorker*, August 30, 2004, http://www.newyorker.com/archive/2004/08/30/040830fa_fact1; De Waal, *Famine That Kills*, 73.
7. Russell Schimmer, "Tracking the Genocide in Darfur," Yale University Genocide Studies Program, Working Paper 36 August 1, 2008, http://www.yale.edu/gsp/publications.
8. Savo Heleta, "Evolution of the Darfur Rebellion—A Revolution in the Making," Nelson Mandela Metropolitan University, Port Elizabeth, South Africa, October 1, 2008, http://www.cmi.no/sudan/resources.cfm?id=112-evolution-of-the-darfur-rebellion-a-revolution-in-the-making.
9. Faris, *Forecast*.
10. Rosemarie North, "Darfur's Refugees in Chad," *Magazine of the International Red Cross and Red Crescent Movement* 2 (2005), http://www.redcross.int/EN/mag/magazine2005_2/22–23.html.
11. "Sudanese Refugees Raped in Chad," BBC News, September 30, 2009.
12. Ban Ki-moon, "A Climate Culprit in Darfur," Washington Post, June 16, 2007, http://www.washingtonpost.com/wp-dyn/content/article/2007/06/15/AR2007061501857.html.

13. Solomon M. Hsiang, Kyle C. Meng, and Mark A. Cane, "Civil Conflicts Are Associated with the Global Climate," *Nature* 476 (August 25, 2011): 438–441.

14. Karen Franken, ed., *Irrigation in the Middle East Region in Figures, AQUASTAT Survey 2008* (Rome: Food and Agriculture Organization of the United Nations, 2009), 31.

15. Jon Podesta and Peter Ogden, "The Security Implications of Climate Change," *Washington Quarterly* 31, no. 1 (2007): 121.

16. Ibid., 122; Gordon R. Sullivan et al., "National Security and the Threat of Climate Change," CNA, 2007.

17. Walter V. Reid et al., *Millennium Ecosystem Assessment, Ecosystems and Human Well-being: Synthesis* (Washington, D.C.: Island, 2005), 174.

18. Franken, *Irrigation in the Middle East Region*.

19. Michael T. Klare, *Resource Wars: The New Landscape of Global Conflict* (New York: Henry Holt, 2002), 161.

20. Steven Solomon, *Water* (New York: HarperCollins, 2010), 408–409.

21. Vandana Shiva, *Water Wars* (Cambridge, Mass.: South End Press, 2002).

22. Godfrey Jansen, "Tussle over the Euphrates," *Middle East International* (February 16, 1990): 12–13; John C. K. Daly, "Turkey's GAP Project: A Mixed Blessing for Neighbors," *Eurasia Daily Monitor* 5, no. 135 (July 16, 2008), http://www.jamestown.org/programs/edm/single/?tx_ttnews%5Btt_news%5D=33807&tx_ttnews%5BbackPid%5D=166&no_cache=1.

23. Lina Ibrahim and Nayla Razzouk, "Syria to Build Dam on Border Running along Orontes River," Bloomberg, January 26, 2011, http://www.bloomberg.com/news/2011-01-27/syria-turkey-to-build-dam-on-border-running-along-orontes-river.html.

24. Podesta and Ogden, "The Security Implications," 122.

25. Jean-Phillip Venot, Francois Molle, and Remi Courcier, "Dealing with Closed Basins: The Case of the Lower Jordan River Basin," *Water Resources Development* 24 (2008): 247–263.

26. Klare, *Resource Wars*, 169.

27. Solomon, *Water*, 402.

28. Ofira Seliktar, "Turning Water into Fire: The Jordan River as the Hidden Factor in the Six Day War," *Middle East Review of International Affairs* 9, no. 2 (June 2005): 57–71.

29. Solomon, *Water*, 402.

30. Alon Tal, "Seeking Sustainability: Israel's Evolving Water Management Strategy," *Science* 313 (2006): 1081–1084.

31. Ethan Bronner, "Israel Holds Peace Talks with Syria," *New York Times*, May 22, 2008, http://www.nytimes.com/2008/05/22/world/middleeast/22mideast.html.

32. S. Solomon et al., eds., *Climate Change 2007: Working Group 1: The Physical Science Basis* (Cambridge, U.K.: Cambridge University Press, 2007), 11.3.3.2, figure 11.5; Oli Brown and Alec Crawford, "Rising Temperatures, Rising Tensions: Climate Change and the Risk of Violent Conflict in the Middle East," International Institute for Sustainable Development, 2009, http://www.iisd.org/pdf/2009/rising_temps_middle_East.pdf.

33. The study assumes an increase in average land temperatures of 2.7° C, which is perhaps a little lower than what I assume throughout this book, depending on what one assumes about the difference between warming over land and warming over water. Give the uncertainties involved, however, the assumptions in this study are close enough to the ones I am making that I am comfortable taking the results at face value. Daisuke Nohara, Akio Kitoh, Masahiro Hosaka, and Taikan Oki, "Impact of Climate Change on River Discharge Projected by Multimodel Ensemble," *Journal of Hydrometeorology* 7 (2006): 1076–1089.

34. Fengjun Jin, Akio Kitoh, and Pinhas Alpert, "Water Cycle Changes over the Mediterranean: A Comparison Study of a Super-High-Resolution Global Model with CMIP3," *Philosophical Transactions of the Royal Society A* 368 (2010): 1–13.

35. Brown and Crawford. "Rising Temperatures."

36. Jon Martin Trondalen, *Water and Peace for the People* (Paris: UNESCO, 2008).

37. The prediction that per-capita water supply of water will fall by 50 percent by 2050 "will likely be exacerbated as climate change make countries hotter and drier." World

Bank, "Middle East and North Africa," 2011, http://web.worldbank.org/WBSITE/ EXTERNAL/COUNTRIES/MENAEXT/0,,contentMDK:20536156~pagePK:14673 6~piPK:226340~theSitePK:256299,00.html.

38. United Nations, "Goal 1: Eradicate Extreme Poverty and Hunger, Fact Sheet," 2010, http://www.un.org/millenniumgoals/poverty.shtml.

39. Belarus, Kazakhstan, and Ukraine all had nuclear weapons left over from the Soviet Union, but these were eventually all transferred to Russia or destroyed. India had long had a nuclear-weapons program and had conducted what it termed a "peaceful nuclear explosion" in 1974. It probably had the capacity to develop nuclear weapons from that time forward and may have done so. In 1998, India conducted its first full-scale weapons test. Pakistan also conducted its own tests in 1998 (in response to India's), indicating that it had the ability to construct nuclear weapons by that time. Andrew Krepinevich, "US Nuclear Forces Meeting the Challenge of a Proliferated World," Center for Strategic and Budgetary Assessments, Strategy for the Long Haul, 2009.

40. Paul Bowers, "Kashmir," International Affairs and Defense, Research Paper 04/28, U.K. House of Commons Library, March 30, 2004.

41. James Heitzman and Robert L. Worden, eds., *India: A Country Study* (Washington, D.C.: U.S. Government Printing Office, 1996).

42. Undala Z. Alam, "Questioning the Water Wars Rationale: A Case Study of the Indus Waters Treaty," *Geographical Journal* 168, no. 4 (December 2002): 341–353.

43. IUCN Water and Nature Initiative, "The Lower Indus River: Balancing Development and Maintenance of Wetland Ecosystems and Dependent Livelihoods," 2003, http://cmsdata.iucn.org/downloads/indus.pdf; World Wildlife Fund, "Indus River Delta-Arabian Sea Mangroves," 2001, http://www.eoearth.org/article/ Indus_River_Delta-Arabian_Sea_mangroves.

44. World Bank, "Pakistan Country Water Resources Assistance Strategy—Water Economy: Running Dry," Report No. 34081-PK, November 22, 2005, 25–26.

45. William Wheeler, "The Water's Edge," *Good Magazine*, July 13, 2009, http://www.good. is/post/the-water-s-edge.

46. Ibid.

47. "Kashmir Is the Jugular Vein of Pakistan: Zulquarnian," *Nation* (Pakistan), February 12, 2010, http://www.nation.com.pk/pakistan-news-newspaper-daily-english-online/ lahore/12-Feb-2010/Kashmir-is-jugular-vein-of-Pakistan-Zulqarnain.

48. Mohammad Jamil, "Looming Threat of Water Wars," *Nation* (Pakistan), February 24, 2009, http://www.nation.com.pk/pakistan-news-newspaper-daily-english-online/colu- mns/25-Feb-2009/Looming-threat-of-water-wars.

49. Wheeler, "The Water's Edge."

50. Ibid.

51. "Future Wars Will Be Fought on Water," *Nation* (Pakistan), September 20, 2008, http://www.nation.com.pk/pakistan-news-newspaper-daily-english-online/ Lahore/21-Sep-2008/Future-wars-will-be-fought-on-water-Dr-Javed.

52. Ibid.

53. "Smash Indian Dams with Atom Bombs, Says Nizami," *Nation* (Pakistan), September 3, 2009, http://www.nation.com.pk/pakistan-news-newspaper-daily-english-online/ lahore/03-Sep-2009/Smash-Indian-dams-with-atom-bombs-says-Nizami.

54. "Future Wars Will Be Fought."

55. "Water Dispute Can Trigger."

56. "The Final Settlement: Restructuring India-Pakistan Relations," Strategic Foresight Group, 2005.

57. "Nigeria,"WorldFactbook,https://www.cia.gov/library/publications/the-world-factbook/ geos/ni.html.

58. Fergus Nicoll, "Nigeria's Ethnic Divisions," BBC News, February 18, 1999, http://news. bbc.co.uk/2/hi/africa/129493.stm.

59. "Climate Change: National Security Threats," Committee on Foreign Relations Hearing.

60. Meg Handley, "The Violence in Nigeria: What's Behind the Conflict?" *Time*, March 20, 2010, http://www.time.com/time/world/article/0,8599,1971010,00.html.

61. Scott Baldauf, "Nigeria Violence: Muslim-Christian Clashes Kill Hundreds," *Christian Science Monitor*, March 8, 2010, http://www.csmonitor.com/World/Africa/2010/0308/Nigeria-violence-Muslim-Christian-clashes-kill-hundreds; "Group: 200 Dead in Nigerian Religious Violence," *Washington Post*, January 20, 2010, http://www.washingtontimes.com/news/2010/jan/20/group-more-200-dead-nigerian-religious-violence.

62. Baldauf, "Nigeria Violence."

63. Princeton N. Lyman, "The War on Terrorism in Africa," in *Africa in World Politics*, 3rd ed., ed. John W. Harbeson and Donald Rothchild (Boulder, Colo.: Westview, 2000).

64. Lyman, "The War on Terrorism."

65. Joe Boyle, "Nigeria's 'Taliban' Enigma," BBC News, July 31, 2009, http://news.bbc.co.uk/2/hi/8172270.stm.

66. Dulue Mbachu, "Nigeria's Taliban-Inspired Uprising in North Sparks Christian-Muslim Divide," Reuters, February 16, 2011, http://www.bloomberg.com/news/2011-02-15/nigeria-s-taliban-inspired-uprising-worsens-religious-divide.html.

67. "Factbox: What Is Nigeria's Boko Haram?" Reuters, December 28, 2010, http://www.reuters.com/article/2012/01/24/us-nigeria-sect-bokoharam-factbox-idUSTRE80N0R620120124.

68. Ibid.

69. Mbachu, "Nigeria's Taliban-Inspired Uprising."

70. U.S. Department of State, "Country Reports on Terrorism 2009," August 2010, http://www.state.gov/j/ct/rls/crt/2009/140881.htm.

71. Through September 2010, Nigeria has exported 1,056,000 barrels of petroleum per day to the United States. This represents slightly more than Venezuela (1,006,000) and almost as much as Saudi Arabia (1,086,000).

72. Joshua B. Busby, "Climate Change and National Security: An Agenda for Action," Council on Foreign Relations, CSR No. 32, November 2007, 9; Sullivan et al., "National Security"; Podesta and Ogden, "The Security Implications," 20.

73. David Smock, "Crisis in the Niger Delta," United States Institute for Peace, September 2009.

74. Stephanie Hanson, "MEND: The Niger Delta's Umbrella Militant Group," Council on Foreign Relations, March 22, 2007, http://www.cfr.org/nigeria/mend-niger-deltas-umbrella-militant-group/p12920; Nina Budina and Sweder van Wijnbergen, "Managing Oil Revenue Volatility in Nigeria: The Role of Fiscal Policy," in *Africa at a Turning Point? Growth, Aid, and External Shocks*, ed. Delfin S. Go and John Page (Washington, D.C.: World Bank, 2008), 427–460.

75. Hanson, "MEND."

76. "Fighting in Nigeria's Delta Getting Desperate," *Economist*, May 28, 2009, http://www.economist.com/node/13745871.

77. "A Bloody Election Omen," *Economist*, October 7, 2010, http://www.economist.com/node/17209786.

78. Baldauf, "Nigeria Violence"; Dulue Mbachu, "Nigeria's MEND Says It Plans Attack on Oil Industry," *Businessweek*, January 18, 2011, http://www.businessweek.com/news/2012-02-06/nigerian-militant-group-mend-says-it-attacked-eni-pipeline.html; Hanson, "MEND."

79. President George W. Bush, *The National Security Strategy of the United States of America* (Washington, D.C.: White House, 2006), 37.

80. President Barack Obama, *National Security Strategy of the United States of America* (Washington, D.C.: White House, 2010), 45.

81. Busby, "Climate Change and National Security," 9.

82. Carter Ham, "Commander's Intent," August 2011.

83. Lyman, "The War on Terrorism."

84. Thomas Fingar, "National Intelligence Assessment on the National Security Implications of Global Climate Change to 2030," House Permanent Select Committee on Intelligence, House Select Committee on Energy Independence and Global Warming, June 25, 2008, 8.

85. "Climate Change Information on Nigeria," Building Nigeria's Response to Climate Change, 2008, http://www.nigeriaclimatechange.org/ccinfo.php.

86. S. H. Schneider et al., "Assessing Key Vulnerabilities and the Risk from Climate Change," *Climate Change 2007: Impacts, Adaptation and Vulnerability. Contribution of Working Group II to the Fourth Assessment Report of the Intergovernmental Panel on Climate Change*, ed. M. L. Parry, O. F. Canziani, J. P. Palutikof, P. J. van der Linden, and C. E. Hanson (Cambridge, U.K.: Cambridge University Press, 2007).

87. Ewah Out Eleri, "Strengthening Energy and Ecosystem Resilience in Nigeria," Sustainable Energy Watch, 2007, http://www.helio-international.org/Nigeria. En.pdf.

88. James Stuhltrager, "Global Climate Change and National Security," *Natural Resources and Environment* 22, no. 3 (2008): 39.

89. Isha Sesay, "Shrinking Lake Chad Turning Farmland into Desert," CNN World, March 2, 2011, http://articles.cnn.com/2011–03–02/world/shrinking.lake. chad_1_lake-chad-lake-region-locals?_s=PM:WORLD.

90. Klaus Paehler, "Nigeria in the Dilemma of Climate Change," Konrad-Adenauer-Stiftung Nigeria Office, July 19, 2007, http://www.kas.de/nigeria/en/publications/11468; U.S. Department of State, "Background Note: Nigeria," April 19, 2012, http://www.state. gov/r/pa/ei/bgn/2836.htm.

91. Stuhltrager, "Global Climate Change," 39.

92. "Climate Change Information on Nigeria."

93. Busby, "Climate Change and National Security," 9; Sullivan et al., "National Security"; Podesta and Ogden, "The Security Implications," 115–138, 20–22.

Chapter 6

1. " Managing the Health Effects of Climate Change," *Lancet* (May 16, 2009): 1693.

2. "Life Expectancy at Birth," World Factbook, https://www.cia.gov/library/publications/ the-world-factbook/rankorder/2102rank.html.

3. "Global Life Expectancy Reaches New Heights but 21 Million Face Premature Death This Year, Warns WHO," World Health Report 1998, http://www.who.int/whr/1998/ media_centre/press_release/en/index2.html.

4. UNAIDS, Report on the Global AIDS Epidemic (2008), 6–16.

5. John M. Barry, *The Great Influenza: The Epic Story of the Deadliest Plague in History* (New York: Viking, 2004).

6. Ibid., 92.

7. Ibid., 18.

8. David A. Koplow, *Smallpox: The Fight to Eradicate a Global Scourge* (Berkeley: University of California Press, 2003).

9. World Health Organization, "Influenza, Fact Sheet No. 211," April 2009, http://www. who.int/mediacentre/factsheets/fs211/en.

10. Flu viruses are classified based on two proteins on their outer skin. The first is called hemagglutinin. Fifteen different forms of this protein have been found, and this accounts for the first part of the names of different viruses: H1, H2, H3, etc. The other protein is called neuraminidase. Nine varieties of this protein have been found, and this provides the second half of the naming system: N1, N2, N3, etc. That is how we get names such as H1N1, H5N1, and so on.

11. Nassim Nicholas Taleb, *The Black Swan: The Impact of the Highly Improbable* (New York: Random House, 2007).

12. Madeline Drexler, *Secret Agents: The Menace of Emerging Infections* (Washington, D.C.: Joseph Henry, 2002), 174.

13. Elizabeth Rosenthal, "Chickens Killed in Hong Kong to Combat Flu," *New York Times*, December 29, 1997, http://www.nytimes.com/1997/12/29/world/chickens-killed-in-hong-kong-to-combat-flu.html?pagewanted=all&src=pm.

14. Michael Greger, *Bird Flu: A Virus of Our Own Hatching* (New York: Lantern, 2006).

15. Pete Davies, "The Plague in Waiting," *Guardian*, August 7, 1999, http://www.guardian. co.uk/world/1999/aug/07/birdflu.

16. Amena Ahmad, Ralf Krumkamp, and Ralk Reintjes, "Controlling SARS: A Review on China's Response Compared with Other SARS-Affected Countries," *Tropical Medicine and International Health* 14, supp. 1 (November 2009): 36–45.
17. Stacey Knobler et al., eds., "Learning from SARS: Preparing for the Next Disease Outbreak," *National Academy of Science* (2004): 117.
18. John Pomfret, "SARS Coverup Spurs a Shake-Up in Beijing," *Washington Post*, April 21, 2003, A01.
19. Chris Buckley, "China Expects Tourism to Grow Rapidly," *New York Times*, October 14, 2003, W1.
20. World Bank, "Influenza A (H1N1) and Avian Influenza (H5N1)," http://web.worldbank.org/WBSITE/EXTERNAL/NEWS/0,,contentMDK:23192033~menuPK:34480~pagePK:64257043~piPK:437376~theSitePK:4607,00.html.
21. Gary Cecchine and Melinda Moore, "Infection Disease and National Security," RAND Corporation, 2006, xiii.
22. Barry, *The Great Influenza*, 145.
23. Anne Underwood and Jerry Adler, "Scary Strains," *Newsweek*, November 1, 2004, http://www.thedailybeast.com/newsweek/2004/10/31/scary-strains.html.
24. Richard A. Cash and Vasant Narasimhan, "Impediments to Global Surveillance of Infectious Diseases: Consequences of Open Reporting in a Global Economy," *Bulletin of the World Health Organization* 78, no. 11 (2000): 1358.
25. Chris Buckley, "China Expects Tourism."
26. Cash and Narasimhan, "Impediments to Global Surveillance," 1358.
27. "Global Alert and Response: Plague," *Weekly Epidemiological Record* 79, no. 33 (August 13, 2004): 301–308.
28. "The history of international public health is littered with examples of states trying to deny, hide and postpone the detection of new viruses." Jody Freeman and Andrew Guzman, "Essay: Climate Change and U.S. Interests," *Columbia Law Review* 109 (October 2009): 1592.
29. Mike Davis, *The Monster at Our Door: The Global Threat of Avian Flu* (New York: New Press, 2005), 105.
30. Thomas Abraham, *Twenty-First Century Plague: The Story of SARS* (Baltimore: Johns Hopkins University Press, 2005), 24.
31. World Health Organization, "Epidemic and Pandemic Alert and Response," 2009, http://www.afro.who.int/en/clusters-a-programmes/dpc/epidemic-a-pandemic-alert-and-response.html.
32. Rosalie Woodruff et al., "Predicting Ross River Virus Epidemics from Regional Weather Data," *Epidemiology* 13 (2002): 384–393; Tarekegn Abeku et al., "Forecasting Malaria Incidence from Historical Morbidity Patterns in Epidemic-Prone Areas of Ethiopia: A Simple Seasonal Adjustment Performs Best," *Tropical Medicine and International Health* 7, no. 10 (October 2002): 851–857.
33. Huei-Ting Tsai and Tzu-Ming Liu, "Effects of Global Climate Change on Disease and Social Instability around the World," Human Security and Climate Change, International Workshop, Oslo, 2005.
34. D. H. Campbell-Lendrum et al., "How Much Disease Could Climate Change Cause?" in *Climate Change: Risks and Response*, ed. A. J. McMichael et al., World Health Organization, 2003; Global Humanitarian Forum, *The Anatomy of a Silent Crisis* (Geneva: Forum 2009: Climate Change, 2009).
35. World Health Organization, "Removing Obstacles to Healthy Development," World Health Organization Report on Infectious Diseases, 1999, http://www.who.int/infectious-disease-report/index-rpt99.html.
36. National Research Council, *Under the Weather: Climate, Ecosystems, and Infectious Disease* (Washington, D.C.: National Academy Press, 2001), 52; S. S. Morse, "Factors and Determinants of Disease Emergence," *Revue Scientifique et Technique* 23, no. 2 (2004): 443, 445; A. S. Khan et al., "Hantavirus Pulmonary Syndrome: The First 100 U.S. Cases," *Journal of Infectious Disease* 173, no. 6 (1996): 1297–1303.

37. Emily K. Shuman, "Global Climate Change and Infectious Diseases," *International Journal of Occupational Environmental Medicine* 2 (2011): 11.
38. World Health Organization, "Malaria, Fact Sheet No. 94," http://www.who.int/mediacentre/factsheets/fs094/en.
39. Ibid.
40. Ibid.
41. Shuman, "Global Climate Change," 16.
42. Paul R. Epstein and Dan Ferber, "Malaria on the Rise as East African Climate Heats Up," *Scientific American*, April 1, 2001, http://www.scientificamerican.com/article.cfm?id=east-africa-malaria-rises-under-climate-change.
43. Ibid.
44. World Health Organization, "Global Alert and Response (GAR): Impact of Dengue," 2011, http://www.who.int/csr/disease/dengue/impact/en.
45. Ibid.
46. Summarizing studies to date on projected climate-change impacts on dengue fever and malaria, noting some projected decreases but more projected increases, see U. B. Confalonieri et al., "Human Health," in *Climate Change 2007: Impacts, Adaptation and Vulnerability. Contribution of Working Group 2 to the Fourth Assessment Report of the Intergovernmental Panel on Climate Change*, ed. M. L. Parry, O. F. Canziani, J. P. Palutikof, P. J. van der Linden, and C. E. Hanson (Cambridge, U.K.: Cambridge University Press, 2007): 409–410.
47. Ibid., 408.
48. Michelle Roberts, "Haiti Cholera 'Far Worse Than Expected,' Experts Fear," BBC News, March 15, 2011, http://www.bbc.co.uk/news/health-12744929.
49. Richard Knox, "Doctors Urge Cholera Vaccine for Haiti, Neighbors," NPR, December 10, 2010, http://www.npr.org/2010/12/10/131950133/doctors-urge-cholera-vaccine-for-haiti-neighbors.
50. World Health Organization, "Cholera, WHO Fact Sheet No. 107," August 2011.
51. Jeffrey Gettleman, "Cholera Epidemic Infects Thousands in Kenya," *New York Times*, December 4, 2009, http://www.nytimes.com/2009/12/05/world/africa/05kenya.html.
52. Roberte Manigat, France Wallet, and Jean-Claude, "From Past to Better Public Health Programme Planning for Possible Future Threats: Case Studies Applied to Infection Control," *Annali dell'Istituto Superiore di Sanità* 46, no. 3 (2010): 232.
53. Michael Emch et al., "Seasonality of Cholera from 1974 to 2005: A Review of Global Patterns," *International Journal of Health Geographics* 7, no. 31 (June 20, 2008), http://www.ncbi.nlm.nih.gov/pmc/articles/PMC2467415.
54. Ibid.
55. Interagency Working Group on Climate Change and Health, Environmental Health Perspective & National Institute of Environmental Health Sciences, "A Human Health Perspective on Climate Change: A Report Outlining the Research Needs on the Human Health Effects of Climate Change," April 22, 2010.
56. Katharine Hayhoe et al., "Emissions Pathways, Climate Change, and Impacts on California," *PNAS* 1010 (August 2004): 12423.
57. Pew Center on Global Climate Change, "Climate Change 101: Understanding and Responding to Global Climate Change," January 2009.
58. Stephanie Vandentorren et al., "Mortality in 13 French Cities during the August 2003 Heat Wave," *American Journal of Pubic Health* 94, no. 9 (2004): 1518–1520.
59. Ibid.
60. Ibid.

Chapter 7

1. Daniel A. Farber, "Building Bridges over Troubled Waters: Eco-Pragmatism and the Environmental Prospect," *Minnesota Law Review* 87 (2002): 851–883.
2. Samuel Fankhauser and Richard S. J. Tol, "On Climate Change and Economic Growth," *Resource and Energy Economics* 27 (2005): 1, 3–6.

3. There is a risk that we could cross a climate threshold or tipping point, after which the harms would escalate extremely quickly and the GHGs in the atmosphere might rise rapidly and beyond our control. To give just one example, areas of permafrost currently store an enormous amount of methane, a powerful greenhouse gas. As temperatures warm and the permafrost thaws, there is concern that the methane will be released, triggering further warming, more melting of the permafrost, and more release of methane, leading to a self-perpetuating "runaway" climate change. In this and other similar scenarios, once we cross a critical threshold, it becomes impossible to stop further warming. At that point, even dramatic reductions in emissions have little effect. Whether such tipping points exist and where are highly uncertain. This means that even if we are concerned about them, incremental reductions in emissions are valuable, because any given increment might be the difference between crossing and not crossing a critical threshold.

INDEX

Osterhaus, Albert, 186
Ottawa, temperatures, 14
Oxford University, Environmental Change
    Institute, 51

Pacific, typhoons, 88
Pakistan
    cholera, 199
    floods, 157
    GDP, 160
    Nazaria-i-Pakistan Trust, 160–61
    nuclear warnings (potential climate wars),
        152–61
    nuclear weapons, 152, 244n39
Palestine Liberation Organization, 148
Palin, Sarah, 232n14
Pandemics. *See also* Illnesses, possible
        aggravation of; Infectious disease
        pandemic, possible effect of climate
        change on
    acknowledge of emergence of pathogen,
        199–200
    Avian flu (1997), 185–88
    The Black Death, 184
    causing of, 193–201
    cholera, 199, 206–7
    crowding and, 194–97
    droughts as cause, 193
    globalization and, 181
    government, role in avoidance of, 197–201
    HIV/AIDS (*See* HIV/AIDS)
    H1N1 virus, 178–79, 191–93
    influenza pandemic of 1918, 174–79 (*See also*
        Influenza pandemic of 1918 *for detailed
        treatment*)
    international institutions, role in avoidance
        of, 197–201
    microorganisms, 194
    migration to avoid, 180, 196
    near misses, modern day, 184–93
    Plague of Athens, 184
    Plague of Justinian, 184
    polio, 197
    prevention systems, weakening of, 181–82
    refugee camps and, 196
    reporting of disease and, 199
    SARS, 188–91, 198–99
    smallpox, 184
    tuberculosis, 174–75
    typhus, 184
Paris, heat wave of 2003, 210
Past climatic changes, 20, 29–36
Persian Gulf War (1990–91), 134
Peru, cholera, 207
Petroleum, Nigeria, 165
Pfeffer, Tad, 83
Phillips, Melanie, 21

Plague of Athens, 184
Plague of Justinian, 184
Plasmodium, 204
Policy
    Greenhouse gas emissions, curbing, 227–30
    responses to climate, 2–3
Polio, 197
Politics
    consensus in scientific community and, 27–28
    denial of climate change, 28–29
Pol Pot, 69
Port Sudan, temperatures, 15
Potomac-Raritan-Magothy aquifer system, 73
Poverty, South Asia, 151–52
Predictions, 2, 4, 17, 20
    future refugees, 66–69
    health, climate change and, 201–10
    land loss, effect on refugees, 67–69
    sea levels, rising, 75–85, 95–96
    war (*See* Climate wars (potential))
Prince of Wales Hospital (Hong Kong), 189
Princip, Gavrilo, 136
Procrastination, 215–17

Queen Elizabeth Hospital (Hong Kong), 185

Rainfall, Africa, 169
RAND Corporation, 193
Refugee camps, pandemics and, 196
Refugees
    Cambodia, 69–70
    Chad, 138
    future refugees, predictions, 66–67
    Hindu, 152–53
    land loss predicted, effect of, 67–69
    Maldives. potential, 70–71
    rising sea levels and, 59, 65–71
Rensselaer Polytechnic Institute, 48
Republican Party, skepticism regarding climate
    change, 27–28, 232n14
Research, personal, 51–52
Rignot, Eric, 83
Rivers, study on the effect of climate change
    on, 150, 243n33
Rodent population, disease and, 203
"Runaway" climate change, 249n3
Russia. *See also* Soviet Union
    climate change, when helpful, 128, 130
    nuclear weapons, 152, 244n39
    World War I, 136
Rwanda, genocide, 136

Sacramento-San Joaquin Delta, 74
Sahel region (Africa)
    drought, 120, 122–25
    famine, 122–25
    map with location of, *123*